Victorian Liberalism

Scholarly and popular interest in Victorian political culture has grown tremendously in recent years. Students of every political complexion have turned to nineteenth-century thought and society as an indispensable pre-condition for coming to grips with today's problems and for assessing the continued validity of our inherited political concepts.

Victorian Liberalism brings together leading political theorists and historians in order to examine the interplay of theory and ideology in nineteenth-century liberal thought and practice. Drawing on a wide range of source material, the authors examine liberal thinkers and politicians from Adam Smith, Jeremy Bentham, and John Stuart Mill to William Gladstone and Joseph Chamberlain. Connections are drawn throughout between the different languages which made up liberal discourse and the relations between these vocabularies and the political movements and changing social reality they sought to explain. The result is a stimulating volume that breaks new ground in the study of political history and the history of political thought.

Victorian Liberalism

Nineteenth-century political thought and practice

Edited by Richard Bellamy

Routledge
London and New York

First published 1990
by Routledge
11 New Fetter Lane, London EC4P 4EE

Simultaneously published in the USA and Canada
by Routledge
a division of Routledge, Chapman and Hall, Inc.
29 West 35th Street, New York, NY 10001

Collection © 1990 Routledge; individual contributions © 1990 the respective
contributors

Typeset in 10/12 Times by LaserScript Limited, Mitcham, Surrey
Printed in Great Britain by TJ Press (Padstow) Ltd, Padstow, Cornwall

British Library Cataloguing in Publication Data

Victorian liberalism : nineteenth-century political thought and practice
   1. Great Britain. Political ideologies: Liberalism, history
   I. Bellamy, Richard
   320.5'1'0941
   ISBN 0-415-01677-0

Library of Congress Cataloging in Publication Data

Victorian liberalism : nineteenth century political thought and practice /
   edited by Richard Bellamy
      p.   cm.
   Bibliography: p.
   Includes index.
   ISBN 0-415-01677-0
1. Liberalism—Great Britain—History—19th century. 2. Political science—Great
Britain—History—19th century. 3. Great Britain—Politics and government—19th
century. I. Bellamy, Richard (Richard Paul)
JA84.G7V53 1989
320.5'12'0941—dc20
89-6298

Contents

Contributors

Richard Bellamy

Richard Bellamy is Lecturer in Political Theory at the University of Edinburgh. His publications include *Modern Italian Social Theory* (Polity Press, 1987) and numerous articles on the history of political thought. He is currently working on a study of liberalism and a short book on French social theory.

Stephen Conway

Stephen Conway is Lecturer in History, University College London, and Editor of the *Correspondence of Jeremy Bentham*, vols viii and ix, as part of the new edition of the *Collected Works*.

Bianca Fontana

Bianca Fontana has held fellowships at King's College, Cambridge, the Institute for the Advanced Study of Humanities, the University of Edinburgh, and the Political Science Department, European University Institute, Florence. She has recently completed a book on *Rethinking the Politics of Commercial Society: The 'Edinburgh Review', 1802–32*, (Cambridge University Press, 1985) and an edition of *The Political Writings of Benjamin Constant* (Cambridge University Press, 1988).

Michael Freeden

Michael Freeden is Fellow and Tutor in Politics, Mansfield College, Oxford. He is the author of *The New Liberalism: An Ideology of Social Reform* (Clarendon Press, 1978), *Liberalism Divided: A Study in British Political Thought 1914–1939* (Clarendon Press, 1986), and *J. A. Hobson: A Reader* (Hyman Unwin, 1988), as well as numerous articles. He is currently writing a book on comparative ideological analysis, as a British Academy Research Reader.

John Gibbins

John Gibbins is Senior Lecturer in Politics and Philosophy at Teesside Polytechnic. He is review editor of *Theory, Culture and Society* and recently completed a doctoral thesis on John Grote. He has edited *Contemporary Political Culture: Politics in a Postmodern Age* (Sage, 1988).

Tim Gray

Tim Gray is Senior Lecturer in Politics at the University of Newcastle upon Tyne. His publications include various articles on Spencer and a book on *Freedom* (Macmillan, 1989). He is co-author of *Burke's Dramatic Theory of Politics* (Gower, 1988), and currently working on a comparison of Spencer's liberalism and that of the New Right.

Christopher Harvie

Christopher Harvie is Professor of British Studies at Tübingen University in West Germany. He is the author of *The Lights of Liberalism: University Liberals and the Challenge of Democracy, 1860–1886* and of several works on Scottish history and politics. He is presently at work on a history of political fiction in Britain.

Alan Hooper

Alan Hooper is Senior Lecturer in Politics in the School of Health and Human Sciences, Hatfield Polytechnic. He has worked on the history of nineteenth-century radicalism in Birmingham, and is increasingly interested in the fortunes of liberalism in the Third World.

John Robertson

John Robertson is a Tutor and Fellow in History at St Hugh's College, Oxford. He has written several articles on Hume and Smith and a recent book on *The Scottish Enlightenment and the Militia Issue* (John Donald, 1985). He is currently working on a comparison of the Scottish and the Neapolitan enlightenments.

Frederick Rosen

Frederick Rosen is Reader in the History of Political Thought, University College London and General Editor and Director of the Bentham Project. He is the author of *Jeremy Bentham and Representative Democracy* (Oxford University Press, 1983) and co-editor with J. H. Burns of Bentham's *Constitutional Code*, vol. 1 (Oxford University Press, 1983).

Chapter one

Introduction

Richard Bellamy

Liberalism is a notoriously elusive notion, largely because it is extremely difficult to circumscribe and define accurately its terms of reference. It has been variously employed to denote an organized political tendency, a cultural allegiance to certain values intrinsic to Western civilization, and the ideology of capitalism. None of these definitions seems particularly satisfactory for our purposes. Many of the figures examined in this volume defined themselves as Radicals and Whigs rather than as Liberals; indeed, the party itself only came into existence mid-way through our period. Yet if party affiliation is too narrow to capture the nature of liberalism, then regarding it simply as 'an attitude to life' based on a commitment to individual freedom and rational enquiry is too broad.[1] This approach quickly degenerates into the absurdity of finding anticipations of liberalism as far back as Socrates, apparently a 'notable liberal of ancient times',[2] or in Christianity, or at the very least identifying it as 'the outstanding doctrine' of 'the last four centuries' of European history.[3] These and analogous views amount to little more than the truism that liberalism, in common with much else, has been the beneficiary of prior intellectual developments, and in particular those revolutions in Western thought associated with the Renaissance and the Reformation which have done so much to shape the modern world.

The third option canvassed above appears more promising in offering a degree of specificity which does not exclude those who frequently adopted the prevalent assumptions of liberalism without subscribing either to a party or even a doctrine labelled unequivocally as liberal. Historically, there are good *prima facie* grounds for linking liberalism with the political and economic transformations associated with the English, French, and industrial revolutions, respectively. For as a consciously espoused set of ideas it increasingly came to describe a new type of social order related to a novel mode of production that was in marked contrast to either feudalism or the ancient republics. From this perspective, liberalism can be identified with the various struggles to safeguard and expand various aspects of individual freedom: from the attack on the arbitrary government of absolute monarchs in the seventeenth century, to the battles against aristocratic privilege, through the movements for parliamentary reform and free trade in the nineteenth century. These conflicts reflected in turn the growing prominence of the middle

1

classes, and the attempt to create a society of economically and politically independent individuals whose qualities mirrored their aspirations and interests.

If liberal theorists sought to come to terms with the social, economic, and political implications of the emergent capitalist system, it would be excessively reductive to regard their writings as contributions to a unitary body of principles dubbed the capitalist ideology. According to this intellectual construct, the liberal agent was a self-interested atomistic individual, driven by a series of self-referential desires to acquire and produce material goods. The aim of liberal politics consisted in allowing the fullest range possible to these passions in order to enable the maximal individual liberty for the production and accumulation of material wealth.[4] Politics was subordinated to the naturally harmonious causal properties of social relations, so that liberalism came to form the philosophical counterpart to *laissez-faire* economics, On the contrary, liberals were haunted by this ethos of egoistic, possessive individualism and strenuously battled against it. A more accurate version of the liberal ideal would consist of a meritocratic society of self-reliant and responsible citizens, co-operating together in pursuit of individual, social, material, and moral improvement. Liberalism incorporated a variety of heterogeneous political languages, and evolved piecemeal over a long period of social change. Intellectual sources as diverse as natural rights doctrines, Whiggism, classical political economy, utilitarianism, evangelical Christianity, idealism, and evolutionary biology all played a part in liberal ideology, modifying its understanding of, and emphasis on, the market mechanism and property ownership. Liberalism may have been the ethos of the bourgeoisie but it cannot be regarded as a narrow economic doctrine. Its hegemonic sway arose from its having broader cultural roots. Notions such as the belief in progress and reason and the emphasis on individual character shaped as well as reflected the economic and social interests of the middle classes, informing their attitude towards the role of the state and the management of the economy. The conceptual, socio-economic, and political elements of liberal doctrine were inextricably interconnected, forming part of a single historical process.

The interdisciplinary approach adopted in this book, which brings together the work of political historians and historians of political thought, aims to capture some of this complexity by offering a broader view of liberalism than studies written from one or other of these perspectives alone usually do. In a variety of ways, each author has endeavoured to chart the interplay between liberal theory and practice in nineteenth-century Britain. The thinkers and politicians examined below are seen as employing and developing various political vocabularies in order to address a particular practical context. Understanding a given liberal theorist involves an appreciation of both the shifting political and social relations and the alterations in intellectual conventions, not just to explain one by the other, but because of the mutual dependence and internal dynamics of both. Instead of a unitary and static liberal ideology, this volume provides an analysis of a variety of liberalisms, stemming from diverse epistemological and political traditions, and explores some of the ways in which they evolved through their interactions with each other and with an emerging mass industrial society.

Adam Smith is frequently regarded as the apostle of *laissez-faire* economic liberalism. However, recent commentators have drawn attention to the important political dimensions of his economic writings deriving from the Whig and civic humanist traditions.[5] As the chapters by John Robertson and Bianca Fontana show, nineteenth-century liberalism was as indebted to these elements of his work as it was to his advocacy of the free market. Central to Smith's politics was his understanding of the transition from feudal to commercial society stemming from his stadial theory of social progress. He maintained that the crucial aspect of this transformation consisted in the change in manners and patterns of behaviour, rather than in any alterations in the form of government. Neither the civic virtues of the city republics, nor the modifying influence of the deferential morality of an aristocratic society based on rank and patronage, were available or appropriate to the market economy. In a commercial system, individuals took up particular economic functions and contributed to the wealth of the nation from motivations of personal gain alone. This circumstance posed a problem, for Smith questioned the self-regulating capacity of market forces. He doubted that people had either the foresight or the self-restraint not to seek to subvert the freedom of the market for their own short-term advantage. For if your orientations were largely egoistic, why should you act in ways injurious to your own interests simply because the results were beneficial, in the long run, to the interests of others? He appreciated that private vices only yielded public benefits given certain structural arrangements which ensured the competitiveness of the system, preserved private property rights, and upheld the fairness of contracts and exchange. Far from being a doctrinaire believer in non-interventionist government, he saw that without the support of the state, these essential regulative structures would wither. The difficulty confronting the political theorist was how to make up for the absence of public spiritedness brought about by the market ethos, so as to ensure that the government did not come under the influence of particular interests seeking to undermine the very system it was required to uphold. For if the dependence of landlords and labourers on rent and wages respectively meant that their interests were generally linked to the prosperity of the country as a whole, Smith's analysis of the mercantile system had revealed that merchants and manufacturers characteristically sought to 'deceive and even to oppress the publick' by persuading governments to grant them corporate privileges to protect their profits.[6]

Robertson argues that Smith's awareness of this conflict of interests formed the basis for his treatment of the relationship between government and the economy. Institutional arrangements were required both to motivate individuals to provide those public services, such as defence, the administration of justice, schools, and a transport system, necessary for any modern society, and to ensure that no group gained control of the state apparatus for their own sectional advantages. Robertson shows how Smith believed that they could be regulated by the economic criteria of the division of labour, competition, and self-interest. At the same time, Smith contended that the resulting economical government would also be a 'free government', providing for political as well as civil liberty. Smith retained a sensitivity to civic republican worries relating to the corrupting influence of luxury on the body politic, the effeminacy of modern manners once the martial virtues were no longer practised, and the importance of political participation to safeguard the freedom of the polity. These concerns were reinforced by Smith's prescient understanding of the alienating and enervating effects of factory work and modern urban life on the labouring classes. Smith hoped that a public system of education would place the lower orders in a position to assert their interests against the anti-social ones of the mercantile class. Once again, the reasoning behind this proposal was economic, the control of government revenue by subjecting the raising of taxation to the consent of these who paid it – a project consistent with the newly-emergent British doctrine of Parliamentary sovereignty.

Bianca Fontana traces the transmission of Smithean ideas to England via the *Edinburgh Review*, and with them the passage from Whiggism to liberalism. Whig doctrine amalgamated a number of other political discourses, combining the Lockean theory of natural rights to life, liberty, and property, with constitutionalist notions of limited monarchy, mixed government, and the balance of interests, republican fears about the effects of luxury on civic virtue and an historicist thesis concerning the need to adapt political institutions to the changing customs of the populace. The constitutional settlement of 1688 came to mark the high-point of such a process of successful adaptation, with Whiggism being gradually turned from an opposition into an establishment ideology, supporting the eighteenth-century ruling oligarchy of the commercial and landed classes. Whereas Smith has been dubbed a 'sceptical Whig',[7] his theory became 'vulgarized' by his more anglicized followers and successors. The Scottish theory of the progress of society remained crucial to the reviewers' understanding of politics, who connected it to the civilizing effects of a wider distribution of property and the disproportionate growth of the 'middling ranks'. However, what had been a discovery for Smith became a nineteenth-century platitude in the works of writers such as the great Whig historian, T. B. Macaulay. A regular contributor to the *Review*, Macaulay's advocacy of constitutional adjustment to admit the middle classes to the franchise so as to reconcile the landowners and capitalists,[8] typified the Whig belief in the necessity of timely reform to meet evolving social circumstances. Behind such arguments lay a desire to protect the position of the landed aristocracy by ensuring a continued balance of interest between the three orders of society. They were concerned that a failure to compromise might result in the middle classes joining with the unpropertied masses, whose lack of a stake in the community would precipitate a revolution akin to the English of 1642–6 or the French of 1789. The 1832 Reform Act, with its limited extension of the suffrage, encapsulated their pragmatic position.

Whiggism is habitually contrasted with another important strand in Victorian

4

liberalism – the Benthamite utilitarianism of the Philosophic Radicals.[9] The Whigs' gradualism and their concern with balance were castigated by the Radicals as the self-serving temporizing of the aristocratic Few, concerned to preserve the privileges of the landed gentry against the legitimate demands of the democratic Many. Although Smith and Macaulay employed notions of utility to explain the spontaneous emergence of a unique set of social institutions out of selfish interests, they did not seek to evaluate the system itself, let alone particular features of it, in utilitarian terms. The Radicals, in contrast, sought to do just this. The formula 'the greatest happiness of the greatest number' rendered individuals rather than groups the locus of interests and suggested that numerical criteria could be applied to assess the suitability of the existing constitutional framework for attaining the desired end. James Mill and Jeremy Bentham deliberately shifted the meanings of key Whig terms to suit their purposes. Thus, when they spoke of the need for 'checks' on self-interest, they meant the need to protect the majority from the actions of a powerful minority, not the importance of achieving an equilibrium between different social orders to preserve the mixed constitution.

Frederick Rosen notes how these features of Benthamism have earned it the reputation of being illiberal. However, Halévy, with whom this line of criticism originated,[10] 'failed to appreciate the significance of Bentham's emphasis on security as a replacement for the traditional idea of political liberty'. Bentham perceived that no political system could guarantee complete freedom for everyone. We require laws because the happiness of some individuals is liable on occasions to come into conflict with that of others. The best that can be achieved is to secure as many people as possible against such incursions so that they can exercise their liberty to maximize their happiness unimpeded. Largely as a result of James Mill's influence, Bentham was convinced that the best means of ensuring that legislation served this purpose was to hold the possessors of efficient power accountable to the body of the people.

Halévy also claimed to have found a second defect in Bentham's reasoning. Bentham's hedonistic psychology posed the problem of how to reconcile humankind's egoistic drives with the requirements of society, to make duty and interest coincide. According to Halévy's influential interpretation, Bentham agreed with Smith in assuming a 'natural harmony of interests' pertained in most economic relations, but was led away from this libertarian insight in his legislative theory, which held that sanctions were required artificially to create such an accord. In fact, no such contradiction existed. Bentham simply followed Smith's insight concerning the need for government to reinforce the framework of order and administration within which individuals pursued their interests. Since state employees frequently escaped market pressures, teachers, civil servants, judges, and prison governors all had to be placed under the necessity of exerting themselves for the general interest by careful institutional design. Smith had recognized also that a major responsibility of government must be the provision of 'certain public works and certain public institutions, which it can never be for the interest of any individual, or small number of individuals, to erect and maintain.'[11] In the growing urban and industrial environment of early Victorian Britain, Benthamite disciples such as Edwin Chadwick increasingly saw that these 'public goods' included the provision of a healthy atmosphere and the control of certain 'externalities' such as pollution. Indeed, Bentham's notion of 'security' brought with it the acknowledgement that health, education, and welfare, no less than real property and wealth, formed preconditions for the exercise of liberty.

Stephen Conway, in chapter 5, details the Benthamite influence on the revolutionary explosion of governmental activity in this period. Two points need stressing in this regard. First, in spite of the dramatic increase in the quantity of government interference, Dicey was quite right not to regard this as a move from 'individualism' to 'collectivism'.[12] Its justification remained impeccably individualist and aimed at maintaining the conditions of genuinely free economic competition. Second, the principles guiding the funding and administration of these new agencies remained the Smithean ones of efficiency and equity. Bentham continued to believe that accountability was best ensured through the purse, that services should be as self-financing as possible, and that those taxes which were levied ought to fall on the most able to pay, be convenient to collect, and should not interfere with the allocative mechanism, or deter individual effort. However, it should be recalled that his belief in the diminishing marginal utility of wealth made him think an ever more egalitarian distribution of resources was possible with the increase of abundance.

John Stuart Mill's critique of Benthamism, and his retrospective endorsement of Macaulay's criticism of his father's *Essay on Government*, added a further twist to the complex intertwining of the languages of liberalism. John Gibbins maintains that Mill's sense of the difficulties attendant upon the 'transitional' nature of English society as it entered the mass industrial age provides the key to understanding his various political positions. Many of these worries were variations upon Whig themes, and Mill's historical insights could just as well be taken from the Scottish conjectural history of John Millar or Smith as from the sociology of Comte or the writings of Guizot and de Tocqueville, as he claimed. As Fontana also notes, Mill's concern that the 'mildness of manners' associated with 'civilization' produced 'moral effeminacy', 'torpidity and cowardice', rendered people 'less heroic', unable to support pain or difficulty or even 'disagreeable ideas', and confined their energies to 'money-getting' so that public service was neglected, echoed earlier civic republican and Country fears. Of course, Mill added specifically nineteenth-century refinements, such as the view that the division of labour created new types of dependency, and the anxiety about the 'tyranny of the majority'. Even more than Smith, he appreciated that the 'salutory influence' of public opinion in a small society was 'lost in the hubbub' of modern cities.[13]

Mill's remedy for these evils was to devise forms of economic co-operation which would revive the value of competition, and to design 'national institutions of education and forms of polity, calculated to invigorate the individual character'. There were two aspects to the Victorian emphasis on 'character'. On the one hand, the insistence on the related virtues of thrift, self-help, and individual effort were directed against the paternalistic ethos of the landed aristocracy. They were treated as a parasitic class whose inherited wealth and income from rents was 'unearned'. Drawing on a number of sources, from the muscular Protestantism of evangelical Christianity to Ricardian economics, liberals counterposed to the aristocratic ideal of a paternalistic society based on land and hierarchical status, and tied together by patronage, the bourgeois ideal of a society of self-made entrepreneurs whose riches and position depended on merit and effort. The campaign to repeal the Corn Laws and the movement for free trade generally epitomized this struggle between the two rival ideals. On the other hand, the language of character was employed to moralize the working classes. According to the Malthusian thinking of classical political economy, the economic surplus did not admit of infinite expansion. The only way for the poor to improve their standard of living was by practising self-restraint, particularly in relation to birth control, so as to avoid glutting the labour market or causing demand to outstrip supply. Moreover, through the spread of bourgeois habits, liberals aimed to pre-empt the threat of a revolt from below and gain an ally against aristocratic privilege. Numerous institutions, from elementary schools and Mechanics' Institutes to friendly societies, co-operatives, and savings banks, were founded to help inculcate the virtues of prudence and self-reliance among the general populace. The extension of the franchise and the spread of democracy at both local and national levels were similarly justified as a means to elevate the lower orders through the practice of self-government and the exercise of civic responsibilities.[14] As Gibbins indicates in chapter 6, Mill's advocacy of both a judicious reform of the electoral system and profit-sharing in industry was designed for the improvement of the character of the masses so as gradually to bring about the co-operation of capital and labour on the basis of a common morality. In this manner, the gospel of self-help was made to apply to all strata of society, promising the prospect of better living conditions for the poor, and the removal of all barriers to the entry of every hard-working citizen into the life-style of the middle classes.

Mill looked on Gladstone as the statesman 'in whom the spirit of improvement is incarnate, and in whose career as minister the characteristic feature has been to seek out things that require or admit of improvement.'[15] The moral earnestness of Mill's vision, his picture of life as a Manichaean struggle between the allure of the lower pleasures and the improving higher ones, of aristocratic unearned privilege versus the self-made man, was quintessential Gladstonianism. In his chapter, Christopher Harvie illustrates Gladstone's achievement in harnessing these sentiments, already strong in middle-class political movements such as the Anti-Corn Law League and the nonconformist culture of skilled manual workers, to the parliamentary Liberal Party. Of course, Gladstone's premises were theological, so that he spoke of the workings of providence rather than the course of history, of salvation and the triumph of righteousness over sin rather than the more secular progress desired by Mill. Yet both shared the belief that conflict and turmoil had to be maintained to avoid stagnation, and that the spread of individual responsibility was the best means of doing this.[16] Gladstone attacked the 'poison' of protectionism and espoused free trade in order to allow God's moral economy to reveal itself. Its providentially arranged system of rewards and punishments moved men to virtue and so elevated the whole of society. Extending the franchise became a matter not of balance or citizen rights, so much as a question of moral entitlement: '[S]elf-command, self-control, respect for order, patience under suffering, confidence in the law and regard for superiors' were the qualities he claimed to find among the 'better part' of the working classes, and which now brought them 'within the pale of the constitution'. [17] The uplifting spirit of the campaigns for parliamentary reform and repeal of the Corn Laws had to be maintained through attacks on the iniquities of foreign powers and the rooting-out of further domestic blocks to individual self-development, such as the power of the Church and landed establishment in Ireland. By such means, Gladstone sought to involve the lower classes in morally enhancing issues rather than gaining their allegiance by pandering, as he would have seen it, to their material welfare. By 1880, his galvanizing of the provinces had turned elections into a recognizably modern affair, with a national campaign fought on clear-cut issues and five-sixths of the constituencies being contested, even if the electorate still fell short of full adult male suffrage. Along the way, he had also introduced those other features of modern politics: charismatic leadership, party machines, and executive government.

Responding to the need of the age for scientific proof of essentially religious doctrines, Spencer sought to justify liberal ideals as immanent laws of organic life. Although his coining of the phrase the 'survival of the fittest' gained him the reputation of being a Social Darwinist, his evolutionary theory drew its support from the Lamarckian model of adaptation to the environment and the inheritance of acquired characteristics, rather than Darwin's thesis of the competitive struggle for existence. Lamarck's view fitted the Victorian notion of the develop-ment of national character through the judicious reward of effort far more easily than Darwin's. In general, Spencer defended *laissez-faire* not because he thought the weakest should go to the wall, but so that people would be forced to adapt themselves through their own efforts and their improvements became 'organic' in the race. For Spencer, the character of a whole society depended on the characters of all its constituent parts aggregated together. Even so, Tim Gray's analysis, in chapter 7, indicates that a large degree of fudging was necessary for Spencer to show that the liberal ideal he advocated was the natural conclusion of the evolutionary process.

Spencer's fully evolved society consisted of a purified form of mid-nineteenth-century market society, largely corresponding to the goals of the provincial nonconformist Radicals of the 1840s to whose ranks he had belonged.[18] The contrast between the 'militant' and 'industrial' stages reflected the liberal commonplace that free trade would abolish war. Spencer envisaged a future society of independent producers who co-operated for their mutual benefit in companies they owned. All workers would start on an equal footing and voluntarily contract into the association, retaining their independence within it. No status barriers would exist – a person's reputation deriving from his actions and the rewards he obtained by them. There would be no special privileges transmitted by birth, even property rights were initially regarded by Spencer as creating inequalities of wealth which frustrated the attempts of later generations to raise themselves through their own efforts. Finally, lack of a hierarchical structure meant that all decisions were made by mutual agreement. Spencer's ideal provided the most complete picture of the mid-Victorian liberal utopia. Rather than being based on 'egoism', it assumed a process of moral change towards 'altruism'. He even hinted at a third stage, 'aesthetic' society, in which work was subordinated to 'higher activities' of a spiritual and intellectual kind.[19]

Spencer was well aware that contemporary reality frequently fell far short of this picture. He admitted that freedom of contract for the wage-earning factory hand 'amounts in practice to little more than the ability to exchange one form of slavery for another',[20] and that '[a] system of keen competition carried on, as it is, without adequate moral restraint is very much a system of commercial cannibalism.'[21] However, he generally treated such aberrations as temporary phases arising from some contrived hindrance to the mechanism of adaptation. Unfortunately for him, his long life meant that he lived to see forms of industrial and social organization that largely contradicted his expectations, while new scientific discoveries discredited his evolutionary theory. In such an environment, his ideas lost most of their plausibility and progressive appeal, and were taken up and twisted to justify a very different style of capitalism from anything he had imagined.

Spencer had attempted to recruit science to the defence of opinions that had originated largely in an evangelical context. However, by the 1880s the naturalist thesis that moral propositions and progress could be derived from a determined course of organic evolution was under attack from a number of directions. For many, it seemed simpler and more coherent to associate them with the exercise of will – a step taken by the British Idealists. Furthermore, ambiguity persisted in much character discourse concerning the degree to which changes in social structure were the cause or effect of alterations in individual morality. Mill had already noted the reciprocal relationship between character and those political institutions fostering its development. T. H. Green now argued that the state had a duty to provide the social preconditions necessary for the attainment of character. He recognized that poverty, bad housing, alcoholism, and unemployment hindered the deprived's capacity for self-development. However, he did not thereby move in the direction of collectivism, as some commentators maintain. He aimed to stimulate self-help and voluntary action, not to substitute for it with government-funded schemes. Richard Bellamy shows in chapter 8, that Green is best seen as providing a self-conscious attempt to express the underlying assumptions and aspirations of Victorian liberalism in philosophical language. Green still blamed the degradation of the masses on the continued effects of 'feudal' habits and arrangements. He justified state intervention to rectify past abuses and to foster the conventional set of liberal attitudes associated with the respectable citizen. His faith in the benefits of a morally regulated capitalist system remained firm. Nevertheless, Green's approach raises the question of the appropriateness of treating character or liberty as an attribute of the individual when the institutions defining liberties and restrictions for a particular society themselves form the capacity of its members for certain types of action. For how autonomous or virtuous are agents whose political environment gives them no option but to be so? This dilemma had particular relevance for Green's views on the drink question and his moralistic approach to social reform generally.

It became increasingly difficult for liberals to portray their own values as transcending class and defining the common good. From the 1880s onwards, a number of changes within British society placed their ideals under a severe strain.[22] There was a noticeable downturn in the rate of economic growth under the impact of the depression of the 1870s and the competition of foreign states, particularly Germany. If real incomes had risen, the distribution of wealth had become more inequitable, with poverty and unemployment attaining unprecedented levels. The surveys of Booth and Rowntree, conducted in London (1889) and York (1899) respectively, revealed that a third of the population in these urban areas had less than the 'minimum necessary expenditure for the maintenance of merely physical health'.[23] The possibilities for social advancement had also declined. Businesses outgrew the small-scale private partnerships run by owner-managers idealized by Spencer. Joint-stock companies managed by professional directors, a form of organization condemned by all the theorists considered so far, became the norm. Even the giant family firms that survived could no longer be adequately controlled at shop-floor level by their owners. The ideal of the self-made man, who rose from manual worker to captain of industry, became an anachronism, even as a myth. The expansion of large enterprises undermined many of the principles of the entrepreneurial ethos characteristic of mid-Victorian liberalism. For the new corporate capitalists the distinction between earned income from capital and unearned income from land did not make much sense, and open competition seemed less in their interest than its limitation by price agreements, amalgamations, and mergers. Finally, the undermining of the Gladstonian 'labourer aristocracy' of skilled workers by new techniques and the decline of older industries threatened the cultural and political ties uniting them to liberalism. During the 1889 dock strike, for example, this trend combined with a socialist revival and led to pressure for the creation of a mass democracy and political representation by an autonomous labour movement rather than the Liberal Party.

Michael Freeden, in chapter 10, and Alan Hooper, in chapter 11, discuss the manoeuvrings of liberal theory and practice as it attempted to respond to these social changes. Freeden describes how the New Liberalism arrived at a broader conception of the role of the state through, to quote Hobson, 'a fuller appreciation of individual liberty contained in the provision of equal opportunities for self-development'.[24] Like Green, they explored the effects of social deprivation on individual character, unlike him, questioning various nostrums of traditional liberalism in the process. The notion of a self-regulating free market, reflecting natural law and epitomizing social justice, was eroded by the economic ills of recurrent capitalist crises with their mass unemployment. Certain dogmas of classical political economy, such as the assumption of a natural equilibrium between supply and demand, the wages fund, and the fear of economic stagnation, began to be rejected, and distributional arrangements gained a certain autonomy from questions of production. The New Liberalism attempt to negotiate a path between 'individualism' and 'socialism' so as to accommodate both working- and middle-class demands at a time when these groups were beginning to realign politically into Labour and Conservative respectively. The most important innovation in this regard was the justification of a limited degree of redistributive taxation on the basis of an irreducible social element in the creation of wealth. This 'unearned' surplus could be used to finance positive measures of welfare relief such as pensions and unemployment benefit without encroaching on the traditional liberal emphasis on individual desert and merit. New forms of social and economic power replaced the earlier emphasis on aristocratic privilege as possible sources of injustice preventing the progress of liberal values throughout society.

In such ways, the New Liberals sought to adapt the old ethical language to meet the imperatives of a collectivist and democratic age. By selective excision and reformulation, they preserved much of the liberal tradition. Biological metaphors, as Freeden observes, greatly aided this attempt. Britain's relative decline was attributed to moral and physical 'unfitness'. However, the fusion of economic and ethical argument proved ambiguous. Social reform remained geared to improving the character and productivity of the individual worker, a policy with potentially disturbing consequences for the mentally, physically, or morally, 'unfit'. Welfare continued to be targeted towards the 'deserving' poor, with the object of helping them contribute to the common good. If liberal intellectuals tended to step back from such conclusions, politicians and businessmen who backed these schemes demanded that social legislation be judged by its tangible benefits for 'national efficiency'. Thus the tension between the Gladstonian view of the state as a moral force, an agent for the maintenance of ethical values between itself, its citizens, and other states, and the economic notion of the state as a material force, a power entitled actively to pursue the prosperity of its citizens, if necessary in conflict with other states, became increasingly manifest. The party split on Irish Home Rule, then the Boer War, imperialism, and tariff reform. The First World War proved an important turning-point, finally shaking the liberal conviction in the progressive dynamic of history as the unfolding of reason and human freedom.

Alan Hooper reminds us that liberalism did not simply move to the left in order to outflank the new working-class movements. For many of its erstwhile supporters, it was much more natural to realign themselves on the right. Indeed, it had been Chamberlain's attempt to build a cross-class coalition with social imperialist policies which had galvanized the Liberals into action on the social question. Chamberlain tried to emulate the German model of the developmental, paternalistic state, although his version of corporatism derived its inspiration from the experience of English Radicalism in his native Birmingham. Radical sources fed the left as well, of course, most particularly via the Fabians and the writings of the Webbs. Chamberlain's rightwards move, along with the remaining Whigs, has often been treated as a personal aberration, a product of his exasperation at Gladstone's frustration of his own career and the Radical Programme with what he perceived as the largely irrelevant cause of Irish Home Rule. However, with a class-based mass electorate placing Victorian values under increasing strain, a businessman like Chamberlain could quite rationally regard the Tories as a better prospect for his policy of protectionism and populist imperialism than a demoralized Liberal Party. The complex reasons underlying the failure of this project are explored by Alan Hooper. Many have regarded it as a movement abhorrent to the ethos of British liberalism. Halévy looked on Chamberlain's measures as indicative of the illiberal and constructivist tendencies he claimed to have found at the philosophical heart of Radicalism. Hooper indicates it would be fairer to note that British society had drastically altered, undermining both the values and the practical context presupposed by the political tradition explored in this book.

To a considerable extent, our understanding of the meaning and importance of key political terms and institutions, such as freedom, social justice, democracy, and the market, still bears the stamp of their liberal origins. Modern conservatives and socialists, as well as self-declared liberals, naturally employ parts of this ideological heritage. Thus, conservatives frequently appeal to the virtues of economic competition and limited government, and socialists to the ideal of a community of self-governing producers. The notion of citizenship within Western democracies is permeated by liberal assumptions concerning the rights and duties of the individual. Yet a return to Victorian values in modern circumstances would be seriously misguided. For much of liberalism has been shaped by aspirations and beliefs which have ceased to command our allegiance and addressed social and political conditions which no longer exist. Within the pluralistic and complex mass societies of today, dominated as they are by imposing structures of corporate and bureaucratic power and an intricate international market, the Victorian moral code of self-improvement has become little more than a useful fiction for justifying forms of oppression and privilege akin to those liberals originally sought to remove. Today, the project of securing individual liberty requires a very different defence and will call for quite different social and political institutions from those imagined by even the most farsighted of nineteenth-century thinkers.[25]

Notes

I am grateful to Louise Dominian, John Gibbins, Paul Smart, and the publisher's anonymous readers for their comments on various versions of this introduction.

1 Throughout this introduction I use liberalism to refer to the broad school of thought, and Liberalism to refer to the doctrine of the parliamentary party. Liberal and liberal are employed in an analogous manner.
2 J. Salwyn Schapiro (ed.), *Liberalism: Its Meaning and History* (Amsterdam, 1958), pp. 14, 94, cited in A. Arblaster, *The Rise and Decline of Western Liberalism* (Oxford, 1984), p. 12. John Gray, *Liberalism* (Milton Keynes, 1986) also adopts the Plato to NATO approach, remarking: 'It is in Pericles, perhaps, that we find the clearest statement of the liberal outlook ...' (p. 3).
3 Harold J. Laski, *The Rise of European Liberalism* (London, 1936), p. 5.
4 The 'possessive individualist' interpretation of liberalism is particularly prevalent among critics on the left, e.g. S. Wolin, *Politics and Vision: Continuity and Innovation in Western Political Thought* (Boston, 1960), ch. 9; C. B. Macpherson, *The Political Theory of Possessive Individualism* (Oxford, 1962); and Arblaster, *Western Liberalism*, although a number of conservatives also share this view, e.g. L. Strauss, *Liberalism: Ancient and Modern* (New York, 1968).
5 See D. Winch, *Adam Smith's Politics: An Essay in Historiographic Revisionism* (Cambridge, 1978).
6 A. Smith, *An Inquiry into the Nature and Causes of the Wealth of Nations*, eds R. H. Campbell, A. S. Skinner, and W. B. Todd (Oxford, 1976), I. xi. p. 10.
7 D. Forbes, '"Sceptical Whiggism", Commerce and Liberty', in A. S. Skinner and T. Wilson (eds), *Essays on Adam Smith* (Oxford, 1975), pp. 179–201.
8 E.g. T. B. Macaulay, review of H. Hallam, *The Constitutional History of England*, *Edinburgh Review*, 48 (September 1828), pp. 167–8.
9 See S. Collini, D. Winch, and J. Burrow, *That Noble Science of Politics: A Study in Nineteenth-Century Intellectual History* (Cambridge, 1983), ch. 3, for a full discussion of the relations between the two traditions, with specific reference to the famous debate between James Mill and T. B. Macaulay over the former's *Essay on Government*. The relevant articles are reproduced in J. Lively and J. Rees (eds), *Utilitarian Logic and Politics: James Mill's 'Essay on Government', Macaulay's Critique, and the Ensuing Debate* (Oxford, 1978).
10 E. Halévy, *The Growth of Philosophic Radicalism*, trans. M. Morris (London, 1928), pp. 17, 33.
11 Smith, *Wealth of Nations*, V.i.c.1.
12 A. V. Dicey, *Lectures on the Relation between Law and Legislation in the Nineteenth Century* (London: 1905), p. 169.
13 J. S. Mill, 'Civilization' (1836), in *Essays on Politics and Society*, I, J. M. Robson (ed.), *Collected Works* (Toronto, 1977), Vol. XVIII, pp. 117–47. For a specific analysis of this article as an illustration of the influence of Whiggish themes on liberalism, see J. Burrow, *Whigs and Liberals: Continuity and Change in English Political Thought* (Oxford, 1988), pp. 77–87, 100–7.
14 The above draws on S. Collini, 'The Idea of "Character" in Victorian Political Thought', *Transactions of the Royal Historical Society*, 5th Series, 35 (1985), pp. 29–50; T. R. Tholfson, 'The Transition to Democracy in Victorian England', *International Review of Social History*, VI (1961), pp. 226–48; idem, 'The Intellectual Origins of Mid-Victorian Stability', *Political Quarterly*, LXXVI (1971), pp. 57–91; and H. Perkin, *The Origins of Modern British Society* (London, 1969), chs VII and VIII.

15 Quoted by J. Morley, *The Life of William Ewart Gladstone* (London, 2nd edn, 1905), I, p. 757, and cited in I. Bradley, *The Optimists: Themes and Personalities in Victorian Liberalism* (London, 1980), p. 200.

16 I owe this comparison between Mill and Gladstone to the article by B. Hilton, 'Gladstone's Theological Politics', in M. Bentley and J. Stevenson (eds), *High and Low Politics in Modern Britain: Ten Studies* (Oxford, 1983), pp. 47–8.

17 W. E. Gladstone, debate on Baine's Bill, *Hansard*, 3rd series, CLXXV (1864), 324–5, cited in Bradley, *The Optimists*, p. 155.

18 See J. D. Y. Peel, *Herbert Spencer: The Evolution of a Sociologist* (London, 1971), esp. chs 1–4.

19 H. Spencer, *The Principles of Sociology*, 3 vols (London, 1876–96), I, p. 563.

20 Spencer, *Principles of Sociology*, III, p. 516.

21 H. Spencer, 'Morals of Trade' (1859), in *Essays Scientific, Political and Speculative*, 3 vols (London, 1891), p. 134.

22 The following paragraph summarizes Perkin, *Origins of Modern English Society*, ch. X.

23 Rowntree's definition of the poverty line, cited in ibid., p. 422.

24 J. A. Hobson, *The Crisis of Liberalism: New Issues of Democracy* (London, 1909), p. xii.

25 The most ambitious attempt to rethink the liberal public sphere remains that of J. Habermas, *Strukturwandel der Öffentlichkeit* (Neuwied-a-Rhein, 1962). My own more modest effort, *Liberalism and the Modern Social Order*, is forthcoming from Polity Press.

Chapter two

The legacy of Adam Smith: government and economic development in the *Wealth of Nations*[1]

John Robertson

'Considered as a branch of the science of a statesman or legislator', Adam Smith wrote in the *Wealth of Nations*, political economy proposes two distinct objects:

> first, to provide a plentiful revenue or subsistence for the people, or more properly to enable them to provide such a revenue or subsistence for themselves; and secondly, to supply the state or commonwealth with a revenue sufficient for the public services. It proposes to enrich both the people and the sovereign.[2]

Distinct as they are, however, the two objects of political economy as Smith here considers it are not necessarily in harmony: reading the *Wealth of Nations*, it emerges that the relation between economic development, 'the progress of opulence', and government, 'the state or commonwealth', presents a major problem. It is Smith's treatment of this problem in the *Wealth of Nations* that I propose to examine, in the conviction that it supplied a foundation-stone of Victorian liberalism.

The problem was not, of course, original to Smith: it has long been one of the staples of economic writing. But it confronted Smith with particular urgency in his own social and intellectual context in eighteenth-century Scotland. At the beginning of the century, the Scots had been required by the Treaty of Union with England to sacrifice their national political institutions to the quest for economic improvement; and the loss, however compensated, continued to cause them misgivings well into the second half of the century. Almost certainly under the stimulus of this experience, moreover, Scottish thinkers had placed the problem of the relation between government and economic development at the centre of their historical and political writings. First in the years preceding the Union, when Andrew Fletcher of Saltoun led a remarkably sophisticated debate on the national predicament, and again in the period of the Enlightenment, at the instigation of David Hume, the Scots had explored the demands which economic improvement makes of government institutions, and had sought to identify which form of government would be best adapted to the needs of a progressive, commercial society. It was this Scottish experience and debate which, I suggest, provided the immediate starting-point for Adam Smith's discussion of government and economic development in the *Wealth of Nations*.

The terms in which Smith's Scottish predecessors had come to grips with the problem were, as I have argued elsewhere, the terms of the civil tradition.[3] Of classical and more specifically Aristotelian genesis, the civic tradition's most authoritative exponents since the Renaissance had been the Florentine Machiavelli and the Englishman James Harrington.[4] The tradition's concepts focused upon the institutional, moral, and material conditions of free citizenship in a political community, viewed in a perspective secular and historical rather than theological and natural. These concepts defined a political community first and foremost by possession of a regular constitution, under which the institutions of civil government and a militia secured the freedom of all citizens to participate in the political life and defence of the community. Primary though the institutional framework was, it none the less depended on further moral and material conditions. If citizens were to take advantage of the freedom to participate given by the constitution, they must be capable of moral virtue, of a commitment to the public good. In turn, fulfilment of this moral condition of citizenship depended on the possession of material independence or autonomy: only those – assumed to be few in number – in a position to satisfy their needs without making themselves dependent on others were capable of the requisite civic virtue. Conversely, failure to observe these material and moral conditions brought corruption. For the Scots, it was precisely this interdependence of the social and moral and the institutional dimensions of citizenship in a political community that made the concepts of the civic tradition so applicable when they sought to relate the demands of material improvement to the continuing institutional requirements of government.

Even so, it was a peculiarly Scottish development of the civic tradition that adapted its terms to the positive pursuit of wealth. Hitherto, thinkers in the tradition had been hostile to wealth, preferring a social regime of Spartan austerity; at best, wealth had been approved as a private pursuit, which citizens should keep strictly separate from their public, political activity. For the Scots of 1700, however, to escape from poverty was a national priority, and Andrew Fletcher took the initiative to adapt civic concepts to the pursuit of wealth as a public good. In a series of economic, social, and political proposals, Fletcher offered to set the pursuit of economic improvement on a classically civic footing. As long as a clear differentiation of citizens from the unfree was maintained, and the participatory institutions of a national parliament and militia were safeguarded, economic improvement could be seen as quite consistent with – indeed, as the key to – Scotland's continuing survival as an independent political community.

Fletcher's particular vision of the Scottish political community may have been swept aside in the Treaty of Union; but the problem he had confronted continued to exercise the thinkers of the Scottish Enlightenment, David Hume first of all. He too deployed the concepts of the civic tradition to treat the problem: but where

Fletcher's ingenious adaptation had preserved the concepts' traditional significance, this was radically altered by Hume. For Hume combined the fundamental civic concepts of citizenship and liberty with very different, individualist principles drawn from the jurisprudential traditions of political thought.

Hume's starting-point was the proposition that wealth was created by the individual's free pursuit of his own interest: in the first instance, therefore, wealth was not a public good. On the contrary, it was precisely the attempts of those in power to appropriate wealth in the name of the public good that created the problem of government and economic development. To avoid that misappropriation of resources, Hume maintained that the priority for government in a commercial society must be to provide the maximum possible security for the individual's person and property, to ensure his freedom from interference. The issue of citizenship, for Hume, arose only on condition that every individual's personal liberty was thus secure. Once that liberty was secure, however, the issue of citizenship would itself acquire a new scope. For as wealth increases and extends through commercial society, so, Hume suggested, more and more of society's members will tend to acquire the material independence and moral capacity that, in civic terms, equip men to be citizens. No longer could citizenship be regarded as the preserve of a few, as Andrew Fletcher had regarded it. The universal provision of individual personal liberty would, in the long run, require a comparably universal extension of the citizen's political liberty.

The modification of civic concepts thus wrought by Hume in formulating the problem of government and economic development is confirmed in his response. Although nowhere in his writings is a solution to the problem explicitly advanced, one may be reconstructed by way of his observations on the history and influence of forms of government. These observations attached ever more importance to the adaptability of forms of government to economic progress. In Hume's view the principles of regular government were first developed by the ancient republics, which had thus been the first to encourage commerce and the arts. Subsequently, the principles of regular government had been assimilated by monarchies; and with the advantages of size, the absolute monarchies of modern Europe must now be supposed better adapted to economic development than the remaining republics, or even than the mixed government of Britain, of whose stability Hume was decidedly sceptical. Those monarchies, however, were still not perfect: their social conventions inhibited the full development of commerce and political liberty.

Inconclusive in themselves, these historical observations on forms of government can then be seen to provide the basis for Hume's own projected 'Idea of a perfect Commonwealth'. A republic in form, this perfect commonwealth was yet deliberately adapted to the circumstances of large states: it would thus achieve the combination of regular government with the advantages of scale required for economic development. At the same time, the principles on which Hume drew to frame this perfect commonwealth are readily identifiable as those of the civic tradition. Hume expressly presented it as an improvement on Harrington's *Oceana*, while its federal structure also recalls Fletcher's proposals. In line with his revision of the concept of citizenship itself, however, Hume had significantly modified the traditional assumptions of civic constitutionalism. In Hume's perfect commonwealth it is clear that priority will be given to securing the individuals's freedom from interference in the pursuit of his own interest; political liberty will be extended only gradually. As Hume made clear elsewhere, moreover, the exercise of liberty in any government will depend on the government's possession of sufficient authority: even in the perfect commonwealth, the freedoms of the individual and the citizen alike presuppose the authority of the government to enforce them. Thus balancing the civic form of liberty against the juridical, and both against authority, Hume's constitutional model represented a synthesis far removed from the strict civic vision of Andrew Fletcher. As a solution to the problem of government and economic development it was at the limits of the civic tradition.

In giving a detailed account of Adam Smith's treatment of the same problem in the *Wealth of Nations*, I shall view it in the light of the preceding Scottish debate, and Hume's contribution in particular. There are two respects, I shall argue, in which Smith developed his analysis beyond Hume's. The first is conceptual. Even more sharply than Hume, Smith recognized the limitations of traditional civic concepts. In formulating the problem of government and economic development, Smith confirmed that the corollary of universal individual freedom would be the eventual universalizing of citizenship and its liberty; at the same time he showed a keener awareness of the obstacles to universal citizenship in the circumstances of commercial society. Smith's solution to the problem went further still, positively discarding the institutional principles of the civic tradition in favour of principles associated with the novel, indigenously British doctrine of parliamentary sovereignty. If Smith thus seems to move beyond the conceptual limits of the civic tradition, however, it is by way of a second, no less important development in the form of his analysis. Compared with Hume's, Smiths's treatment of the problem of government and economic development in the *Wealth of Nations* is remarkable for its directness and coherence. Instead of considering the problem under the separate heads of commerce and government, Smith integrated the economic and political in one systematic analysis. Both in formulation and in resolution the problem became explicitly and straightforwardly one of 'political economy'.

Emphasizing these two features of Smith's analysis, my interpretation runs counter to the prevailing historical approach to 'Adam Smith's politics'. In the view first taken by Duncan Forbes, and recently reinforced by Donald Winch and Knud Haakonssen, Smith's political arguments should be understood primarily in the framework of natural jurisprudence.[5] My contrary assertion of a civic dimension in Smith's political arguments is, as I have indicated, a strictly qualified one.[6] It does not exclude but presupposes Smith's use of jurisprudential concepts.[7] It also presents Smith as far removed from the traditional civic perspective of Andrew Fletcher. Not only is it clear that Smith follows and extends Hume's revision of the traditional civic account of the material and moral conditions of citizenship; it is very much my argument that he looks outside the civic tradition for his constitutional principles. Nevertheless, Smith's treatment of the problem of government and economic development cannot be understood if jurisprudential concepts alone are taken to provide the determining framework of his thought. Smith may, like Hume, insist on the juridical freedom of the individual; but he also reiterates Hume's concern that government provide as well for the political liberty of citizens. Recognizably a civic concern in Hume, this is still so for Smith. However, the extension of political liberty in commercial society may have to be balanced against the need to ensure the individual's juridical freedom, Smith continues to insist on its importance, and hence on the importance of citizenship. If, as indeed I argue, Smith moves beyond the civic tradition, it is only after having at once affirmed and transformed these, the tradition's fundamental concepts of liberty and citizenship.

A second difference with the current jurisprudential approach to Smith's politics is implicit in this paper's suggestion that the relation between government and economic development is discussed in the *Wealth of Nations* by the integration of political with economic analysis within 'political economy'. Holding that the *Wealth of Nations* was, in Bagehot's phrase, but 'the enduring particular result' of 'a comprehensive and diffused ambition',[8] exponents of the jurisprudential approach have been content to regard the political arguments of the work as more or less fragmentary and underdeveloped. Their coherence, it is supposed, is to be established not within the *Wealth of Nations*, but in the context of Smith's larger project of a 'science of the legislator'.[9] In support of such an approach to the *Wealth of Nations*, moreover, there is Smith's own view of the work. It should be seen, Smith explained in 1790, at the very end of his life, as a partial fulfilment of the promise he had made in 1759 to follow the *Theory of Moral Sentiments* with 'an account of the general principles of law and government'. The *Wealth of Nations* covered the principles of revenue, police and arms; but Smith still intended to complete the account by writing 'the theory of jurisprudence'.[10] As for the particular problem of government and economic development, it was treated in the *Wealth of Nations* as a problem of 'political economy' considered as a 'branch of the science of a statesman or legislator'.

Faced with Smith's own word on the relation of the *Wealth of Nations* and its 'political economy' to his greater design, my challenge to the jurisprudential approach again needs careful qualification. It is not my intention to deny that the political arguments of the *Wealth of Nations* may be profitably and consistently related to the arguments of Smith's other works. Still less is it to detract from the scope of Smith's intellectual ambition, the grandeur of his vision of his lifework. But that ambition was, after all, unfulfilled, that lifework never completed. The *Wealth of Nations* was the only major work Smith actually published after the *Theory of Moral Sentiments*. Once he had done so, he appears to have devoted the greater part of his remaining energy to revising those two works, not to writing the theory of jurisprudence.[11] However much Smith still cherished his 'comprehensive and diffused ambition', it was to the enduring of the particular results that he himself gave priority. In these circumstances, it does not seem necessary to give overriding weight to Smith's declarations of larger intent. It is not only permissible but preferable to begin with what he achieved and completed, and to work outwards from the *Wealth of Nations* to his larger enterprise, in so far as that can be reconstructed.

Such is the approach of this paper. It is simply my contention that when the political arguments of the *Wealth of Nations* are studied in relation to the same work's economic principles, they can together be understood independently of their place in any large enterprise.[12] Far from being fragmentary and underdeveloped, those arguments have in the *Wealth of Nations* a coherence of their own within the analytical framework of 'political economy'. This political economy Smith might still introduce as 'a branch of the science of a statesman or legislator'. But the course of his subsequent analysis of the specific problem of government and economic development indicates that it is a branch which has become internally self-sufficient, and capable of direct application by the legislator. To approach the *Wealth of Nations* as a coherent, substantially independent work, is, moreover, not only in line with Smith's own priorities: it is to see the work as it was seen by most of its subsequent nineteenth-century readers. Indifferent to the *Theory of Moral Sentiments* and unaware of the contents of the Lectures on Jurisprudence, almost all of its Victorian readers encountered the *Wealth of Nations* on its own, and understood it in ignorance of its place in Smith's larger project. By tying Smith's achievement too closely to a particular intellectual inheritance, the modern jurisprudential approach has made it unnecessarily difficult to understand his work's subsequent impact. But if students of politics and political economy, and, still more, statesmen and legislators came in the nineteenth century to revere the *Wealth of Nations* as a source of liberal doctrine, it was, I suggest because there Smith confronted the great problem of government and the economy and offered to resolve it in one coherent set of arguments, the arguments of political economy. Comprehensive and self-sufficient, the *Wealth of Nations*, not the unwritten 'science of the statesman or legislator', was the foundation of Victorian liberalism.

Smith began his analysis of the relation between government and economic development from the same ground as Hume. His point of departure was the conviction that the individual's self-interested pursuit of wealth – the natural desire of 'bettering our condition', in the words of the *Wealth of Nations* – is the motor of the progress of society as a whole.[13] At the same time, Smith assumed that the cultivation of self-interest depended upon the security of property: and hence, again like Hume (and almost every other thinker in the jurisprudential tradition), he identified government's provision of that security through the institutions of justice and defence as the necessary condition of society's progress. Necessary though it thus is, however, the relation between government and economic development is also potentially problematic. In language rather more categorical than Hume's, Smith contended that 'the whole, or almost the whole public revenue, is in most countries employed in maintaining unproductive hands'. Should those 'unproductive' hands multiply unnecessarily, their demands may so encroach upon the funds necessary to maintain productive labour that economic development is checked and, before long, reversed.[14] Smith, it is true, immediately went on to proclaim his confidence that 'the uniform, constant, and uninterrupted effort of every man to better his condition' is frequently sufficient to sustain 'the natural progress of things towards improvement, in spite both of the extravagance of government, and of the greatest errors of administration'.[15] Nevertheless, underlying the *Wealth of Nations* is a conviction that in the course of improvement there is an intensified pressure on those in government to frustrate the natural enterprise of society.

This conviction is rooted in an analysis of the deepening conflict of interests within commercial society. Here Smith broke ground untilled by Hume. Where his predecessor thought only broadly of factions from interest, Smith analysed commercial society in specific economic terms, identifying the fundamental interests within it by their different sources of revenue or income. The 'three great, original and constituent orders of every civilized society, from whose revenue that of every other is ultimately derived' are those who live by rent, those who live by wages, and those who live by profit – respectively the landowners, the labourers, and the employers of stock or capital.[16]

Smith explained that the interests of the first two of these orders, the landowners and the labourers, ought to be strictly connected with the general interest of society, since the real level of both rent and wages will tend to increase with the growth of the real wealth of society. Only the employers of stock, whose profit can be increased without a simultaneous increase in the wealth of the nation, have an interest which can conflict with that of society at large. Unfortunately, however, landowners and labourers are presently no match for this third order in the knowledge and assertion of their own interests. The natural indolence of landowners, whose revenue costs them neither labour nor care, too often renders them ignorant of their interest and quite incapable of foreseeing the consequences of any public regulation. As for labourers, their condition and education commonly leave them incapable either of comprehending the interest of society, or of understanding its connection with their own. The capitalist merchants and master-manufacturers, by contrast, are well aware of their own interest, and fully prepared to impose it at the expense of society's. They have, Smith observed, 'generally an interest to deceive and even to oppress the publick'.[17]

The proof of Smith's charge against the third order lay in 'the mercantile system'. The better to maintain their profits, Smith demonstrated, merchants and manufacturers characteristically seek to persuade government to grant them an array of corporate privileges, fiscal concessions, preferential trading regulations, and colonial monopolies, even though these distort the natural distribution of resources between the different sectors of the economy and encroach upon the freedom of other producing classes. In the event of such privileges and mono-polies being challenged by foreign rivals or colonial subjects, moreover, the merchants and manufacturers also expect government to divert its own resources to the defence of their particular interest. Smith's prolonged assault on this system in Book IV of the *Wealth of Nations*, the rhetorical centrepiece of the entire work, is usually understood as the expression of a straightforward commit-ment to economic liberalism. When, however, the mercantile system is seen as the outcome of the manipulation of government by the trading interest, it is clear that simply ensuring men's natural economic liberty will not be enough. To prevent the improper regulation of economic activity and minimize the diversion of resources from all branches of productive enterprise, it will in addition be necessary to ensure that government itself cannot be subverted by the anti-social interest of the capitalist order.

Dismissive though Smith initially was of the capacity of the other two orders of commercial society to stand up to the merchants and manufacturers, there are passages elsewhere in the *Wealth of Nations* indicating that he did not altogether exclude the possibility. Both landowners and labourers have the potential, at least, to play a constructive part in public life. In the case of the landowners, there is, as Phillipson has pointed out, a suggestive distinction between great land-owners of long-established family and lesser country gentlemen and farmers.[18] The former Smith criticized sharply as inclined to cling to social privileges, such as the right of entail, for their political benefit, even though such privileges impede the fully economic development of the land.[19] Country gentlemen and farmers, on the other hand, Smith commended as 'of all people, the least subject to the wretched spirit of monopoly'. They generally seek neither to keep improvements to themselves, nor to combine against the public.[20] This section of the landowning class, therefore, might well be called upon to offset the subversive influence of the capitalist order on government.

It should be noted, however, that Smith did not think it wise to allow a landed any more than a mercantile interest actually to preponderate in government. The doctrine of Physiocracy, to which he turned his attention once he had finished with the mercantile system, shows that it is quite possible to overvalue the contribution of agriculture to economic development; and while he did not suggest that any government had yet been persuaded to adopt the doctrine, the consequence of one deluded into doing so could be little less damaging than the effects of the mercantile system.[21] On its own, therefore, no section of the landowning order can be regarded as a completely reliable alternative to the capitalist.[22]

What, then, of the second great order of commercial society, the labouring? At first sight, Smith's further remarks on the condition of labourers offer no hope at all. He was very far from sharing Hume's apparent confidence in the beneficent impact of commerce on the moral and political capacity of the common people. Instead, Smith followed up his comment in Book I on the ignorance of the labourer with an ominous diagnosis in Book V of the degradation and 'mental mutilation' consequent upon the full development of the division of labour. His employment reduced to a few simple, monotonous operations, the labourer, Smith asserted, 'generally becomes as stupid and ignorant as it is possible for a human creature to become'. Incapable of just judgement in even the ordinary duties of private life, he is quite unable to judge the interests of his country, or to defend it in war. 'His dexterity at his own particular trade seems, in this manner, to be acquired at the expense of his intellectual, social, and martial virtues.'[23]

This damning judgement needs, however, to be set in the context of other observations on the material and juridical condition of the labouring class in commercial society. Right at the outset of the *Wealth of Nations*, Smith identified the object of economic development as the achievement of 'universal opulence'; and he insisted particularly on the benefit of this to the labourers themselves. Sharing in a 'general plenty', they enjoy not only the necessaries of life, but an unprecedentedly wide variety of household goods.[24] Later Smith observed that almost all the common people in modern commercial society also possess liberty in their own labour. It was, to be sure, by no means inevitable that the attainment of such freedom should accompany economic development; nevertheless it had done so in Western Europe.[25] The labouring class had thus been able to add material self-sufficiency to juridical independence: and for Smith – as for Hume – these were precisely the two conditions of a full participation in social life.

Such conditions are presupposed in the discussion of the social virtues of justice and benevolence in the *Theory of Moral Sentiments*. Accurate and precise sentiments of justice, Smith there observed, are not to be expected from a people living in conditions of rudeness and barbarism. It is the emergence of property and a system of ranks which fosters the most complete sense of justice and the desire for order.[26] But given the limited, retributive character of Smith's concept of justice, still more significant is the virtue of benevolence, discussed in a passage added to the sixth edition of the work. In primitive, pastoral societies, Smith commented, benevolence is chiefly felt towards members of one's family or tribe, for this is the association most necessary for common defence. Once the authority of law is sufficient to give perfect security to every individual, however, the family tie soon narrows, and the range of benevolence extends to neighbours, colleagues, benefactors, and social supervisors.[27] It extends also, Smith went on, to the institutions of society and, in general, to the 'love of our country'. As Smith then defined it, the love of our country

> seems, in ordinary cases, to involve in it two different principles; first, a certain respect and reverence for that constitution or form of government which is actually established; and secondly, an earnest desire to render the condition of our fellow-citizens as safe, respectable, and happy as we can. He is not a citizen who is not disposed to respect the laws and to obey the civil magistrate; and he is certainly not a good citizen who does not wish to promote, by every means in his power, the welfare of the whole society of his fellow citizens.[28]

Smith, of course, made no explicit connection between this analysis of the general conditions of moral sentiment and the analysis of the particular orders of commercial society, including the labouring, developed in the *Wealth of Nations*. But the *Theory of Moral Sentiments* gives no reason to suppose that a labouring class enjoying material self-sufficiency and juridical independence would be unable to cultivate the virtues of justice and benevolence. Could a remedy for the 'mental mutilation' of the division of labour be found, therefore, it would benefit not only the labourer himself, but society as a whole. Liberating the moral potential of the labouring class, it would yet enable it to play its part in public life – and so join the landowners in countering the anti-social designs of merchants and manufacturers.

The outcome of the *Wealth of Nations'* novel analysis of the conflict of interests in commercial society is thus, I suggest, a fresh formulation of the problem of government and economic development. At once restating and developing Hume's, Smith's formulation consolidates the revision which Hume had made of the traditional civic perspective. To Smith as to Hume, wealth is first of all an individual not a public good: securing for the individual the greatest possible freedom from government interference is accordingly the first condition of economic development.[29] At the same time, Smith followed Hume in supposing that the progress of commerce, bringing sufficiency and independence to all ranks, including the lowest, ought in the long run to universalize moral and political capacity. Far from accepting the traditional civic presumption that the producing section of society would be immutably excluded from citizenship, Smith reaffirmed Hume's conviction that in conditions of opulence all should ultimately be free to participate in public life. Still more clearly than Hume, furthermore, Smith insisted on the consequent interdependence of the forms of liberty in commercial society. It is the establishment of universal liberty under the law, the jurisprudential form of liberty, which makes possible the general cultivation of the virtues of justice and benevolence required for the ultimate universalization of the traditionally civic liberty to participate. In turn, liberty under the law will itself come to be fully secured only by the universal exercise of the freedom to participate: ensuring a balance of influences upon government, general participation will prevent the abuse of its power by particular interests. Specifically, the participation of the two orders whose interests coincide with society's, landowners and labourers, should then serve to check the anti-social interest of the order of stockholders.

At this point, however, Smith gave his reformulation of the problem of government and economic development a final original twist. Desirable as it is, the future participation of all in the public life of commercial society cannot be counted upon. Given the habitual indolence and ignorance of landowners, and the increasing degradation of labourers, there is on the contrary every likelihood that the freedom to participate will be monopolized by the very mercantile order whose influence it is supposed to forestall. Unless, therefore, the political alienation of the first two orders of society can be remedied, and landowners and labourers induced to act as citizens, the provision of civic, participatory liberty will simply facilitate the efforts of the third, capitalist order to encroach upon the individual freedom of everyone else. Without positive measures to release the liberty of all to participate, in short, it will not be possible to secure the maximum freedom for all under the law.

Smith's primary solution to the problem he had thus reformulated is developed in Book V of the *Wealth of Nations*. Cast in institutional terms, it is a solution, I shall argue, that differs from Hume's in being framed in line with explicitly economic principles, and in embodying constitutional principles foreign to the civic tradition.[30]

Formally, Book V is a discussion of the expenses and revenue of the 'Sovereign or Commonwealth', and Smith's first concern was simply with efficient government. As far as possible, he argued, the organization of defence, justice, and the public revenue should be subject to economic standards of performance. In the case of defence, the relevant economic principle is that of the division of labour. A commercial society, Smith maintained, should rely on a standing army of professional soldiers rather than a part-time militia, because the former will cause less disruption of productive economic activity, while facilitating the acquisition of the complex skills of modern warfare.[31] In the administration of justice, the principles of self-interest and competition are applicable as well. Not only should the judiciary be a separate, specialist profession; judges should be rewarded on the basis of the number of suits decided; there ought to be competition between courts; and the cost ought to be met as far as possible by charging a fixed fee for plaintiffs.[32] Likewise, in the provision of public works as much scope as possible should be given to the self-interest of their undertakers, and wherever practicable a charge should be paid by those who benefit by their use.[33] Finally, Smith urged that public revenue should be raised by taxation rather than by borrowing, since in the long run a system of public credit removes the incentive to invest productively.[34] Taxation itself, he added, should be levied according to the four maxims of equity, certainty, convenience, and administrative economy.[35]

If the prescription of efficient, economical government was Smith's first, it was not his only concern in Book V. Simultaneously, he was at pains to insist that the outcome of his recommendations would also be 'free government'. He made the point with particular emphasis in recommending a standing army. 'Men of republican principles' might be jealous of such an army as dangerous to liberty. But, Smith replied,

> where the sovereign is himself the general, and the principal nobility and gentry of the country the chief officers of the army; where the military force is placed under the command of those who have the greatest interest in the support of the civil authority, because they have themselves the greatest share of that authority, a standing army can never be dangerous to liberty.

25

On the contrary, a standing army may enable the sovereign to dispense with any discretionary power to check disorder, and tolerate a much larger degree of popular freedom.[36] The proposal of a separate, specialist judiciary had similarly positive implications for liberty. Smith held the judges' independence of the executive to be the essential condition of the impartial administration of justice, on which 'the liberty of every individual, the sense which he has of his own security in turn depends'.[37] By comparison, Smith made little of the political advantages of taxation over public credit; but he did observe that reliance on taxation creates a healthy incentive to end a war as soon as there ceases to be 'a real or solid interest' to fight for.[38] Implicitly, it is clear that taxation can only be levied equitably and economically if it has the consent of the taxpayers.

Free government, however, also makes demands on the members of commercial society. Specifically, in Smith's view, it requires them to be educated. Discussing education under the head of public works and institutions, Smith argued that it should be provided at public expense only for the common people, since these had not the means or inclination to obtain it for themselves.[39] Nevertheless, he was also insistent that the requirement of education be imposed upon all classes since it formed an indispensable qualification for public life. For those of 'middling or more than middling rank and fortune', he recommended the introduction of some sort of probation 'to be undergone by every person before he was permitted to exercise any liberal profession, or before he could be received as a candidate for any honourable office of trust or profit.'[40] At a lower level, premiums and examinations should be used to encourage the common people to take education; and to these inducements should be added compulsory military exercises after the Greek and Roman example.[41]

Such military exercises, Smith acknowledged, might add little to a modern society's defence, but they had other advantages. Above all, by maintaining the martial spirit of the people they would take the first essential step towards remedying the 'mental mutilation' they suffered as a consequence of the division of labour. Broadening his argument, Smith went on to offer an explicitly political justification for educating the inferior ranks. The more instructed the common people are, he claimed, the less liable they are to the delusions of enthusiasm and superstition, and the more decent and orderly in their behaviour. Feeling themselves more respectable, they are more likely to gain the respect of their lawful superiors, and to respect them in turn. They will be better able to see through 'the interested complaints of faction and sedition', and hence will be less apt to be misled into wanton opposition to government. And

> in free countries, where the safety of government depends very much upon the favourable judgement which the people may form of its conduct, it must surely be of the highest importance that they should not be disposed to judge rashly or capriciously concerning it.[42]

These successive arguments in Book V were a direct response to the problem of government and economic development. At the most obvious level, Smith's prescriptions for economical government confront head on the 'unproductive' character of institutions. Whenever possible, they suggest, the necessary diversion of resources should be regulated by subjecting government itself to the natural discipline of economic life. Yet simultaneously, Smith's conviction that his proposals would also result in 'free government' may be seen to meet the further, underlying, political dimension of the problem, created by the conflict of interests within commercial society. It is not enough, his arguments indicate, to contain the diversion of resources: the institutions of government should be positively framed to secure the liberties of society.

To begin with, liberty under the law should be secured by ensuring a significant degree of autonomy to the essential institutions of justice and defence. An independent judiciary offers a first line of defence for individual freedom; a specialist standing army a second, in so far as it enables government to do without a discretionary power to override the law. The autonomy of these institutions should be qualified, however, by provision for a certain freedom to participate, to ensure that they yet remain responsive to society at large. In particular, to prevent the army from being made an instrument of arbitrary rule, it should be commanded by 'the principal nobility and gentry in the country', those who have 'the greatest interest in the support of the civil authority'. And more generally, to prevent the squandering of the public revenue which supports the various branches of government, taxation should be subject to consent. But simply to provide the opportunity to participate is by itself insufficient: free government must further command participation by means of education. Requiring that the middle and upper ranks be qualified before holding office, and imposing an elementary education and military exercises upon the lower, government should actively encourage the extension of the capacity for political liberty at every level of commercial society. In this way, it may be inferred, free government would rectify the indolence and ignorance which inhibit the landowning and labouring classes from asserting the identity of their interests with society's – and so release them to counter the influence of the mercantile order which needs no encouragement to impose its particular, anti-social interest.

This solution to the problem of government and economic development was not arbitrarily advanced. As Smith made clear by the historical and comparative analyses which prefaced each of his major recommendations, it was framed within a comprehensive theory of social development, distinguishing the commercial stage from its predecessors. The general features of this historical or 'stadial' theory are now well known, but it is perhaps in the context of the present problem that its application to commercial society is clearest.[43] Specifically, the theory enabled Smith to isolate two critical features of the relation between government and economy at the commercial stage of development.

First, it showed that where, in primitive societies, the relation was loosely articulated, in a commercial society it must be one of close interdependence. In both the hunting and the pastoral stages of development, every man is naturally a warrior and defence consequently costs the sovereign nothing. Even in the early agricultural stage men are free to serve in summer, and any cost of war, can be paid out of hoards.[44] In a commercial society, by contrast, men are disinclined to leave productive employment for military service, and the expense of war is great, while the very wealth of society attracts acquisitive neighbours.[45] The means of defence, in short, become less readily available, just as the need for it increases. The same is true of justice, whose administration becomes more extensive and costly as the demand for its services grows.[46] If commerce thereby requires a much more precise balance between the needs of government and the economy than hitherto, it also indicates the methods of attaining it. Simply by the application of the principle of the division of labour, commercial societies can provide for their defence at the least possible cost, and at the same time assure themselves of military superiority over their primitive neighbours.[47] Likewise, no more speedy, inexpensive, and accountable system of justice can be envisaged than one which adopts commercial standards of specialization and competitiveness. The complexity of commercial society may give the problem of institutions an unprecedented urgency, but it also, on Smith's theory, makes possible its definitive solution.

What the stadial theory makes no less clear, however, is, second, the dependence of that solution on human initiative. In primitive societies with crude and rudimentary institutions, economic, civil, and military needs are combined as a matter of course.[48] In a complex commercial society, by comparison, the process of adaptation is by no means automatic. As Smith pointed out, the operation of the division of labour in the organization of defence does not occur in the natural course of economic development: it must be introduced by 'the wisdom of the state'.[49] Far from being guaranteed by any 'invisible hand', the harmonization of government and economy in commercial society is, Smith believed, the task of the legislator.[50]

So direct and systematic a response to the problem of government and economic development marks a clear advance on Hume's treatment of the same subject. Hume's response, I indicated, was indirect, and has to be reconstructed by way of his observations on the history of forms of government and their success in encouraging commerce. These historical observations can then be seen as the basis for his projection of a model or perfect form of government whose institutions also matched the requirements of a fully commercial society. In the *Wealth of Nations*, by contrast, the problem is given an explicit solution, consistent with the main lines of the economic analysis already developed in the work. The institutions of commercial society should be framed in accordance with the economic principles appropriate to that stage of development, in a way that simultaneously furthers the ends of free government. Given these criteria, it is then the responsibility of the legislator to render theory into practice, and in due course to reform existing institutions. The problem, in short, is resolved within the framework in which Smith introduced it – that of political economy, with the legislator being required to act directly upon political economy's prescriptions.[51] The very coherence and directness of Smith's solution does, however, leave one aspect of his response less clear than was the case with Hume: the constitutional principles informing the prescribed model of free government. To identify these principles, therefore, it is still necessary to examine Smith's historical commentary on particular forms of government. This will reveal that Smith's solution differed from Hume's, not only in form, but also in conceptual content.

For the purposes of historical analysis in his Lectures on Jurisprudence, Smith had reduced the forms of government to two, the monarchical and the republican. In a monarchy the three parts of the sovereign power, the legislative, the judicial, and the power of making peace and war, are vested in one person. In a republican government the several powers are committed to a greater number: if to 'the nobles or men of rank', it is an aristocracy; if to 'the whole body of the people conjunctly', it is a democracy.[52] This distinction recurs in the *Wealth of Nations*: but the assessment of different forms of government is there much more closely related to the economic performance of the societies for which they are responsible.

Smith acknowledged in his Lectures that the ancient world had produced the first examples of 'regular government' in the city-states of Attica, formed to protect the infant trade and agriculture of the Greeks from the predatory nomads surrounding them.[53] There, and again in the *Wealth of Nations*, Smith also admitted a measure of subsequent economic development in antiquity, despite the harm done by the system of slavery.[54] Nevertheless, Smith was distinctly unwilling to allow that there had been a positive relation between ancient governments and their economies. Quite apart from the maintenance of slavery, ancient institutions of justice and defence were never properly adapted to economic needs. Smith was especially critical of the classical republics. They did not satisfactorily separate the judicial from other governmental powers;[55] and as they grew wealthy, they were unable to reform their characteristic military organization, the city militia.[56] If anything, the later military monarchy of the Roman Empire had performed better than the republics, for it had at least secured regular civil justice. But the imperial armies had been commanded by men whose interest was not necessarily connected with the support of the constitution of the state; and there had been no countervailing civilian political institutions. The idea of representation being, as Smith observed, 'unknown in ancient times', the participatory assemblies of the republic had been unable to cope with the great increase in the numbers of Roman citizens: nothing, therefore, survived to limit the absolute power of the emperors in public affairs.[57]

Smith had no doubt of the superiority of modern over ancient governments. The separation of the judicial from the executive power was now widespread, and it could be taken for granted that all the great nations of Europe enjoyed the regular administration of justice.[58] Standing armies too were now kept by almost all the great powers, and the opulent and civilized nations were therefore secure against their poor and barbarous neighbours.[59] Only the proliferation of national debts gave cause for disquiet, the more so as they were usually accompanied by oppressive taxation.[60] These developments had affected both the republican and the monarchical forms of government; but Smith attached more significance to the achievement of the monarchies.

The republican form of government might seem to be 'the principal support of the present grandeur of Holland', since by according the merchant aristocracy a share in government along with the nobility, it made them more willing to bear the heavy taxation needed to preserve the country from the sea as well as its enemies.[61] But Smith also remarked that while merchant aristocracies might be fitted to administer a mercantile project like the Bank of Amsterdam, they were not fitted to be sovereigns of great states. He evidently sensed Holland's relative economic and political decline as a great power.[62] There was in comparison no question of France's status as a great power; and Smith emphasized that its government was free in so far as its judicial institutions secured personal liberty under the law.[63] He was, however, sceptical of the possibility of reforming the wasteful and oppressive financial administration of the country;[64] and as a result his final assessment of the French monarchy was deliberately balanced. If France was 'certainly the great empire in Europe which, after that of Great Britain, enjoys the mildest and most indulgent government', its was a government which nevertheless still belonged to 'a gradation of despotism'.[65]

The British, it is clear, was one government with no part in this 'gradation'. Of no other existing government, indeed, was Smith so positive in his judgement: he seems to have believed that Britain's institutions came closer than any to satisfying the criteria of free government in a commercial society. The administration of justice, in England if not in Scotland, was competitive and efficient, and the separation of powers as secured by the appointment of professional judges for life.[66] Defence was entrusted to a standing army and navy, with the English militia and sizeable merchant and fishing fleets in reserve; and the peace-time military establishment was more moderate than that of any European state which could pretend to rival Britain in wealth and power.[67] The national debt was certainly a burden, and Smith warned that although at present it seemed to be supported with ease, it could not necessarily be supported for ever. But he also repeatedly acknowledged that the British system of taxation was more equitable and less oppressive than any other.[68] And this, he suggested, was largely due to the unique relation which had been established in Britain's constitution between taxation and consent through representation.[69]

Yet if the system of taxing by consent through representation was unique constitutional asset, it was also at the heart of Britain's present crisis, the crisis which, even as Smith wrote the *Wealth of Nations*, seemed to throw into the balance the country's future as a commercial power – the conflict with the North American colonies. As Smith was well aware, taxation was at least as much an issue in the dispute with the colonies as the regulation of trade. Moreover, he believed that taxation, unlike trade, was an issue on which Britain was not altogether in the wrong. There was every justification for the colonies paying, not only for their own defence, but also their share in support of the general government of the empire. Equally, however, there was every reason to doubt whether the colonies could be brought to raise the appropriate revenue. The colony assemblies could not be managed to do so voluntarily, and would resist paying by requisition, even if it was clear that their contribution could be no more than their due proportion. Management was almost impossible because, although modelled on the House of Commons, the colonial assemblies were, as Smith put it, more 'republican, in form – more equally representative, and accordingly more open to the influence of their constituents. For their part, members of the assemblies enjoyed a status as leaders of the colonial communities which would be lost if they were to submit to requisitions from Great Britain.[70] In the existing state of colonial and British representation, therefore, deadlock was inevitable.

As early as 1776, Smith recognized that war would be no solution to this impasse, since the cost of the permanent subjection of the colonies would be prohibitive. But equally, it was clear that Britain could not be expected to agree to a voluntary separation at once. Smith therefore offered a solution which tackled the problem of representation directly: he proposed a scheme for full imperial union with the colonies and the mother country represented in a single parliament. Taxation would be in proportion to representation, which would be determined by wealth and population. In such a parliament, Smith was confident, a proper degree of management could be achieved without undermining the colonial representatives' ultimate dependency on their constituents. At the same time, the leading men of the colonies would gain a sufficiently large field for their ambition, thereby delivering the colonies from 'those rancorous and virulent factions which are inseparable from small democracies'. The colonies could also look forward to the removal of the seat of government to America, when, as could be expected in due course, their contribution to imperial revenue overtook that of Britain. As for the original British constitution, it would, Smith claimed, be 'completed' by such a union, and indeed seemed 'imperfect' without one.[71]

Smith self-deprecatingly described this proposal as 'a new Utopia', and he concluded the *Wealth of Nations* with a hard-headed exhortation to Britain's rulers to give up the empire and accommodate their future designs to 'the real mediocrity of her circumstances'.[72] Yet even when defeat had forced Britain's rulers to do just that, and Smith himself came to revise the work for its third edition in 1784, the proposal remained.[73] Such adherence to a 'utopian' and by then clearly outdated scheme appears puzzling – unless perhaps Smith regarded it as having rather more than a narrowly practical significance. That this may indeed have been the case is suggested by comparison with his treatment of the commercial issues raised by the American conflict.

Andrew Skinner has argued that his purposes in devoting so much attention to those issues were chiefly doctrinal. Smith, it can be seen, was little concerned with providing a comprehensive review of the commercial matters actually in dispute between Britain and the colonies, still less with influencing the immediate direction of policy. Rather, he would marshal all the evidence of the folly of commercial regulations and monopolies which the American case provided in order to illustrate his theoretical critique of the mercantile system.[74] In much the same way, I would argue that a paradigmatic purpose may be detected in Smith's analysis of the constitutional dimension of the crisis. The question of America could be represented as an excellent example, not only of the danger of mercantile restrictions, but also, more generally, of the problem of institutions and economic development.

If Britain and America could be envisaged as one united, imperial society, it should be clear that they would together enjoy unequalled economic opportunities. Britain was already the most advanced nation in Europe, while America had a possibly unique chance to develop according to what Smith termed 'the natural progress of opulence'.[75] To realize such economic potential, of course, required that the empire be endowed with appropriate political institutions, and that the burden of maintaining them be equitably distributed. But these conditions could, at least in theory, be met. The requisite institutions of justice and defence now existed in Britain, and the principle of taxation by representative consent was established in the constitution. All that was needed to develop the economic potential of the two countries to the full, therefore, was the extension of those institutions to the colonies, and the translation of the principle of taxation by representative consent into a constitutional framework adapted to the colonies' growing resources and aspirations: thus the purpose of the scheme of Atlantic empire. Effectively matching the criteria of Smith's model of efficient and free government in a commercial society, the proposal exemplified the solution to one of the central analytical problems of his political economy.

So resumed, what does Smith's commentary on particular forms of government – past, present, and projected – reveal of his constitutional principles? It should at least be clear that they were not of the same historical derivation as Hume's. By contrast with Hume, who believed that the classical republican form of government, with all its flaws, had been responsible for the initial development of commerce and the arts, Smith denied that that form of government had possessed any of the particular judicial, military, and representative institutions appropriate to a commercial society. Instead, Smith suggested that it was in the modern world, and specifically in the civilized monarchies, that the requisite institutions had first emerged. If Smith thus ascribed a greater institutional originality to modern monarchy, he was also more insistent on its limitations. Where Hume supposed that the civilized monarchies of Europe had significantly improved upon the republican principles they inherited, Smith still considered them to belong to 'a gradation of despotism'. Their achievement in the spheres of justice and defence was offset, he believed, by their reliance on oppressive and wasteful system of public finance.

Smith's divergence from Hume is even clearer in relation to the existing government of Britain. Hume had accepted the conventional view of Britain as a mixed government, combining monarchic with republican features. But far from sharing the common admiration for this unique mixture, Hume had been severely sceptical of its continued stability. In the long run, Hume judged mixed government to be less likely to cope with the pressures of economic development than civilized absolute monarchy, which compensated for its lack of political liberty by its capacity to ensure regular justice and to override the financiers. Little of this scepticism survives in Smith's observations of British government, however. By-passing debate over the strengths and weaknesses of mixed government, Smith simply noted the extent to which Britain already possessed what he identified as the requisite institutions for a commercial society. Here alone had the independence of the judicial power been properly secured and military organization adapted to the nation's needs; and in the system of taxation by representative consent, Britain enjoyed a constitutional asset not found in any of the continental monarchies. So well formed, indeed, did Smith believe British government to be, that he only had to project its perfection in an imperial parliamentary union with America to provide a paradigm of free government in a commercial society.

It is precisely this readiness to set aside Hume's reservations over the government of Britain, I now suggest, that holds the key to Smith's constitutional principles. For his assessment of particular British institutions implies that Smith no longer found it necessary to think exclusively in terms of mixed government. In approving of an independent judiciary, it is true, Smith does not seem to have gone beyond the principle of the separation of powers, which was compatible with mixed government.[76] But his treatment of the two other institutions he singled out for commendation, the standing army and the system of representative, parliamentary consent for taxation, shows him to have moved onto ground where one still subscribing to the doctrine of mixed government could not readily follow.

This is clearest in the case of the standing army. In the perspective of mixed government, as Hume had had to acknowledge, to entrust defence to professional soldiers was necessarily to give the monarch a preponderant weight in the constitution. Smith, however, saw no such danger. Brushing aside the objections of men of 'republican principles', he would argue that an army subordinate to the sovereign and commanded by the leading classes in society is a strength rather than a threat to liberty. Less obvious, but, it can be argued, not less critical, was Smith's departure from the mixed government view of parliamentary representation. According to that view, parliament should be considered the republican element in the constitution, from which, as Hume recognized, it was but a short step to regarding members of parliament as delegates, bound by the instructions of their constituents.[77] Smith, however, can be seen to have rejected this interpretation of the representative relation in his discussion of Britain's imperial crisis. It was, he observed, because of the 'republican' influence of electors over the members of the American colonial assemblies that these were so unmanageable. Diminishing such influence was the object of his scheme of imperial parliamentary union. What was needed to secure the principle of parliamentary consent on an imperial basis, he argued, was a directly proportional relation between representation and taxation; but this should not be confused, as it was liable to be in the doctrine of mixed government, by a view of representation as delegation.

In renouncing the mixed government view of the British constitution in these two respects, Smith may be seen to have taken advantage of distinct, alternative constitutional principles. From the beginning of the century, political commentators of 'Court' or 'Whig' persuasion had sought both to defend the standing army on the self-same grounds of subordination to civil authority and integration into the social hierarchy, and to distinguish representation from delegation, denying the legitimacy of instructions. When Hume wrote in the mid-century, such arguments were not yet in the ascendant; but by 1776, the outbreak of the American rebellion, and the publication of the *Wealth of Nations* they had won general acceptance among the parliamentary classes. By adopting them, it is important to note, Smith did not commit himself exclusively to the Court or Whig viewpoint, with its uncompromising hostility to the claims of the colonists. Nor did he commit himself to an alternative general theory of the constitution. Both the standing army and the distinction between representation and delegation were, in principle, closely tied to the concept of parliamentary sovereignty.[78] But as it was of the essence of parliamentary sovereignty that it evolved piecemeal, adoption of its subordinate principles did not necessitate explicit reference to the concept itself. It was enough that alternative principles on which to assess the British constitution were available, permitting Smith to break free of the doctrine of mixed government to which Hume reluctantly still felt bound.

And not only the doctrine of mixed government. Smith was also free to dispense with the more general body of constitutional principle of which that doctrine had been a particular, local variant: the civic tradition. Once again, comparison with Hume is telling. Diagnosing the precariousness of mixed government, and yet acknowledging the lack of political liberty under continental absolute monarchy, Hume had fallen back on fundamental constitutional principles of the civic tradition to frame an 'Idea of a perfect Commonwealth'. However radically Hume can be seen to have modified the traditional significance of civic principles to accommodate the social consequences of economic development, the principles themselves remained. In the *Wealth of Nations*, by contrast, those civic principles are conspicuous by their absence. Evidently they were no longer needed. Viewing British government in terms more appropriate to parliamentary sovereignty than to mixed government, there was no reason to doubt its superiority over any other existing form. It had improved upon the strengths of the monarchies in justice and defence; it had evolved a unique system of representative parliamentary consent for taxation: as a result its institutions were better adapted than all others to economic development. True, it was not yet flawless. In the long term, it would require radical reform to ensure that representation was properly proportional to taxation (and to support the consequent extension of the electorate, the provision of public education for the lower ranks would have to be generalised). But such reform could occur within the present constitutional framework. Smith, therefore, had no occasion to invoke civic principles, no occasion to write an 'Idea of a perfect Commonwealth'. To exemplify his idea of free government, he had only to project the perfection of British government.[79]

From that final vantage-point, Smith may be thought to have moved quite beyond the limits of the civic tradition, previously reached by Hume. It has already been argued that, by his formulation of the problem of government and economic development, Smith confirmed and extended his predecessor's revision of the traditional social and moral premises of political community. But the implication of his response to the problem went still further, questioning whether it was worth even attempting a corresponding revision of civic constitutional principles. To enable the legislator in a commercial society to meet the institutional demands of economic development, it appeared to Smith simpler to begin to define the concept of free government anew, on principles displayed in the British constitution.

To regard Smith's constitutional arguments as a straightforward progression beyond Hume's would, of course, be misleading. Contingent historical circumstances – the later maturing of Smith's political thought, the changing context of British constitutional debate – were what made possible Smith's break with the doctrine of mixed government, and thence with civic constitutional principles. It would indeed be an insular, Whiggish view that saw the rejection of civic principles in favour of those of parliamentary sovereignty as 'progress'. At the same time, it is important to emphasize once more that it was not Smith's purpose in the *Wealth of Nations* to elaborate a complete constitutional doctrine. Given the critical importance he attached to the relation between government and economic development, he could not avoid a reckoning with political and constitutional theory. But in the solution as in the formulation of the problem, that reckoning is conducted in integral relation with the economic analysis of the *Wealth of Nations*. Whatever the status of political economy as 'a branch of the science of a statesman or legislator', within the *Wealth of Nations* itself it is political and constitutional principles which are rendered a branch of political economy. To keep Smith's adoption of the principles of parliamentary sovereignty in proper perspective, therefore, it should be recognized that those constitutional principles have themselves been assimilated into political economy.

To say this, however, is not to qualify Smith's achievement, but to identify one of its most original aspects. It was the assimilation of the indigenous British constitutional principles of parliamentary sovereignty into political economy which, perhaps more than anything, gave the *Wealth of Nations* its subsequent impact, and made it a canonical text for Victorian liberalism. The legislators of nineteenth-century Britain who held the sovereignty of parliament and the laws of the market to be the touchstones of government and economy may have been indifferent to Adam Smith's own grander political vision; theirs may not be the appropriate vantage-point for an historian wishing to understand Smith's

35

enterprise as a whole.[80] But those legislators' open acknowledgement of the author of the *Wealth of Nations* in particular was not misplaced. The constitutional and economic principles on which they acted are already present in the political economy of the *Wealth of Nations*. That enduring work is, after all, rather more Gladstonian in character than it has lately been fashionable to admit.

Notes

1 This is a revised version of a paper first published as 'Scottish Political Economy beyond the Civic Tradition: Government and Economic Development in the *Wealth of Nations*', in *History of Political Thought*, IV, 3 (1983), pp. 451–82. I am most grateful to the editors and publishers of this journal for permission to republish.

2 *An Inquiry into the Nature and Causes of the Wealth of Nations*, (1776), R. H. Campbell, A. S. Skinner, and W. B. Todd (eds), 2 vols (Oxford, 1976), Book IV, Introduction. Throughout this paper I shall use the reference system common to the Glasgow edition of the *Works and Correspondence of Adam Smith*. The other works in the edition to be cited are: *The Theory of Moral Sentiments* (1759), D. D. Raphael and A. L. Macfie (eds) (Oxford, 1976); *Lectures on Rhetoric and Belles Lettres* (Report of 1762–3), J. C. Bryce (ed.) (Oxford, 1983); *Lectures on Jurisprudence* (Reports of 1762–3 and 1766), R. L. Meek, D. D. Raphael, and P. G. Stein (eds) (Oxford, 1978); and *The Correspondence of Adam Smith*, E. C. Mossner and I. S. Ross (eds) (Oxford, 1977).

3 John Robertson, 'The Scottish Enlightenment at the Limits of the Civic Tradition', in I. Hont and M. Ignatieff (eds), *Wealth and Virtue. The Shaping of Political Economy in the Scottish Enlightenment* (Cambridge, 1983). The following six paragraphs summarize this paper's argument.

4 J. G. A. Pocock, *The Machiavellian Moment* (Princeton, NJ, 1975).

5 Duncan Forbes, 'Sceptical Whiggism, Commerce and Liberty', in A. S. Skinner and T. Wilson (eds), *Essays on Adam Smith*, (Oxford, 1976); Donald Winch, *Adam Smith's Politics. An Essay in Historiographic Revision* (Cambridge, 1978); Knud Haakonssen, *The Science of a Legislator. The Natural Jurisprudence of David Hume and Adam Smith* (Cambridge, 1981).

6 Another to have argued for the importance of a civic component in Smith's thought is Nicholas Phillipson, in 'Adam Smith as Civic Moralist', in Hont and Ignatieff (eds) *Wealth and Virtue*. Phillipson's emphasis, however, is upon Smith's use of the moral concepts associated with the civic tradition. In so far as the resulting interpretation allows Smith a politics at all, it appears to accept the jurisprudential framework.

7 On the general desirability of a convergence between the civic and the jurisprudential approaches, see J. G. A. Pocock, 'Virtue, Rights and Manners: a Model for Historians of Political Thought', *Political Theory*, 9 (1981), reprinted in J. G. A. Pocock, *Virtue, Commerce and History* (Cambridge, 1985).

8 Walter Bagehot, 'Adam Smith as a Person' (1876), in *Biographical Studies* (London, 1889), p. 249.

9 For confident affirmations of this position, see Duncan Forbes, 'Natural Law and the Scottish Enlightenment', in R. H. Campbell and A. S. Skinner (eds), *The Origins and Nature of the Scottish Enlightenment* (Edinburgh, 1982); and Donald Winch, 'Adam Smith's "Enduring Particular Result": A Political and Cosmopolitan Perspective', in Hont and Ignatieff (eds), *Wealth and Virtue*.

10 *Theory of Moral Sentiments*, Advertisement (added in the 6th edition, 1790), and VII. iv. 37 for the original promise. See also Smith's remarks on his uncompleted projects

in a letter of 1785: *Correspondence of Adam Smith*, no. 248, to the Duc de la Rochefoucauld, 1 November 1785.

11 Though it is not known how much of this projected work was included in the papers that were destroyed on Smith's orders just before his death, there is no evidence that it was anywhere near completion.

12 In this paper I take the 'economic' principles of the *Wealth of Nations* to be simply the principles of the market economy. This is not, of course, to assume that the principles of the market economy were without historical antecedents of their own, or that such antecedents lay only in earlier economic writing. Whatever those antecedents, however, the formal presentation of the principles of the market economy in the *Wealth of Nations* is in distinct and largely autonomous terms. On the relation between the economic argument of the *Wealth of Nations* and its antecedents, see I. Hont and M. Ignatieff, 'Needs and Justice in the *Wealth of Nations*', Introductory Essay to *Wealth and Virtue*.

13 *Wealth of Nations* II. iii. 28; IV. vii. c. 88; even if as Smith also observed in the *Theory of Moral Sentiments*, material acquisition itself is largely delusory as a source of individual happiness: I. iii. 2.1.

14 *Wealth of Nations*, II. iii. 30.

15 Ibid., II. iii. 31.

16 Ibid., I. xi. 7.

17 Ibid., I. xi. 8–10.

18 Phillipson, 'Adam Smith as Civic Moralist', *Wealth and Virtue*.

19 *Wealth of Nations*, III. ii. 4–7.

20 Ibid., IV. ii. 21.

21 Ibid., IV. ix. 49.

22 It may be added that Smith did not elaborate on the identity of the 'country gentlemen and farmers' referred to at IV. ii. 21, and the category of 'country gentlemen' in particular remains imprecise throughout the *Wealth of Nations*. In Book, III, Smith insisted that a commitment to agricultural improvement could be relied on only in those whose holding was sufficiently small for them to farm it directly: the examples he cited were the yeoman and tenant farmers of England and, best of all, the independent small proprietors of North America. With the exception of those who had formerly been merchants, 'country gentlemen' were by contrast described as 'timid' undertakers: III. ii. 20, III. iv. 3, 19. Later, in Book V, Smith recommended that the tax system should specifically discourage improvement by landowners whose estates were of a size to require bailiffs if they were to be farmed directly: V. ii. c.15. To claim, as Phillipson does in 'Adam Smith as Civic Moralist', that Smith put his faith in a 'gentry' seems therefore to strain the evidence.

23 *Wealth of Nations*, V. i. f. 50.

24 Ibid., I. i. 10–11.

25 Ibid., III. iii. 5; III. iv. 4.

26 *Theory of Moral Sentiments*, VII. iv. 36; II. ii.

27 Ibid., VI. ii. 1.12–20.

28 Ibid., VI. ii. 2.1–11.

29 This is as far as analysis of Smith's treatment of the problem is usually taken: see e.g. L. Billet, 'Political Order and Economic Development: Reflections on Adam Smith's *Wealth of Nations*', *Political Studies*, XXIII (1975), pp. 430–41.

30 I do not deny that, as Phillipson argues in 'Adam Smith as Civic Moralist', Smith also struggled persistently to identify the terms of an ethical solution to the conflict of interests in commercial society. The success of the enterprise, however, appears doubtful. Smith might indeed ask in the *Theory of Moral Sentiments*:

What institution of government could tend so much to promote the happiness of mankind as the general prevalence of wisdom and virtue? All government is but an imperfect remedy for the deficiency of these. (IV. ii. 1)

But the prospect of the 'general prevalence' of wisdom and virtue is almost certainly utopian. Even in individuals, Smith acknowledged, the qualities of wisdom and virtue are exceptionally difficult to discern (ibid., VI. ii. 1.20).

It seems to me, therefore, that the judgement of one of the first commentators to notice the problem of conflicting interests, Joseph Cropsey, still stands: failing the idea of a social or moral 'natural aristocracy', Smith fell back on a solution in institutional terms. *Polity and Economy. An Interpretation of the Principles of Adam Smith* (The Hague, 1957), pp. 67–70.

31 *Wealth of Nations*, V. i. a. 8–25.
32 Ibid., V. i. b. 20–2.
33 Ibid., V. i. c–g.
34 Ibid., V. iii. 47–56.
35 Ibid., V. ii. b. 2–7. Cf. for the above paragraph, A. S. Skinner, *A System of Social Science. Papers relating to Adam Smith* (Oxford, 1979), pp. 211–16.
36 *Wealth of Nations*, V. i. a. 41.
37 Ibid., V. i. b. 25.
38 Ibid., V. iii. 50.
39 Ibid., V. i. f. 52–3.
40 Ibid., V. i. g. 14.
41 Ibid., V. i. f. 54–9.
42 Ibid., V. i. f. 60–1.
43 The pioneering work on Smith's stadial theory was done by R. L. Meek, culminating in his *Social Science and the Ignoble Savage* (Cambridge, 1976); but Meek's focus on the theory's application to primitive societies may have encouraged an unnecessary scepticism over its relevance to commercial society, exemplified in Lindgren, *Social Philosophy of Adam Smith*, pp. xiii, 68. Andrew Skinner has provided a more balanced account of the theory: 'A Scottish Contribution to Marxist Sociology?', in I. Bradley and M. Howard (eds), *Classical and Marxian Political Economy. Essays in Honour of R. L. Meek* (London, 1982). See also the lengthy discussion of stadial theory in Haakonssen, *Science of a Legislator*, chs 7–8, although Haakonssen's concern is with the theory's place in the reconstruction of Smith's theory of jurisprudence, not with its actual significance in the *Wealth of Nations*.
44 *Wealth of Nations*, V. i. a. 2–7; V. ii. 1–2.
45 Ibid., V. i. a. 8–10, 15.
46 Ibid., V. i. b. 24.
47 Ibid., V. i. a. 39.
48 Ibid., V. i. a. 2–7; b. 12.
49 Ibid., V. i. a. 14. On Smith's theory, in other words, the economic 'base' does not straightfowardly and reductively determine the institutional 'superstructure'. To the contrary, the theory indicates that the rational, economic, and free ordering of institutions will come about only as a result of conscious choice.
50 Beyond distinguishing him from 'that insidious and crafty animal', the politician (IV. ii. 39), Smith did not elaborate on the character of the legislator in the *Wealth of Nations*. Subsequently, revising the *Theory of Moral Sentiments* for its sixth edition in 1790, Smith incorporated there a discussion of the role and attributes of the 'statesman', treating him as a legislator. While the responsibility is described in appropriately lofty tones, it is none the less important to note that the statesman was to proceed gradually.

Some general, and even systematical, idea of the perfection of policy and law, may no doubt be necessary for directing the views of the statesman. But to insist upon establishing, and upon establishing all at once, in spite of all opposition, everything which that idea may seem to require, must often be the highest degree of arrogance.

Smith went on to condemn in particular the arrogance of individual 'imperial and royal reformers', *Theory of Moral Sentiments*, VI. ii. 12–18. (This reference to 'imperial and royal reformers' casts doubt on the suggestion of his editors, Raphael and Macfie (p. 231, n. 6), that Smith was thinking of the French Revolution when he added this passage.)

It seems clear that Smith's reference to the statesman or legislator in the singular was meant to be figurative: what he had in mind was not the founding law-giver of classical myth, but the institution of law-making or legislation as the means to reform the other institutions and practices of government.

51 The importance of the legislator in Smith's political thought has been emphasized by Winch, in *Adam Smith's Politics*, pp. 130–3, and in his subsequent article 'Science and the Legislator: Adam Smith and After', *The Economic Journal*, 93 (1983); by Haakonssen, *Science of a Legislator*, pp. 97–8, 188–9; and by J. H. Burns, 'Scottish Philosophy and the Science of Legislation', *The Royal Society of Edinburgh*, Occasional Papers (1985), pp. 20–4. With the exception of Winch, 'Science and the Legislator', however, these view the legislator's role in relation to the application of the prescriptions of jurisprudence. Without denying this more ambitious role, what I would emphasize (with Winch) is the immediate practical responsibility given the legislator in the *Wealth of Nations* for carrying out the prescriptions of political economy.

52 *Lectures on Jurisprudence* (A), iv. 1–3; (B), 18–19.

53 Ibid., (A), iv. 56–74.

54 Even in his strongest criticism of ancient slavery, Smith still conceded the achievement of considerable prosperity: *Wealth of Nations*, IV. ix. 47; cf. *Lectures on Jurisprudence* (A), iii. 105–11, 139–47.

55 Although the Roman republic registered a significant advance on its Greek predecessors in this respect, Smith still does not appear to have regarded the Roman praetors as fully professional judges. Cf. *Wealth of Nations*, V. i. b. 24 and V. i. f. 44 with the digression on the absence of legal argument from precedent in antiquity in Smith's *Lectures on Rhetoric and Belles Lettres*, ii. 198–203.

56 *Wealth of Nations*, V. i. a. 29; more fully, *Lectures on Jurisprudence* (A), iv. 76–87.

57 *Wealth of Nations*, V. i. a. 41; IV. vii. c. 77; also *Lectures on Jurisprudence* (A), iv. 97–9.

58 *Wealth of Nations*, V. i. b. 24 and V. iii. 7, 10 (which imply that the development of national debts presupposed the availability of regular justice).

59 Ibid., V. i. a. 37–9.

60 Ibid., V. iii. 57–8.

61 Ibid., V. ii. k. 80.

62 Ibid., V. ii. a. 4, 7; V. ii. k. 79.

63 Ibid., V. i. b. 20.

64 Ibid., V. ii. j. 7 and k. 77; V. iii. 35–6.

65 Ibid., V. ii. k. 78; V. i. g. 19. Cf. this paragraph with Forbes, 'Sceptical Whiggism, Commerce and Liberty', *Essays on Adam Smith*, pp. 188–97.

66 *Wealth of Nations*, V. i. b. 21; cf. *Lectures on Jurisprudence* (A), v. 5.

67 *Wealth of Nations*, V. i. a. 20; IV. ii. 24 and IV. v. a. 27; V. iii. 92.

68 Ibid., V. ii. k. 66; V. iii. 58.

69 Ibid., IV. vii. b. 51. Further discussion of the system of securing consent by representation in Britain is to be found in the *Lectures on Jurisprudence*. To refute Locke's proposition that consent for taxation is a necessary condition of all allegiance,

Smith had been careful to point out to his students how much the formal relation between taxation and consent was peculiar to Britain, and even then was still largely 'metaphorical'. *Lectures* (A), v. 134–5 and (B), 94–5. Nevertheless, Smith made equally clear the extent to which Britain's 'rational system of liberty' depended on parliamentary control of government finance. Parliament had been able to establish this control at the end of the seventeenth century by exploiting the fortunate absence hitherto of a standing army and the dissipation of the crown's own ordinary revenues. In consequence, parliament, and the House of Commons in particular, now effectively regulated both the civil and the military expenditure of the crown; and Smith emphasized that the Commons owed its predominance, not only to its powers to initiate money bills and impeach ministers, but also to the authority which its members derived from the people they represented, and whom they had to satisfy at frequent elections. *Lectures* (A), iv. 168–79, v. 1–2; (B), 61–3.

70 *Wealth of Nations*, IV. vii. b. 51; c. 67–74.
71 *Wealth of Nations*, IV. vii. c. 66, 75–9; V. iii. 90. Cf. Winch, *Adam Smith's Politics*, ch.7, 'The Present Disturbances': but Winch takes Smith's central concern to be with management rather than representation.
72 *Wealth of Nations*, V. iii. 68, 92.
73 At least one friend had urged its removal, in markedly patronizing tones:

> there are some pages about the middle of the second volume where you enter into a description about the measures we ought at present to take with respect to America, giving them a representation etc. which I wish had been omitted, because it is too much like a publication for the present moment. In subsequent editions when publick measures come to be settled, these pages will fall to be omitted or altered.

Correspondence of Adam Smith, no. 151; Letter from the Rev. Hugh Blair, 3 April 1776.
74 Skinner, *A System of Social Science*, ch. 8, 'Mercantilist Policy: the American Colonies'.
75 *Wealth of Nations*, III. iv. 19–20.
76 On occasion, moreover, he could still describe the British constitution in general terms as a mixed government: *Wealth of Nations*, IV. vii. c. 78.
77 Hume appreciated that British MPs were not delegates obliged to receive instructions from their constituents; but he does not seem to have regarded the distinction between delegation and representation as a critical one. A balance between the two was part of the mixture of British government; and in a passage included in his *Essays* between 1742 and 1760, he dismissed the controversy over instructions as 'very frivolous': 'Of the First Principles of Government', *Philosophical Works*, III, pp. 112–13.
78 As indeed was the independence of the judiciary, in that judges were removable only by parliamentary impeachment.
79 Oddly, it is just in this comparison of Smith's project of imperial parliamentary union with Hume's 'Idea of a perfect Commonwealth' that Winch, and now also Phillipson, have identified a resemblance between the institutional principles of the two thinkers: *Adam Smith's Politics*, pp. 172, 178–80; 'Adam Smith as Civic Moralist', *Wealth and Virtue*, pp. 194–7. But the point it not so much the resemblance as the contrast between the two models. For in referring to the 'American' application of both models, Winch forgets that Hume's appealed to those Americans who sought to elaborate a sophisticated republican alternative to parliamentary sovereignty; Smith, by contrast, offered the perfection of parliamentary sovereignty.

Forbes too has aligned Smith's constitutional thinking with Hume's, on the different grounds that Smith subscribed to 'the commonplace Blackstonian view' of the British constitution as a mixed government, 'Sceptical Whiggism, Commerce and Liberty',

Essays on Adam Smith, p. 186. But this is also misleading. Not only can Smith himself be seen to have adopted specific principles associated with the doctrine of parliamentary sovereignty; but Blackstone's *Commentaries* contain resounding general affirmations of the same doctrine. Even if Blackstone throughout (and Smith occasionally, in the *Wealth of Nations*) continued to think of the British constitution in terms of mixed government as well as parliamentary sovereignty, the resulting constitutional doctrine was still markedly different from Hume's more strictly civic view, which had no place for the concept of sovereignty. This difference is clearly brought out by Burns, 'Scottish Philosophy and the Science of Legislation', pp. 14–15.

Haakonssen offers an interesting analysis of the way in which Smith combined the concepts of sovereignty and the division of powers in his Lectures – and also points to Smith's reported description of the constitution as 'a happy mixture of all the different forms of government properly restrained': *Science of a Legislator*, pp. 130–3, 169–70; *Lectures on Jurisprudence* (B), 63. Through reliance on the Lectures, however, Haakonssen misses the diminished importance of the classical account of forms of government in the *Wealth of Nations*, and the bringing to the forefront of the principles of parliamentary sovereignty.

80 Winch, *Adam Smith's Politics*; 'Adam Smith's "Enduring Particular Result"', *Wealth and Virtue*. But see now the concluding remarks of R. F. Teichgraeber III, '"Less abused than I had reason to expect": the Reception of the *Wealth of Nations*, in Britain 1776–90', *Historical Journal*, 30,2 (1987), p. 366.

Chapter three

Whigs and Liberals: the *Edinburgh Review* and the 'liberal movement' in nineteenth-century Britain

Bianca Fontana

The contribution of the group of Scottish-educated intellectuals who, from 1802, were associated with the *Edinburgh Review* is generally regarded as one of the pioneering sources of nineteenth-century British liberalism. Their writings and activities are currently identified with the popularization of Smithian and later, Ricardian political economy; with the promotion of free trade policies, and of various issues of reform such as popular education and the suppression of religious discrimination; and with the struggle for the reform of parliament and the extension of the suffrage. They are, in other words, closely associated with all the representative ideological attitudes and political battles that characterized the progress of the 'liberal movement' in early and mid-nineteenth-century Britain.

In an often cited retrospective assessment of the merits and impact of the *Review*, one of its founders wrote:

> To appreciate the value of the *Edinburgh Review* the state of England at the period when that journal began should be had in remembrance. The Catholics were not emancipated. The Corporation and Test Acts were unrepealed. The Game Laws were horribly oppressive; Steel Traps and Spring-Guns were set all over the country; Prisoners tried for their Lives could have no Counsel ... Libel was punished by the most cruel and vindictive imprisonments. The principles of Political Economy were little understood. The Laws of Debt and Conspiracy were upon the worst footing. The enormous wickedness of the Slave Trade was tolerated. A thousand evils were in existence which the talents of good and able men have since lessened and removed.[1]

Thus this identification of the *Edinburgh Review* with the cause of reform and with liberal ideas was made explicit from the start by the reviewers themselves. It was, perhaps more significantly, endorsed by their political enemies, by that section of the British public opinion that, soon after its appearance, came to see the journal as a dangerous 'incendiary' publication. It was subsequently confirmed and perpetuated by those intellectuals of later generations who liked to see themselves as the spiritual heirs of the *Review*.

Writing about one of the founders of the *Review*, Sydney Smith, Walter Bagehot observed:

Sydney Smith was liberalism in life. Somebody has defined liberalism as the spirit of the world, It represents its genial enjoyment, its wise sense, its steady judgment, its preference of the near to the far, of the seen to the unseen; it represents too its shrinking from difficult dogma, from stern statement, from imperious superstition.[2]

As an influential self-representation, if nothing more, the association of the *Edinburgh Review* with the cause of reform and with the supposed ethos of liberalism needs to be taken seriously, and cannot be set aside as the creation of a simplistic, misleading, and superficial historiography. Yet as soon as one attempts to define it more rigorously, or to test it against the content of specific political issues, it proves discouragingly problematic and elusive.

I

Did what we call the 'liberalism' of the *Edinburgh Review* consist in its allegiance to a political party, in its commitment to a specific programme of reform, or in the popularization of a given political ideology? There seems to be some degree of plausibility in each of these hypotheses. And yet each appears quite unsatisfactory, and they all run into some sort of interpretative difficulty. No doubt the success of the *Edinburgh Review* was very closely associated with the process of transformation and realignment of the Whig Party after the crisis brought about by the French Revolution and Charles Fox's death.[3] But the relation of the group of young Scottish intellectuals to the party of which they became the official '*idéologues*' was, from the start, a critical and complex one. The very phrase 'sceptical' or 'philosophic Whiggism' (this too a self-definition)[4] currently used to describe the reviewers' political outlook, indicates their distance from traditional Whig ideology.

The peculiarities of their position have often been illustrated:[5] although they subscribed to the Whig ideals of English liberty and the defence of the constitution, they were much less preoccupied with piety towards the heritage of the Glorious Revolution than they were with the problems raised by the development of modern commercial society. Formed by the teaching of Dugald Stewart, they were deeply influenced by Adam Smith's and David Hume's writings, and inherited from the latter his 'sceptical' distance from traditional party allegiance.[6]

Significantly, other Scottish intellectuals who shared a similar background ended up in different political camps: this was the case of James Mill and Walter Scott.[7] Henry Brougham himself, whose life and activities were so closely associated with the fortunes of the Whigs, had initially considered the possibility of making a career with the Tories, but opted for the Whigs on purely contingent and opportunistic grounds. The relations between the reviewers and the party were always tense and ambiguous. The *Review*'s editor, Francis Jeffrey, fought hard to retain a reasonable measure of independence from the official party 'line'.

Henry Brougham and Francis Horner, who became Members of Parliament and 'professional' advisers to the Whig grandees, did succeed in exercising a certain influence upon their aristocratic patrons, but their position in the Whig rank and file always remained subordinate, and they never gained access to the party's leadership.[8]

Not only was there an obvious tension between the aristocratic nature of the Whig Party and the social background of the reviewers, all of whom came from the urban, professional bourgeoisie or the petty gentry, there was also, more relevantly, a predictable conflict between the traditional character of the party as a machine for the reproduction of an area of aristocratic interest and influence, and the Scottish theories which placed the growth of the 'middling ranks' and of middle-sized fortunes at the heart of the progress of modern commercial society.[9]

Much has been written to show how the 1832 Reform Bill took shape as a fragile and uneasy compromise between these various conceptions of the desirable social basis for political opposition.[10] It was, in some sense, the impossibility of reconciling them, of assimilating the old aristocratic party to that party 'in the country, in public opinion' to which the *Review* made appeal, which formed the background to the decline of the Whigs in the 1830s and 1840s.[11]

If the relations between the *Edinburgh Review* and the Whig Party were ambivalent, the measures of reform which they endorsed in the first decades of the nineteenth century formed an even more confusing and contradictory picture. On some issues of practical policy the political economists held conflicting views, and the teaching of the Scottish school could offer no straightforward prescriptions: this was the case with the choice of whether to support the agrarian or the industrial interest; the debates over the degree to which state intervention in the economy was thought to be desirable; and in discussions of the problems of population and technological progress. On some occasions when the reviewers fought ostensibly to defend the principles of political economy, as in the debate over the resumption of cash payments and the gold standard, their views had little or no impact upon political decisions. The necessity to adapt their views from time to time to the contingent circumstances and strategies of parliamentary struggle multiplied the inconsistencies in their position. Thus it would be impossible, for example, to claim that the *Review* ever expressed unambiguous support for free trade, or opposed without reservation the growth of executive power and state bureaucracy.

As to the parliamentary reform of 1832, there is plenty of evidence to suggest that the issue was taken up by the Whigs and promoted by the *Review* at a late stage, and for largely contingent reasons; and that the reform proposal itself was hastily designed along improvised and tentative lines. The bitter competition over the years which opposed the Scottish Whigs to the Philosophic Radicals in their role as advocates of reform had a far from negligible influence in determining the timing, shape, and content of their approach to the various reform issues.[12]

Finally, if we try to locate the 'liberalism' of the reviewers, not in their support of the party of the opposition nor in a specific political programme, but in the ideology which inspired them, we again find ourselves on slippery ground. It is quite possible to describe accurately enough the intellectual background of the group and the impact of their encounter with English cultural life and politics upon their early Scottish education. Undoubtedly the *Review* owed its initial success to its monopoly over a unique kind of academic learning and to a style of criticism that was very distinctive and quite unlike any other form of contemporary political journalism. But if one were to look for a consistent theory of society, of historical change and political action, one would find a set of extremely broad assumptions, potentially leading in quite different directions.

At the centre of the theoretical vision of the Scottish Whigs was their commitment to the values of commercial society and modernity; and, as a direct consequence of this, the preoccupation with the maintenance of political stability in advanced and economically developed states. This commitment to modernity implied the rejection of feudal and paternalistic values, and the belief in the validity of the scientific understanding of the laws of the market and of 'scientific' politics – in other words, what was currently described as 'political economy' in the broadest sense of the term. The persuasion that commercial society was not a passing stage; that there was no escape back into some more archaic, egalitarian or paternalistic order; that, on balance, it was a more promising form of social organization – more conducive to general welfare and political liberty – than any previous other; that the existing political system should be modified and reshaped to accommodate its characteristics and its requirements – all of these beliefs clearly distinguished the reviewers' position from a number of other current political traditions and idioms.

Yet the adoption of the approach of political economy left open and undetermined several crucial questions. The belief in the superiority of commercial over ancient or feudal society did not imply an especially optimistic vision of the modern condition. It produced and favoured the growth of public education but did not exclude nostalgia for more aristocratic or elitist cultures. It acknowledged the inevitable growth of inequality, but did not explain how the conflicts which inequality would create within society itself should be dealt with. It suggested that modern society was moving rapidly towards a greater distribution of wealth and consequently a wider political participation; but it did not decree the speed at which this process was to take place, and left open the question of whether it should be promoted or delayed. It rejected as utopian all ideas of perfectibility and progress which did not take into account the constraints of scarcity and the division of labour; but was necessarily vague as to how binding and inflexible those constraints would prove in the long run. It established the existence of a natural affinity between commercial society and free representative government; but did not exclude the possible success of authoritarian policies. It disposed of the ideal of virtue inherited from the civic humanist tradition; but it left open the question of what forms of moral commitment would bind the citizens of a modern commercial state to their community.

This is not to imply that the reviewers themselves did not hold views about all of these questions, though these were often vague, differed considerably between themselves, and naturally changed through time. It means simply that the social theory, or family of social theories, to which they subscribed, allowed in principle for a very wide range of political choices and positions. This was even more apparent throughout the 1830s and 1840s, when the condition of the labouring poor and the growing class conflict within British society became a more dominant and generalized preoccupation than it had been ever before.

On the whole, there was something paradoxical in the relation which the reviewers entertained with the tradition of political economy. When they emigrated to London at the turn of the century, the young Scottish Whigs were in possession of what was undoubtedly a very exclusive and specialist knowledge of the subject. Through Dugald Stewart (whose lectures on moral philosophy and political economy were published only posthumously, in the 1850s) they had learnt a distinctive blend of the Physiocratic and Smithian doctrines, in which the views of the major writers were extensively illustrated and discussed.[13] When they started the *Review* and entered their political careers, they were in a position to capitalize on this knowledge by popularizing it, and gradually turning it into a vital part of political jargon. Familiar as they were with the analytical weaknesses of Smith's work, when new contributions to the subject were advanced by outsiders like David Ricardo, they were better placed than most to appreciate their importance, and assimilate them within the Smithian tradition. Yet this privileged familiarity with political economy did not remain their property alone. The reviewers were not the exclusive disseminators of Smithian doctrine into nineteenth-century English political culture. Although their contribution to the assimilation of political economy within the current political idiom was pioneering and probably decisive, the idiom itself was soon shared by other groupings and forces within parliament and the British press. Moreover, as time went by, the reviewers themselves felt increasingly alienated from what they perceived as the excessively specialist and dogmatic development of political economy effected by the Benthamite and Ricardian schools.

In conclusion, the difficulty in defining the position of the reviewers in terms of their ideological background is that what one finds there is extremely general, and that it overlaps significantly with the views and the beliefs of other competing political groupings.

II

The somewhat elusive and hesitant nature of the liberalism of the Scottish Whigs becomes even more apparent if one considers the question of the legacy of the *Edinburgh Review* to mid-nineteenth-century British culture. Here again, one is confronted with the paradox that the *Review* seems, on the one hand, extraordinarily influential, while on the other its influence is vague, diffuse, and difficult to place anywhere on the political map.

It is in general unsurprising that the migration of the Scottish intellectuals to England should result in the gradual loss of their original cultural identity. Unsurprising first because their education had been deeply embedded in the experience of the Scottish urban elites and of Scottish university teaching, and, in a sense, survived for an extraordinarily long time after its transplanting into an entirely different cultural milieu.[14] Secondly, if the reviewers skilfully exploited their Scottish training, they were also always fugitives from it. Their journals and correspondence were full of ironic remarks about the style and peculiarities of Scottish academic culture. They did not spare themselves or their masters in mocking mercilessly the compulsive Scottish passion for metaphysics, the constant resort to interminable historical reconstructions, the habit of leisurely and relentless philosophical reasoning on every conceivable subject. Their cult of Hume as the only genuinely cosmopolitan intellectual figure in the Scottish tradition and the only one to have had a significant impact upon English thought reinforces this impression.

No doubt their attitude towards their Scottish origins was profoundly ambivalent and – as in the case of Walter Scott – it allowed for a considerable amount of nostalgia. But the project of assimilation within English culture was always clear and unmistakable. It was also extremely successful. The *Review* was in this sense a decisive contribution to the Anglicization of Scottish culture as much as to its promotion.

Thirdly, if it was highly idiosyncratic and provincial, the Scottish intellectual background had also, within itself, a strong cosmopolitan vocation and was, to all effects, very open and receptive. The habit of systematic philosophical reasoning went together with a strong aversion towards any closed system of belief or dogmatic attitudes. Notoriously, the reviewers were driven to a frenzy of irritation and dislike when confronted with Bentham's writings and with the sectarian stance of the Philosophic Radicals. It was only too natural, then, that the Edinburgh grouping should gradually lose its distinctive identity. Even though, after Jeffrey's resignation in 1829, the new editor, Macvey Napier, managed to preserve most of the *Review*'s style and character, this result was only achieved by the employment of skilful professional journalists. It did not derive from the continuing existence of a close-knit group of people moved by a common political project.

The gradual dispersion of the Whigs in the years following the passing of the First Reform Bill accentuated this lack of political and ideological continuity. In this respect, it is interesting to compare the position of the most representative *Edinburgh Review*er in the second generation, Thomas Babington Macaulay, with that of two major contemporary intellectual figures for whom the *Review* was also an important point of reference, Thomas Carlyle and John Stuart Mill.

Macaulay began his association with the *Review* in 1825. In the following years he assisted Henry Brougham in his attempts to promote, through the *Review*, popular support for Canning's coalition government of 1827. By 1830, thanks to a series of brilliant political essays – the most successful of which was his attack on James Mill's *Essay on Government*[16] – he had worked himself into Lord Lansdowne's pocket borough of Calne. His rapid promotion to a parliamentary seat, – which aroused Brougham's immediate jealousy, proved especially well timed. Throughout the debate on the First Reform Bill, which found the Whigs unprepared, Macaulay helped to supply and popularize the arguments for parliamentary reform. That he represented a wise investment for the party is shown by the fact that the same arguments – or a weaker version of them – were still being used half a century after in the debate on the 1867 Reform Bill.[17]

Macaulay's career, his writings, and his journalistic style can be regarded as the perfect embodiment of the message of the *Edinburgh Review*. His success confirmed a pattern that had characterized the experience of the journal's founders – that of the promotion of talent to public life through the patronage of the enlightened section of the aristocracy. His writings were a successful blend of traditional Whig rhetoric with the historicism of the Scottish school. The belief in the inevitable progress of commercial society dictated the necessity for timely reform, and the adjustment of existing political structures to the needs of the modern industrial nation. It also offered, on the same basis, a warning against the danger of too rapid or too radical institutional changes. His style reproduced at its best the rhetorical technique which had decreed from the start the success of the *Edinburgh Review*. Following the example set by Francis Jeffrey (whose articles he claimed to know by heart), Macaulay sought the reader's complicity in demolishing, through what looked like plain, solid common sense, the supposed prejudices and false reasonings of his opponents. Much was, of course, achieved through facile, sensational, polemical effects, the legitimacy of which Macaulay defended, in a letter to Napier, by recalling the ephemeral nature of journalism:

> Now for high and grave works – a history, for example, or a system of political and moral philosophy – Doctor Johnson's rule, that every sentence which the writer thinks fine ought to be struck out, is excellent. But periodical works like ours, which, unless they strike at first reading, are not likely to strike at all, whose whole life is a month or two, may, I think, be allowed to be sometimes even viciously florid. Probably in estimating the real value of any tinsel which I may put upon my articles, you and I should not materially differ. But it is not by his own taste, but by the taste of the fish, that the angler is determined in his choice of bait.[18]

But the most important feature of this style of criticism was the rejection of any ostentatious intellectualism and the adoption of the sensible, balanced viewpoint of the common reader, of moderate and well-informed public opinion *par excellence*.

Where Macaulay embodied successfully and without any apparent tensions the spirit of the *Review*, showing how this could survive, as it were, *in vitro*, the conditions and aspirations which had created it, Thomas Carlyle's relation with the *Review* was a critical and problematic one. Like Macaulay, Carlyle was 'discovered' by the editor, Francis Jeffrey, who was impressed by the vividness and originality of Carlyle's literary talents. Like Macaulay, he was considered as a possible successor to Jeffrey when he was about to retire in 1829. But his association with the *Review* was not an easy one. His writing was certainly impressive, but was also highly idiosyncratic, and resisted the editor's practice of adapting each contributor's style to the rest of the journal. His interest in German culture, although initially welcomed, soon appeared overpowering, and was thought to aggravate his natural propensity to obscurity. In the end though still convinced of Carlyle's superior talents, Jeffrey gave up all hopes that he might learn to write for the readers of a periodical.[19]

For all these reasons, it is generally assumed that Carlyle's most famous contribution to the *Review*, 'The Signs of the Times', published in 1829[20] was, in some sense, an editorial mistake: a brilliant piece that appeared, through some oversight, in the wrong journal. On first reading, Carlyle's apocalyptic picture of the 'Mechanical Age' – the age dominated by machinery 'in every outward and inward sense of that word' – seems at odds with Macaulay's equally famous defence of the modern industrial condition in his review of Southey's *Colloquies on Society* (1830).[21] Yet the difference between the two articles is one of tone rather than of content. In both, modern society is presented as an historical reality from which there is no escape. In his critique of Southey Macaulay did not attempt to deny the material strictures and spiritual uneasiness which arose from the modern condition, but rather stressed the futility of seeking refuge from them in sterile nostalgia, in an appeal to an imaginary past, or in simple recrimination.

In Carlyle's essay the picture of modern society was also two- sided: the writer was divided between the spiritual impoverishment of the age on the one hand, and admiration for its conquests, and faith in its capacity for improvement, on the other:

> Neither, with all these evils more or less clearly before us, have we at any time despaired of the fortunes of society. Despair, or even despondency, in that respect, appears to us, in all cases, a groundless feeling .... However it may be with individual nations ... the happiness and greatness of mankind at large have been continually progressive. Doubtless this age also is advancing. Its very interest, its ceaseless activity, its discontent, contains matter of promise. Knowledge, education are opening the eyes of the humblest; are increasing the number of thinking minds without limit. This is as it should be; for not in turning back, not in resisting, but in resolutely struggling forward, does our life consist.[22]

Carlyle's depressing portrayal of the intellectual features of modern society: the reduction of literature and science to popular digests; the division of knowledge into specialized disciplines; the limiting – technical and instrumental – approach to politics and reform; the all-powerful rule of the periodical press – in other words, the impoverishment of individual experience and the loss of humanistic elitist culture, were all themes which had been frequently discussed in the *Review*, especially in Jeffrey's writings.[23]

I am not arguing here that Macaulay's and Carlyle's positions were identical, nor that they ultimately pointed at converging political views. What I wish to suggest is, rather, that they can be placed within the same perspective on modern commercial society; that they were formulated in compatible idioms; and that they could both be regarded in this respect as the expression of the *Review*'s distinctive approach.

A similar argument can be made for John Stuart Mill's position. Mill's relation with the *Review*, unlike Carlyle's or Macaulay's, was not that of a contributor or sympathizer, but that of a severe critic and political opponent. In 1824 the eighteen-year-old Mill assisted his father, James, in the preparation of two articles on 'Periodical Literature', which were published in the first two issues of the *Westminster Review*.[24] (John Stuart drafted the second of the two articles and supplied the material for both, though with characteristic modesty he attributed the merit of the authorship entirely to his father.) With these essays the newly-born radical journal marked its distance from the two leading political periodicals of the time, the Whig *Edinburgh Review*, and its imitator and competitor, the Tory *Quarterly Review*, edited by Walter Scott. The general argument in the articles was that the two journals were the expression of the 'sinister' interests of two competing factions of the British aristocracy: the conservative, which held the executive power; and the Whig opposition, which tried to win the support of public opinion in order to oust the Tories. Predictably, Mill's attack was more aggressive and critical of the *Edinburgh* than it was of the *Quarterly*. In his view, by following what appeared to be a middle course between the defence of the interests of the aristocracy and the protection of the rights of the people, the Whig journal created the deceptive impression of a will for progress and reform while in fact always stopping short of taking a clear stand on any issue. Thus, in Mill's reconstruction, the *Edinburgh*'s attitude was characterized by

a disposition to compromise, to say a little for aristocracy, a little for the people alternatively, and always to give up so much of every important question, as to avoid an irreparable breach, either with one side or with the other.[25]

The Whig contributors to the *Edinburgh Review* justified their willingness to compromise by arguing that it was necessary to 'yield in small things for the sake of the great ones'.[26] But what were the great ones? In Mill's view, they were never made explicit and were never seriously confronted. In this way, his analysis attacked the *Edinburgh* precisely for what was most distinctive about it: its efforts to find a middle course, its vocation for moderation, its claim to represent independent public opinion. As he gradually dissociated himself from the positions of the Utilitarians, John Stuart Mill relaxed his judgement on the *Edinburgh*: we know, for example, that he sided with Macaulay rather than with his own father in the dispute over the *Essay on Government*. However, in a retrospective assessment in the *Autobiography*, he still described the articles on 'Periodical Literature' as an entirely appropriate and very successful attack upon the supposed reformism of the Whigs.[27]

If Mill was firm and explicit in his opposition to Whig journalism, his article on 'Civilization', which appeared in the *London and Westminster Review* in 1836,[28] could have been printed in the *Edinburgh* alongside the essays by Macaulay and Carlyle cited above, without causing any surprise to the reader. His treatment of the issues of progress and civilization followed the same lines. In the article he made a distinction between two notions of civilization. The first was that of civilization in the more restrictive sense of material improvement – what distinguished modern, technologically and economically advanced societies from primitive ones. Civilization in this sense was both necessary and desirable. It was not, however, in itself sufficient to guarantee the progress of the second form of civilization, that which consisted in spiritual improvement, education, taste, and feelings of commitment to a given political community. The first form of civilization, Mill argued, had to some extent developed independently or even at the expense of the second. The growth and more widespread distribution of wealth and knowledge had resulted in the loss of importance of individuals, and consequently of individual spiritual energy, independence, and commitment, in favour of anonymous, and relatively passive, masses of people.

Mill's conclusions, however, were optimistic. He expressed the belief that not only was material civilization inescapable, but that it would be possible, in the long run, to exploit its advantages and counteract its negative effects:

> Is there, then, no remedy? Are the decay of individual energy, the weakening of the influence of superior minds over the multitude, the growth of charlatanerie and diminished efficacy of public opinion as a restraining power – are those the price we necessarily pay for the benefit of civilization; and can they only be avoided by checking the diffusion of knowledge, discouraging the spirit of combination, prohibiting improvements in the arts of life, and repressing the further increase of wealth and production? Assuredly not. Those advantages which civilization cannot give – which in its uncorrected influence has even a tendency to destroy – may yet coexist with civilization; and it is only when joined to civilization that they can produce their fairest fruits.[29]

The building of a spiritually and morally 'civilized' society could only be achieved through the promotion of truly popular education and wider political participation, and by using, rather than rejecting, the resources of material progress.

There is no room here to discuss the wide and complex issue of the influence of Scottish culture on John Stuart Mill's thought – an influence undoubtedly more important and decisive than Mill's own reconstruction of his intellectual development, as sketched in the *Autobiography* and in the essays on Bentham and

Coleridge, would lead us to believe.[30] In his case, as indeed in Carlyle's,[31] the impact of French and German Romanticism has been generally overestimated at the expense of the earlier, more subtle presence of the Scottish historical tradition. What is relevant for the purpose of this essay is, first, that it seems extremely difficult to establish a clear continuity or discontinuity between the tradition of sceptical Whiggism and some representative products of mid-nineteenth century English 'liberal' culture. Second, that if this is true of writers who were relatively close to the idiom and themes of reflection of the *Edinburgh Review*, it must be even more so in the case of the major 'reforming' enterprises that were only remotely connected with it, like the Society for the Diffusion of Useful Knowledge, the Board of Trade, and the Anti-Corn Law League.

It can, of course, be argued that to talk of the 'influence' of a particular intellectual tradition is in itself necessarily vague and misleading. But even if one accepts this, one is still left with the problem of what constituted the identity of the *Edinburgh Review* in the eyes of its contemporaries and in those of the following generations. Was there ever a real historical object which corresponded to Matthew Arnold's contemptuous picture?

> the great middle class liberalism, which had for the cardinal points of its belief the Reform Bill of 1832, and local self-government, in politics; in the social sphere, free-trade, unrestricted competition and the making of industrial fortunes; in the religious sphere, the Dissidence of Dissent and the Protestantism of Protestant religion.[32]

III

In a letter written on 23 March 1820, Robert Peel asked his correspondent, John Wilson Crocker:

> Do not you think that the tone of England – of that great compound of folly, weakness, prejudice, wrong feeling, right feeling, obstinacy, and newspaper paragraphs, which is called public opinion – is more liberal – to use an odious but intelligible phrase, than the policy of the Government? Do not you think that there is a feeling, becoming daily more general and more confirmed – that is, independent of the pressure of taxation, or any immediate cause – in favour of some undefined change in the mode of governing the country?[33]

This passage is illuminating, first, because the writer confirms the 'intelligibility' of the 'odious' phrase 'liberal'. Second, because he locates its meaning in the gap and opposition between critical public opinion on the one hand, and the current practice of government on the other. His suggestion was, in other words, that the main dividing-line was not between competing interests, parties, political strategies, or ideologies, but rather between the desire to maintain the status quo and a general aspiration to change embodied in and articulated by free opinion and the press.

The importance of raising public opinion at this juncture was by no means an especially new phenomenon. In different historical contexts, public opinion had been regarded, in the absence of constitutional guarantees, as the moderating force which kept the despotism of *ancien régime* governments within acceptable boundaries. In particular, the notion of public opinion played a central role in the Scottish theories of the growth of commercial society and the middling ranks.

Yet undoubtedly the development of the periodical press and of the means of popular education was perceived, at the beginning of the nineteenth century, as a factor of paramount importance, one which changed radically the character of British culture and political life. There was general agreement on this point, an agreement shared by those who regarded the newly-acquired power of the press as a positive conquest, an instrument of improvement and a guarantee of political freedom, and by those who saw it as a sign of irreparable decadence and a threat to individual spiritual autonomy.

Like the judgements expressed on the progress and merits of modern commercial society, the *Review* voiced both these views. Thus we find Macaulay in his review of Hallam, complacently observing that the gallery where the reporters sat (a place, incidentally, where he was known to spend a lot of his time) had become 'a fourth estate of the realm'.[34] Bagehot, for his part noted with satisfaction that, in creating the *Edinburgh Review*, Jeffrey had 'invented the trade of editorship'. Before him, he observed, an editor was 'a bookseller's drudge'; since then he had become 'a distinguished functionary'.[35] In contrast, Carlyle deplored the tyranny of the press and the general spiritual decadence which accompanied it, by claiming that:

> The true Church of England, at this moment, lies in the editors of its newspapers. These preach to the people daily; weekly; admonishing kings themselves; advising peace or war, with an authority which only the first Reformers, and a long-past class of Popes, were possessed of; inflicting moral censure; imparting moral encouragement, consolation, edification; in all ways diligently administering the Discipline of the Church.[36]

Jeffrey, himself, returned frequently to the themes of the impoverishment of knowledge, its separation into narrowly specialist compartments, its reduction to commonplace, instrumental approaches. He conjured up the picture – so vividly captured in Thomas Love Peacock's satires – of a culture in which encyclopaedias and penny tracts had replaced the study of the classics, ephemeral intellectual fashions succeeded one another, and in which the leading viewpoint was no longer that of the philosopher or the scholar, but that of the *épicier*, the ordinary middle-class reader.[37]

What was captured in these now optimistic, now dismayed comments on the development of the press was not merely the growth in the size and shift in the social background of the readership – even though the increase in the sales of the *Edinburgh Review* from 700 to over 10,000 copies within a few years constituted a striking indication of change. There was also a significant evolution in the style of literary and political criticism, once again pioneered by the *Edinburgh*, into what Bagehot called 'a middle species of writing'.[38] That tendency to find a middle way between opposing sides, which the young Mill had stigmatized as a lack of intellectual seriousness and moral consistency in the reviewers, was not only a political choice in the same way as Macaulay's skilful appeal to the reader's common sense and complicity was not merely a rhetorical device. The content and the style of the new periodical press were at one with each other. The novel type of critical writing coincided with the 'modern', 'liberal' approach to politics.

This coincidence was stressed by Bagehot when he argued that Whiggism was not a political credo, but a 'character', an intellectual attitude – fairness of mind, a 'defined neatness of the second order' – and successfully embodied in the *Review*.

> The kind of writing suitable to such minds is not the elaborate, ambitious, exhaustive discussion of former ages, but the clear, simple, occasional writing of the present times. The opinions expressed are short and simple; the innovations suggested are natural and evident; neither one nor the other require more than an intelligible statement, a distinct exposition to the world; and this reception would be only impeded by operose and cumbrous argumentation.[39]

Bagehot's identification of liberalism with a style of criticism – more generally with the function of the press – was no doubt largely self-referential.[40] His essay on the reviewers was written as a celebration of the kind of political journalism to which he himself had given a crucial contribution. Thus his highly sentimental picture of public opinion and the role of newspaper editors is clearly of its age and hence a subject for historical curiosity.

But the more general suggestion, offered by Michel Foucault in one of his lectures at the Collège de France, that liberalism should be seen not as a set of given policies and ideological beliefs, but as a form of systematic and focused criticism of the practice of government, deserves to be taken seriously.[41] The advantage of this reading of the term 'liberalism' (if indeed one wishes to continue to use this 'odious phrase' at all) is that, on the one hand, it can accommodate the unevenness and discontinuities of the nineteenth-century reform movement. As a criticism of governmental activity this could, in fact, reflect different interests and competing projects of change without losing its sense and purpose. It expressed itself through whatever idioms were available to highlight the errors and limits of current policies. Moreover, as a critique, it was bound to be parasitical upon whatever administrative practices it was trying to alter, and was liable to be modified and shaped by them in turn. Its eclecticism, in other words, was dictated by the very nature of critical activity. On the other hand, the existence of converging efforts to modify the status quo could justify the impression, captured in Peel's letter, of a unity of purpose and of the existence of a major dividing-line between government and opposition, establishment and public opinion.

If the criticism of government was essentially eclectic, the idioms it used had to appear theoretically more sophisticated and organized than those embodied in the current practices of administration. Political economy and the 'science' of politics presented themselves as rigorous and systematic (scientific, as opposed to piecemeal and customary) approaches to the issues of government and reform.

Writing in the *Edinburgh Review* in 1827, Henry Brougham observed that the old categories of Loyalist and Jacobin, Court and Country, Tory and Whig, had been replaced by those of 'Liberal' and 'Illiberal'.[42] The suggestion that liberalism is better seen in terms of an eclectic, and yet systematic opposition to the practice of government does not advance far beyond this kind of broad distinction. It does not offer an especially novel or revealing interpretation of what we already know about nineteenth-century British politics. But it can help us cut away some of the dead wood of empty and misleading classifications and definitions. It is an invitation to bridge the gap between the complexity of the picture we are trying to reconstruct on the one hand, and the limits of our generalizations on the other.

Notes

1 Sydney Smith, *Works* (Boston, 1854), pp. 3–4, cited in John Clive, *Scotch Reviewers: the 'Edinburgh Review', 1802–1815* (London and Cambridge, Mass., 1957), pp. 86–7.
2 Walter Bagehot, 'The First Edinburgh Reviewers', in Norman St John Stevas (ed.), *The Collected Works of Walter Bagehot*, 11 vols (London, 1965), vol. 1, p. 318.
3 See A. Foord, *His Majesty's Opposition 1714–1832* (Oxford, 1964); A. Mitchell, *The Whigs in Opposition 1815–1830* (Oxford, 1967); J. J. Sack, *The Grenvillites 1801–1829* (Urbana, Illinois, 1979); F. O'Gorman, *The Whig Party and the French Revolution* (London, 1967).
4 Henry Cockburn, *Memoirs of the Life of Lord Jeffrey*, 2 vols (Edinburgh, 1852), vol. 1, pp. 11–12.
5 In addition to John Clive's work cited above, see B. Fontana, *Rethinking the Politics of Commercial Society: the 'Edinburgh Review', 1802–1832* (Cambridge, 1985).
6 Duncan Forbes, *Hume's Philosophical Politics* (Cambridge 1975).
7 See Duncan Forbes, 'James Mill and India', *Cambridge Journal*, (5 October 1951), pp. 19–53; and 'The Rationalism of Sir Walter Scott', (7 October 1953), pp. 20–35.
8 A. Aspinall, *Lord Brougham and the Whig Party* (Manchester, 1927); C. New, *Life of Henry Brougham to 1830* (Oxford, 1961); an important source on Brougham's early political attitudes is R. H. M. Buddle Atkinson and G. A. Jackson (eds), *Brougham and his Early Friends: Letters to James Lock, 1798–1809*, 3 vols (London, 1908); on Horner see L. Horner (ed.), *Memoirs and Correspondence of Francis Horner*, 2 vols (1843). On the Whig leadership, see Michel Roberts, 'The Leadership of the Whig Party in the House of Commons from 1807 to 1815', *The English Historical Review*, 1 (October 1935), pp. 620–38.
9 Duncan Forbes, 'Scientific Whiggism, Adam Smith and John Millar', *Cambridge Journal*, 7 (August 1954), pp. 643–70; I. Hont and M. Ignatieff (eds), *Wealth and Virtue: Political Economy in the Scottish Enlightenment* (Cambridge, 1985).

10 See: J. R. M. Butler, *The Passing of the Great Reform Bill* (London, 1914, repr. 1964); O. F. Christie, *The Transition from Aristocracy 1832–1867* (London, 1927); D. C. Moore, *The Politics of Deference, a Study of Mid-nineteenth-century English Political System* (New York, 1976); Norman Gash, *Politics in the Age of Peel, a Study in the Technique of Parliamentary Representation 1830–1850* (London, 1953).

11 Donald Southgate, *The Passing of the Whigs 1832–1886* (London, 1962); Norman Gash, *Reaction and Reconstruction in English Politics 1832–1852* (Oxford, 1965).

12 D. Winch, 'The Case of Good Government: Philosophic Whigs versus Philosophic Radicals', in J. Burrow, S. Collini, and D. Winch, *That Noble Science of Politics* (Cambridge, 1983), pp. 91–126; William Thomas, *The Philosophical Radicals: Nine Studies in Theory and Practice 1817–1841* (Oxford, 1979).

13 Sir William Hamilton (ed.), *The Collected Works of Dugald Stewart*, 10 vols (Edinburgh, 1854–60), vols 8 and 9.

14 N. Phillipson, 'The Pursuit of Virtue and University Education: Dugald Stewart and Scottish Moral Philosophy in the Age of the Enlightenment', *The University in Society, Past, Present and Future*, a conference to celebrate the 400th Anniversary of the University of Edinburgh (Edinburgh, 1983).

15 L. Horner (ed.), *Memoirs of Francis Horner*, vol. 1, pp. 108–9.

16 T. B. Macaulay, 'Mill's *Essay on Government*: Utilitarian Logics and Politics', *Edinburgh Review*, 49 (October 1829), pp. 159–89; 'Bentham's Defence of Mill: Utilitarian System of Philosophy', *Edinburgh Review*, 49 (June 1829), pp. 273–99; 'Utilitarian Theory of Government and "the Greatest Happiness Principle"', *Edinburgh Review*, 50 (October 1829), pp. 100–24.

17 The best study of Macaulay's Whiggism is John Burrow, *A Liberal Descent: Victorian Historians and the English Past* (Cambridge, 1981); see also John Clive, *Thomas Babington Macaulay – the Shaping of the Historian* (London, 1973).

18 T. B. Macaulay to M. Napier, 25 January 1830. M. Napier (ed.), *Selections from the Correspondence of the late Macvey Napier Esq.* (London, 1879), p. 77; cited in Clive, *Macaulay*, p. 113.

19 J. A. Froude, *Thomas Carlyle,* 2 vols (London, 1882), vol. 2, pp. 54–9.

20 Thomas Carlyle, 'Signs of the Times', *Edinburgh Review*, 49, (June 1829), pp. 439–59; repr. in *Critical and Miscellaneous Essays*, 7 vols (London, 1869), vol. 2, pp. 230–52.

21 *Edinburgh Review*, 50 (January 1830), pp. 528–65; repr. in *Critical and Historical Essays*, 2 vols (London, 1856), vol. 2, pp. 98–121.

22 T. Carlyle, *Critical and Miscellaneous Essays*, vol. 2, pp. 250–1.

23 See for example his review of Mme de Staël's *De la littérature*, 'Mad. de Staël – sur la Litérature' [sic], *Edinburgh Review*, 21 (February 1813), pp. 1–50. See also Peter F. Morgan, *Jeffrey's Criticism*, (Edinburgh, 1983), Introduction, pp. 1–19.

24 James Mill, 'Periodical Literature: *Edinburgh Review*', *Westminster Review*, 1 (January 1824), pp. 206–49; John Stuart Mill, 'Periodical Literature: *Edinburgh Review*', *Westminster Review*, 1 (April 1824), pp. 505–41; repr. in J. M. Robson and J. Stillinger (eds), *Collected Works of John Stuart Mill, Autobiography and Literary Essays*, vol. 1 (Toronto, 1981), pp. 291–325.

25 J. S. Mill, *Autobiography and Literary Essays*, p. 293.

26 Ibid., p. 315.

27 J. S. Mill, *Autobiography* (London, 1873), pp. 92–4.

28 J. S. Mill, 'Civilisation', *London and Westminster Review* (3 and 25 April 1836), pp. 1–28, repr. in J. M. Robson and A. Brady (eds), *Essays on Politics and Society*, in *The Collected Works of John Stuart Mill* (Toronto, 1977), vols 18 and 19, vol. 18, pp. 117–47. See on this article B. Fontana, 'Democracy and Civilization: John Stuart Mill and the Critique of Political Economy', *Economies et Sociétés*, 20 (March 1986), pp. 3–24.

29 J. S. Mill, *Essays on Politics and Society*, pp. 135–6.
30 J. H. Burns, 'The Light of Reason: Philosophical History in the Two Mills', J. M. Robson and M. Laine (eds), *James and John Stuart Mill: Papers of the Centenary Conference* (Toronto, 1976), pp. 3–20.
31 I am indebted to John Burrow for this suggestion. On Carlyle and Scotland, in addition to Froude, *Thomas Carlyle*, see Jan Campbell, *Thomas Carlyle* (London, 1974).
32 Matthew Arnold, *Culture and Anarchy: an Essay in Political and Social Criticism* (London, 1869), pp. 36–7.
33 Lewis J. Jennings (ed.), *The Correspondence and Diaries of the Late Right Honourable John Wilson Crocker*, 2 vols (New York, 1884), 1, pp. 155–6, cited in J. Clive, *Thomas Babington Macaulay*, p. 101.
34 T. B. Macaulay, *Critical and Historical Essays*, p. 95.
35 W. Bagehot, 'The First Edinburgh Reviewers', *Works*, 1, p. 332.
36 T. Carlyle, 'The Signs of the Times', *Critical and Miscellaneous Essays*, 2, p. 248.
37 T. L. Peacock, 'The épicier', in H. F. B. Brett-Smith and C. E. Jones (eds), *Works of Thomas Love Peacock*, 10 vols (London, 1924–5), pp. 293–4; see also G. Davie, 'The Social Significance of the Scottish Philosophy of Common Sense', The Dow Lecture 1972 (Dundee, 1973).
38 W. Bagehot, 'The First Edinburgh Reviewers', *Works*, 1, p. 323.
39 Ibid., pp. 321–2.
40 J. Burrow, 'Sense and Circumstances: Bagehot and the Nature of Political Understanding', in J. Burrow, S. Collini, and D. Winch, *That Noble Science of Politics*, pp. 161–81.
41 Unfortunately, due to the unclear status of the copyright of Foucault's works, these lectures are at present accessible only in the form of 'unofficial' tape-recordings and it is impossible to give a proper reference. I can only acknowledge the source.
42 H. Brougham, 'State of Parties', *Edinburgh Review*, 46 (1827), p. 431.

Chapter four

The origin of liberal utilitarianism: Jeremy Bentham and liberty[1]

Frederick Rosen

I

'The definition of liberty', wrote Jeremy Bentham in 1776, 'is one of the corner stones of my system: and one that I know not how to do without.'[2] At the time, he was assisting his friend, John Lind, in the latter's critique of Richard Price's influential pamphlet, *Observations on the Nature of Civil Liberty, the Principles of Government and the Justice and Policy of the War with America* (1776).[3] Price's conception of liberty might best be described as Lockean. Like Locke, he defined liberty in terms of power, and also linked it with law and reason.[4] But Price discarded both the framework of natural law and the moderate tone that characterized Locke's discussion of liberty in the context of the preservation of life, liberty, and property. In place of Locke's emphasis on consent, he conceived liberty in a more radical fashion in terms of self-determination and self-government, and defined civil liberty as 'the power of a *Civil Society* or *State* to govern itself by its own discretion; or by laws of its own making, without being subject to any foreign discretion, or to the impositions of any extraneous will or power'.[5]

Even though Price's argument was the subject of considerable controversy during the passionate debate over American independence, especially as his conception of political liberty envisaged some form of self-government and widespread participation by the people, one of its main virtues lay in the coherent way in which it was able to link individual with civil and political liberty. On both levels liberty was conceived as self-government or self-direction without impediment from outside forces.

Many of those who criticised Price at this time simply equated the existing British constitution with civil liberty and saw in Price's pamphlet confusion, if not subversion.[6] The utilitarian response, at least in Richard Hey's pamphlet, tended to define liberty more narrowly as the absence of restraint, and then conceived of civil liberty in terms of a legal system justified by the principle of utility.[7]

One difficulty with this approach was that, for the individual, liberty meant the absence of restraint, while for civil society, liberty depended on the imposition of restraints. This apparent contradiction was explained by the argument that the restraints justified by utility actually enlarged freedom by preventing some people from interfering in the affairs of others. Nevertheless, this argument tended to confuse liberty with utility and led William Paley, using a utilitarian argument, to make the paradoxical assertion that a person imprisoned under a law that brought great benefits to society might have lost his personal liberty but not his civil liberty.[8]

It is important to note that Bentham rejected not only Price's Lockean approach but also the utilitarian conceptions of Hey and Paley. Bentham's own idea of liberty evolved during this period of Lind's debate with Price. In the letter to Lind, quoted above, he referred to 'a kind of discovery' which he believed he had made, namely, 'that the idea of Liberty, imported nothing in it that was positive: that it was merely a negative one: and that accordingly I defined it "*the absence of restraint*".'[9] For various reasons Bentham revised his definition to include constraint as well as restraint, and finally settled on the definition of liberty as the absence of coercion. He found the idea of liberty as the absence of restraint too narrow as it failed to take into account the more positive constraints which he believed were also deprivations of liberty.[10]

In arguing that the idea of liberty was a wholly negative idea, Bentham implicitly ruled out not only a utilitarian conception of civil liberty but also any notion of civil and political liberty conceived in terms of law:

> Liberty then is neither more nor less than the absence of coercion. This is the genuine, original and proper sense of the word liberty. The idea of it is an idea purely negative. It is not any thing that is produced by positive Law. It exists without Law, and not by means of Law.[11]

If liberty and law were incompatible, Bentham could not easily formulate conceptions of civil and political liberty which, for most writers, were based on the operation of law. Those civil arrangements, for example, that depended on the laws to protect the individual's rights to property were, for Bentham, based ultimately on the threat of coercion and hence on the deprivation of liberty. In his view these arrangements could not be described as enhancing liberty.

As Bentham saw no easy link between individual and civil liberty, like that present in Locke's and Price's theories, and as he was unwilling to depict liberty as another way of using utility, he decided to abandon the whole attempt to link the two spheres. For clearer notions of civil and political liberty he turned to Montesquieu who, in *L'Esprit des lois*, had defined political liberty in terms of security.

> The political liberty of a citizen is a tranquillity of mind arising from the opinion each person has of his safety [*sûreté*]. In order to have this liberty, it is necessary that the government be so constituted that a citizen need not fear another citizen.[12]

L'Esprit des lois contains a number of definitions of liberty or instances where liberty is invoked. At some points Montesquieu seems to follow Locke, for example in defining liberty in terms of doing what the law permits.[13] Yet the conception of political liberty in terms of security had the effect, at least on Bentham, of freeing conceptions of liberty from the approach of Locke. Nevertheless, Bentham differed from Montesquieu in more rigorously limiting the definition of liberty to the absence of coercion, while using 'security' in place of ideas of civil and political liberty rather than in definitions of these ideas. The use of the concept of security enabled Bentham to take a fresh and original look at the notions traditionally explored by others from Lockean or utilitarian perspectives.

Although in Hobbes and Locke the idea of security played an important role as the major object sought in the formation of civil society, those writers did not link it directly with liberty. Nevertheless, Montesquieu's insight and Bentham's development of his idea revealed a close connection between security and liberty. Security is often conceived as being *against* something: houses are secured against burglars by installing latches, locks, and alarms. Society is secured against invasion by developing a strong defence system, and against famine by the provision of sufficient supplies of food and a distribution network. In securing *against*, freedom is often created – securing a house against burglars creates freedom from interference by burglars. Not all instruments of security create freedom, but freedom can be established through the use of security. Security in this context is two-dimensional: it manifests the instruments of security and the freedom and well-being created by their use. What Bentham saw and what was fundamental to the development of his conception of liberty was that the instruments of security were the crucial elements in the traditional notion of civil and political liberty, rather than the definitions of these terms themselves. In other words, to establish freedom from interference by burglars, one must concentrate on the development of good locks and alarms. Bentham's move to replace notions of civil and political liberty with the concept of security would enable him to concentrate on the instruments of security. Neither of the two utilitarians, Hey and Paley, had approved of Montesquieu's formulation of political liberty as security. Hey found Montesquieu's conception confusing as he seemed to have confused liberty first with a right to liberty and then with its effects, namely security and tranquillity of mind.[14] Paley referred to the idea of civil liberty as security as 'neither so simple nor so accurate' as his own account, though he admitted that it was closer to 'common discourse'.[15] He also believed that it encompassed too many and different ideas of civil liberty to be worth while.[16]

That Bentham rejected the move to conceive of civil and political liberty in terms of simple calculations of utility and, in addition, found that the emphasis on security was rejected by some contemporary utilitarians, is of some importance in understanding the significance of liberty in his utilitarian system. As security, liberty played the most fundamental role as the main end of legislation, and as a component of the principle of utility itself. Security established the framework within which each person could realize his or her own happiness. Security pointed to the pains against which every human sought protection. 'It has been shown that the happiness of the individuals, of whom a community is composed, that is their pleasures *and their security*, is the end and the sole end which the legislator ought to have in view.'[17] Security was even more fundamental than this passage suggests, because without security, and especially security of expectation, on which the continued existence of the individual's hopes and projects depended, there could be little pleasure and even less happiness.[18] For without security of expectation few of the pleasures of civilized life could be enjoyed, and those of a simpler existence would be fleeting and always under threat.

The legislator, for Bentham, could not maximize the pleasures of each individual in a society, or even respond to each person's wishes and desires, as he could not possibly know what gave pleasure, and if he did, he would be unable to satisfy everyone. What he could do, however, was provide for their basic security, so that they were able to maximize their own choice of pleasures and establish a way of life which brought them happiness.

Without entering into the complexities of Bentham's utilitarian theory, it is important to see how security provides the framework within which each individual lives. That framework might be called a framework of civil and political liberty. Its importance to Bentham may be seen in the fact that he was not satisfied with the simple calculation of the consequences of actions in approaching the complex problems of law and politics. The legislator acted indirectly; he established the framework of security through law, a framework whose value was judged initially by the liberty each person had to pursue his own pleasures so long as he did not harm the interests of others. At the level of the civil law, the legislator secured rights to property, prevented interference, simplified titles and judicial proceedings, and enhanced competitiveness in commercial transactions. At the level of criminal law, he secured the individual against crime with a rational criminal code and a strong and effective police force and judiciary. At the level of constitutional law, the legislator aimed to provide security against misrule.

II

Let us consider in greater detail Bentham's idea of constitutional liberty. In the early *Fragment on Government* he raised the question of how free government might be distinguished from despotic government. He rejected the simplistic view that rulers in a despotic state had greater power than those in a free state and argued that the distinction 'turns upon circumstances of a very different complexion'.[19] Free government, he believed, depended

> on the *manner* in which that whole mass of power, which, taken together, is supreme, is, in a free state, *distributed* among the several ranks of persons that

are sharers in it:– on the *source* from whence their titles to it are successively derived:– on the frequent and easy *changes* of condition between govern*ors* and govern*ed*; whereby the interests of the one class are more or less indistinguishably blended with those of the other:– on the *responsibility* of the governors; or the right which a subject has of having the reasons publicly assigned and canvassed of every act of power that is exerted over him:– on the *liberty of the press*; or the security with which every man, be he of the one class or the other, may make known his complaints and remonstrances to the whole community:– on the *liberty of public association*; or the security with which malecontents may communicate their sentiments, concert their plans, and practise every mode of opposition short of actual revolt, before the executive power can be legally justified in disturbing them.[20]

It is not clear if this list was meant to be suggestive rather than exhaustive. It is fair to say, however, that the 'circumstances' do not constitute a set of conditions, necessary or sufficient, for the existence of free government, as they are too general to function in this manner. What he seems to have listed here are the factors to be taken into consideration in establishing free government. The last two – liberty of the press and liberty of public association – were directly linked to constitutional liberty as security against misrule. Nevertheless, one might have expected Bentham to have argued that liberty of the press was important because it enabled people to reach the truth and to develop responsibly as mature citizens within society, and that such developments would advance the greatest happiness of the greatest number. But such an expectation would betray an ignorance of Bentham's approach. His argument was, in fact, different in referring to the security each person should have to make known 'complaints and remonstrances' to the community. The reason Bentham's approach differed from the one which might be expected is that he was not concerned directly with maximizing happiness, but indirectly with providing security against misrule and hence freedom for individuals to maximize their own happiness. This was the framework of security which would prevent misrule. Bentham did not deny that liberty of speech was important for other reasons, but he was primarily concerned with preventing misrule as part of his conception of a free state. The same response may be given to his reference to liberty of public association. This 'liberty', as he noted, constituted a framework of security within which 'malecontents may communicate their sentiments, concert their plans, and practise every mode of opposition short of actual revolt, before the executive power can be legally justified in disturbing them.' The consequence of this arrangement was the prevention of misrule, and through the prevention of misrule, the reduction of pain and consequently the increase in happiness.

At the time of the French Revolution, Bentham moved beyond this listing or cataloguing of various expedients to prevent misrule and began to construct a theory of constitutional liberty.[21] He now decisively rejected the theory which he had inherited from Montesquieu and his follower, Jean DeLolme:

The true efficient cause and measure of constitutional liberty or rather security is the dependence of the possessors of efficient power upon the originative power of the body of the people.

A spurious efficient cause and measure that has been hitherto commonly substituted to the one above mentioned is the division of the mass of political power by the allotment of different branches of it to different hands.[22]

Bentham presented three main arguments against the doctrine of the division of power. First, he argued that if rulers were already accountable to the people, no additional security was gained by dividing power. Where historically the division of power had been useful, it was because the different parties in conflict had appealed to the people generally for help in their struggle. 'As they quarrelled,' he wrote, 'they appealed to the people: as the appeal spread and the people availed themselves of it, the people gained liberty.'[23] The division of power did not in itself establish constitutional liberty, but where there was conflict, the people were able to benefit from existing divisions to enhance their liberty. However, once accountable government was established no such division would be necessary. Second, with the division of power it was possible that minority rule would replace that of the majority. This development might not be immediately apparent, as one justification for the division of power was that it required a broader consensus for agreement than a simple majority. But Bentham argued that the division gave minorities a veto on legislation. He did not believe that the sacrifice of majority to minority rule was a desirable quality in government, and he nearly always saw evil consequences in it. Third, he argued that where there was no opposition among those who possessed divided power, the system was entirely without effect.[24] Any measure might be adopted unless there was some popular accountability, and it is accountability to the people and not the division of power which had the greater effect.

In place of the division of power, Bentham thus emphasized the accountability of the rulers to the ruled, not only as a good in itself but also as a means of establishing constitutional liberty. He expressed this link with liberty almost as a mathematical proportion: 'Constitutional liberty depends upon and is proportioned to the dependence of the possessors of efficient public power upon the will of the body of the people, in virtue of the originative power they possess.'[25] At the time of the French Revolution, Bentham briefly developed a theory of constitutional democracy which included such securities as a widespread suffrage, an elected assembly, frequent elections, freedom of the press, and of association, and other practices which were widely regarded by reformers as characteristics of a system of constitutional liberty.[26] Bentham included these various practices in his theory because he believed that they would prevent misrule and secure the individual from arbitrary and despotic government. In the *Constitutional Code*, he expanded the notion of security to include not only securities against misrule but also securities for appropriate aptitude, with the latter developed from the framework of the former.[27] If, as a security for appropriate aptitude, Bentham advocated a system of education and competitive examination for potential civil servants, this system was designed to prevent misrule by ignorant and incompetent public officials appointed on the basis of family connection, bribery or some other form of corruption as opposed to merit. Similarly, the 'pecuniary competition system', which enabled equally qualified appointees to compete for official posts at the lowest salaries, was designed to reduce the potentially despotic power of government to impose heavy taxes for the sake of paying inflated salaries to civil servants. His fully developed account of securities for appropriate aptitude was a complex system for preventing misrule set forth within the framework of a constitutional democracy.[28]

III

Bentham's later writings on parliamentary reform and constitutional democracy clearly established his as the first liberal utilitarian. During the 1820s, when his international reputation was at its highest, he was regarded as a liberal, and indeed, addressed his own writings on constitutional democracy 'to all nations and all governments professing liberal opinions'.[29] When his follower, Edward Blaquiere, proposed in 1820 to establish closer links between liberal thinkers throughout Europe through a *bureau de correspondance*, he immediately linked Bentham and his friends in England, Benjamin Constant and colleagues in France, Etienne Dumont in Geneva, and men leading the liberal struggles in Spain, Naples, and Portugal as the key figures in this association.[30]

Although I have called Bentham the first liberal utilitarian, he was never a liberal ideologue. His main interest was in the development of a philosophical theory of law and government with the notion of liberty as security at its heart. Nevertheless, he advanced numerous ideas which would become central to the liberal creed of the nineteenth century: liberty of speech and the press, liberty of association, freedom of trade, freedom to emigrate from one country to another, support for the rule of law, faith in public opinion, and freedom from arbitrary and despotic government which was not accountable to the people. But his orientation towards theory has led some commentators to misjudge Bentham and, especially in the twentieth century, Bentham has been criticized as an opponent of liberty. They have generally developed two sorts of arguments: the first has attacked Bentham's role in the development of liberal thought; the second has contended that whatever Bentham's intentions might have been, experience since his time has shown a clear threat to liberty from the political institutions required to sustain democracy and national security. The institutions and practices which Bentham thought should go together in expanding liberty (as security) have turned out, on this view, to be the greatest threat to liberty.

The most influential critique of Bentham's role in the development of liberal thought may be found in Elie Halévy's *La Formation du radicalisme philosophique*, where Halévy depicted Bentham as introducing into liberal thought an authoritarianism which was at odds both with the 'Whig' doctrine that preceded it and with contemporary radical and democratic thought.[31] For Halévy, liberalism in this period meant a devotion to liberty and emancipation, to such principles as the social contract (through which resistance might be justified) and the division of power (as the bulwark against despotism), support for the American Revolution, and the acceptance of the principle of commercial liberalism. As Bentham apparently rejected many of these ideas, Halévy saw in his writing this authoritarian tendency. Halévy's criticisms were subtle and complex and can only be discussed briefly here.[32] On one level, he read Bentham in terms of French philosophical and political categories. Montesquieu was the main source of liberalism, and English followers of Montesquieu (e.g. Burke) were considered Whigs. Whoever rejected or criticized Montesquieu's depiction of the British constitution as a system of political liberty, criticized or rejected liberalism. Helvetius was regarded as a utilitarian and also as an advocate of despotism. Anyone who rejected or criticized Montesquieu on utilitarian grounds was considered at best a Tory follower of Hume, or at worst sympathetic to despotism. Finally, whoever advocated democracy, advocated 'Jacobinism' which supposedly posed a dire threat to constitutional liberty.

Because Bentham criticized Montesquieu, was a utilitarian, and supported representative democracy, he was considered by Halévy as an authoritarian in politics. Halévy saw this tendency in two aspects of Bentham's critique of Montesquieu. The first, as we have seen, was the rejection of the doctrine of the division of power and its replacement by Bentham with a doctrine of legislative supremacy; and the second was Bentham's critique of Montesquieu's belief that the current British judicial system contained valuable guarantees of the liberties of those accused of crime.

Even though Halévy knew that Bentham took his conception of liberty as security from Montesquieu, he none the less argued that liberty was not one of the four ends of Bentham's theory of legislation. He also argued that Bentham did not consider liberty as instrumental to bringing about the greatest happiness – 'his philosophy is essentially a philosophy written for legislators and men engaged in government, that is to say for men whose profession it is to restrict liberty.'[33] Halévy obviously failed to appreciate the significance of Bentham's emphasis on security as a replacement for the traditional idea of political liberty, and he especially failed to see that Bentham's emphasis on security gave liberty a special place in his utilitarian system. As a result, his reading of Bentham's critique of Montesquieu's doctrine of the division of power did not recognize that Bentham was attempting to replace one notion of political liberty with another. Where Halévy saw legislative supremacy and potential despotism, Bentham saw legislative dependence, security against misrule, and hence liberty. Bentham also believed that numerous aspects of the British judicial system, which Montesquieu in theory had praised, did not provide sufficient security for the individual and he sought to replace these with others. Whatever the value of his suggestions, the key point was that they were suggestions set forth within the framework of political liberty as security. The argument that Bentham wrote for legislators whose object was to restrict liberty was largely irrelevant, especially as Bentham's conception of civil and political liberty led to a concentration specifically on legislation which would act as securities against misrule.

In his writings on representative democracy, Bentham displayed a consistent distrust of the exercise of political power. Ruling elites possessed the means to oppress the people and were sorely tempted by 'sinister interest' to do so, unless prevented by the structure of the constitution and the pressure of the people themselves. Though he believed that rulers needed ample power to rule, for without such power they could not fulfil the wishes of the people, the power they had must be secured against misrule. Bentham emphasized the importance of publicity and public opinion, as well as law, to achieve this end, and Halévy criticized him for placing too much reliance on publicity and especially on public opinion. [34] But Bentham argued that rulers alone could not be relied on to reform the law for the simple reason that rulers were tempted to use the law to benefit themselves. The pressure of public opinion was, for Bentham, of crucial importance as a counterforce to the 'sinister interest' of rulers, despite the existence of legal remedies. Nevertheless, when he became a democrat, he never argued that the voice of the people carried some kind of transcendent authority. The power of the people was limited, but if law was not available to prevent misrule, public opinion was.[35]

The second type of critic of Bentham's commitment to liberty may not have doubted that he intended to advocate liberty, but has concluded that his or similar theories have not achieved this object. Their criticisms have varied widely. Some have seen in Bentham's advocacy of democracy, security, or even utility, major threats to individual liberty. For some of these, an 'omnicompetent' legislature fulfilling the will of the people, with the other branches of government clearly subordinate, has evoked the spectre of 'democratic despotism'.[36] Others have argued that an emphasis on security may threaten liberty in requiring massive state power and the redistribution of wealth. Such an emphasis has evoked the spectre of the totalitarian state organized for efficient production while stamping out individualism, eccentricity, and, most of all, dissent.[37] Utilitarianism itself has been thought to threaten individual liberty by emphasizing the happiness of the greatest number and rejecting the primacy of individual rights, thus evoking the spectre of the tyranny of the majority.[38] Still others have seen in Bentham's account of human psychology and motivation a shallow and somewhat mechanical view of the individual psyche which is at variance with deeper conceptions of individual development and creativity; this shallow view of the human condition, it is believed, found its institutional form in the Panopticon or National Charity Company.[39]

These criticisms are only plausible if Bentham's arguments are removed from the historical and philosophical contexts in which they were set forth. Although Bentham attempted to construct systematic theory, he was greatly, if indirectly, stimulated by the dramatic events which occurred during his long life. His liberalism developed in the contexts of the American struggle for Independence, the French Revolution, the massacre at Peterloo, and the liberal struggles in Spain and Portugal, all of which affected him profoundly and provided important lessons for his theory. Although he initially opposed the Lockean ideas with which Price justified the American struggle, Bentham came to admire the development of constitutional democracy in America.[40] He especially appreciated the success of the Americans in combining an extensive suffrage with security of property as convincing proof that no practical obstacle existed to the extension of suffrage in Britain.[41] His reaction to the French Revolution made him suspicious of all revolutionary change, and especially of the rhetoric of abstract rights and general claims to liberty.[42] Although he fully recognized that the people must resist when faced with unremitting despotic rule and enslavement, he had little confidence in revolution to achieve some sort of individual and political emancipation.[43] His experience of the revolutionary period led him to insist on gradual change based on an overall security of expectation for each individual in society. The massacre at Peterloo reinforced his growing view that political power must be accountable to the people and that changes must be made urgently in Britain to achieve this accountability. With Francis Place he extended his interest in reform to include important initiatives in expanding political participation beyond the narrow circle of middle-class reform.[44] The periods of liberal rule in Spain and Portugal (1820–3), and the emergence of new states in Latin America and Greece, in which considerable interest was taken in Bentham's ideas not only as a philosopher but also as a codifier of law, encouraged him to conceive the utopian vision of a liberal constitutional democracy based on a rational system of codified law supported by an enlightened and educated public opinion.[45]

The commitment to political democracy, to gradual reform based on security of expectation and to an extension of suffrage and participation to as many members of society as possible may have involved a rejection of some ideas traditionally associated with liberty, but in their place he developed new ideas, stimulated by the dramatic events of this period, within a framework of liberty conceived in terms of security. Bentham was both a critic and a follower of what might be called the Lockean tradition in political thought. Without giving up his commitment to liberty, he saw that Locke's theory, even in so radical a form as it appeared in Price's pamphlet at the time of the American Revolution, was either confused or inappropriate to the political conditions which had evolved by the early nineteenth century. He thought that Locke's emphasis on the preservation of property as the object of civil society was such that 'the poor in a body [are] a community which the rich in a body are entitled to make slaves of and for ever treat as such.'[46] The revolutionary period had abundantly shown that the security of the rich depended upon the security of the poor and, as such, security could not be restricted to that of property already acquired. Bentham argued for a gradual redistribution of wealth (largely through a tax on inheritance), which would provide minimal security for the poor and would create a society in which the possessions of the rich would not be threatened. Furthermore, as Bentham could easily see, Price's conception of civil liberty as self-determination, though Lockean in origin, was both vague and dangerous. Indeed, Bentham, emphasizing reform rather than revolution, was a worthy follower of that moderation which Locke had built into his conception of liberty. Yet, Bentham's concentration on security – on the instruments of good government – enabled him to move beyond the Lockean conception of the minimal state towards one more appropriate for a modern democratic society where security would be conceived more widely in terms of education, health, and welfare as well as real property and wealth.

If Bentham did not wish to legislate a preference for poetry to push-pin (a form of billiards), he also insisted that the pleasures and preferences of each individual in a society were due equal respect and protection so long as the pursuit of pleasure by some did not interfere with the enjoyment of others. He was especially willing to reduce the restrictions, enforced by religious doctrine and the common law, which limited the harmless pleasures that might be shared between consenting adults.[47] But he concentrated on the relief of pain, and in providing security at this level, he did not need to probe deeply into the human psyche to understand some deeper springs of intellectual and spiritual emancipation. He left such activities to individuals themselves, though the framework he established enabled his utilitarian disciple, J. S. Mill, to develop a conception of liberty which would meet even these aspirations.[48]

Notes

1   I am indebted to members of the Bentham Project and to various editors of volumes in the *Collected Works* for assistance in many forms. My thanks are also due to Professor J. H. Burns for sharing with me his recent work on Bentham's *Fragment on Government*. A generous grant from the Suntory Toyota International Centre for Economics and Related Disciplines (STICERD), London School of Economics and Political Science, has supported the research for this essay.

2   J. Bentham, *Correspondence*, ed. T. L. S. Sprigge (London, 1968), (*CW*), I. 309. The abbreviated reference to *CW* is to the *Collected Works of Jeremy Bentham* (London, 1968– in progress).

3   For an account of Bentham's relationship with Lind and the debate with Price, see H. L. A. Hart, *Essays on Bentham* (Oxford, 1982), pp. 53–65. The best analysis of Price's concept of liberty is in D. O. Thomas, *The Honest Mind, The Thought and Work of Richard Price* (Oxford, 1977), pp. 152ff, 188ff.

4   See John Locke, *An Essay Concerning Human Understanding*, Bk II, ch. xxi. 8, 15, 51; *Two Treatises of Government*, II, 22–3, 57.

5   R. Price, *Observations on the Nature of Civil Liberty* (London, 1776), p. 3.

6   See, for example, *Licentiousness Unmasked; or, Liberty Explained* (London, n.d. [1776 or 1777]), pp. 5, 8.

7   R. Hey, *Observations on the Nature of Civil Liberty and the Principles of Government* (London, 1776), pp. 8, 55–6, 61; see also the later pamphlet: *Happiness and Rights. A Dissertation upon Several Subjects Relative to the Rights of Man and his Happiness* (York, 1792).

8   *The Principles of Moral and Political Philosophy* (1785), in *The Works of William Paley, D.D.*, 5 vols, ed. A. Chalmers (London, 1819), I. p. 394.

9 *Correspondence (CW)*, I. 310.
10 See Bentham's critique of Hey's concept of liberty as the absence of restraint at U[niversity] C[ollege], lxix. 57–68. See also Hey, *Observations on the Nature of Civil Liberty*, p. 9 n.
11 UC, lxix. 44. See also UC, lxix. 148.
12 Charles Secondat, Baron de Montesquieu, *L'Esprit des lois*, xi. 6.
13 Ibid., xi. 3.
14 Hey, *Observations on the Nature of Civil Liberty*, p. 35.
15 Paley, *The Principles of Moral and Political Philosophy*, I. 395.
16 Ibid., I. 396–7. I am grateful to Professor William Gwyn of Tulane University for first calling my attention to Paley's discussion of security.
17 *An Introduction to the Principles of Morals and Legislation*, ed. J. H. Burns and H. L. A. Hart (London, 1970), *(CW)*, III.1, p. 34 (author's italics).
18 See the excellent account of security, and especially security of expectation, in G. J. Postema, *Bentham and the Common Law Tradition* (Oxford, 1986), pp. 147ff. See also P. J. Kelly, *Utilitarianism and Distributive Justice: Jeremy Bentham and the Civil Law* (University of London, PhD thesis, 1988).
19 *A Comment on the Commentaries and A Fragment on Government*, ed. J. H. Burns and H. L. A. Hart (London, 1977), iv. 24, p. 485.
20 Ibid.
21 For another more extensive list drafted for a chapter in Bentham's essay on 'Indirect Legislation', see UC, lxxxvii. 102–26, written in approximately 1782.
22 UC, cxxvi. 8. Bentham's essay was entitled 'False Principle Division of Power' and will be included in a volume of his political essays, written at the time of the French Revolution. See J. Bentham, *Essays on French and British Political Reform 1788–95*, ed. M. H. James (forthcoming in *Collected Works*).
23 UC, cxxvi. 11.
24 UC, cxxvi. 9.
25 UC, clxx. 168.
26 See M. H. James, 'Bentham's Democratic Theory at the Time of the French Revolution', *The Bentham Newsletter*, X (1986), pp. 5–16.
27 See *Constitutional Code*, Vol. I, ed. F. Rosen and J. H. Burns (Oxford, 1983), *(CW)*, pp. 39–41, 117–33, 168–70, 419–37.
28 See F. Rosen, *Jeremy Bentham and Representative Democracy, A Study of the Constitutional Code* (Oxford, 1983), pp. 55–75.
29 *Constitutional Code*, Vol. I; *(CW)*, p. 1.
30 E. Blaquiere to E. Dumont, November 1820, Dumont MSS, 74/83–8, Bibliothèque Publique et Universitaire, Geneva.
31 3 vols, Paris, 1901–4. The three volumes were translated (without the extensive annotation) in *The Growth of Philosophic Radicalism*, trans. M. Morris (London, 1928). Reference will be given first to the French original and then to the English translation in round brackets with quotations taken from the translation.
32 Halévy's study of Philosophic Radicalism has been examined more fully in F. Rosen, 'Elie Halévy and Bentham's Authoritarian Liberalism', *Enlightenment and Dissent*, 6 (1987), pp. 59–76, from which this material has been taken.
33 Halévy, *La Formation du radicalisme philosophique*, I. p. 131 (74).
34 Ibid., III. p. 189 (411).
35 See Rosen, *Jeremy Bentham and Representative Democracy*, pp. 19–54.
36 See, for example, P. Schwartz, 'Jeremy Bentham's Democratic Despotism', in R. D. Collison Black (ed.), *Ideas in Economics* (London, 1986), pp. 74–103.
37 See, for example, I. Berlin, *Four Essays on Liberty* (Oxford, 1969), pp. liv–lv.
38 See, for example, D. G. Long, *Bentham on Liberty: Jeremy Bentham's Idea of Liberty*

in Relation to his Utilitarianism (Toronto, 1977), p. 105; R. Nozick, *Anarchy, State and Utopia* (New York, 1974), pp. 28–9, 39–41; J. Rawls, *A Theory of Justice* (Oxford, 1972), pp. 22ff.

39 See, for example, D. Long, *Bentham on Liberty*, pp. 216ff; G. Himmelfarb, 'The Haunted House of Jeremy Bentham', in *Victorian Studies* (London, 1968), pp. 32–81; C. Bahmueller, *The National Charity Company* (Berkeley, Calif., 1981).

40 See H. L. A. Hart, *Essays on Bentham*, pp. 53–78.

41 See F. Rosen, *Jeremy Bentham and Representative Democracy*, pp. 35–6. Bentham's own discussions of American practice may be seen in numerous passages in *Constitutional Code*, Vol. I (*CW*), as per index.

42 See 'Anarchical Fallacies' (Bowring, ii. 489–534); J. H. Burns, 'Bentham and the French Revolution', *The Transactions of the Royal Historical Society*, 5th series, xvi (1966), pp. 95–114. References to 'Bowring' are to *The Works of Jeremy Bentham*, ed. J. Bowring, 11 vols (Edinburgh, 1843).

43 See UC, cxiii. 70 (24 May 1822).

44 References to Peterloo are few but none the less striking. See, for example, Bowring ii. 276, 470n, viii. 474, ix. 140, x. 532. For Bentham's links with early working-class reformers, see M. Umekawa (Aichigakuin University), 'Bentham and Wade in 1818' (unpublished paper). I am also indebted to Ms Jacqueline Lugg for sharing with me her research on Bentham, William Thompson, and Thomas Hodgskin.

45 See *Codification Proposal, addressed by Jeremy Bentham to All Nations Professing Liberal Opinions* (London, 1822) (Bowring, iv. 535–94); *Constitutional Code*, Vol. I, (*CW*), pp. xiff.

46 *Deontology, together with A Table of the Springs of Action and Article on Utilitarianism*, ed. A. Goldworth (Oxford, 1983), (*CW*), p. 315.

47 See L. Crompton, *Byron and Greek Love: Homophobia in 19th-Century England* (London, 1985), pp. 12–62, 251–83, 383–6.

48 See F. Rosen, 'Bentham and Mill on Liberty and Justice', in G. Feaver and F. Rosen (eds), *Lives, Liberties and the Public Good* (London, 1987), pp. 121–38.

Chapter five

Bentham and the nineteenth-century revolution in government

Stephen Conway

In the period approximately encompassed by the years 1830 and 1870, British governmental activity underwent a notable change. Central government, while reducing its regulation of commerce with other nations – the Corn Laws were repealed in 1846 and the Navigation Acts in 1849 – increased its involvement in other areas, particularly in social administration.[1] To take just some of the well-known examples: the Poor Law was remodelled to bring it under central supervision; factories and mines were subjected to regulations limiting or prohibiting the employment of certain types of labour and making mandatory the adoption of new safety procedures; general public health legislation was passed; police forces were established throughout the land; and state participation in education was inaugurated. These reforms, besides broadening the role of the state, created new posts and new administrative machinery. But with the acceptance of additional responsibilities, a more thoroughgoing reform of central administration itself was thought necessary, and it was in these years that the first steps were taken to replace patronage in the civil service with competitive examinations.

Viewed together, these developments have been seen as constituting a 'nineteenth-century revolution in government' – a revolution that initiated the process of government growth that eventually led to the 'quasi-collectivist' welfare state of the twentieth century.[2] Perhaps, as some historians have suggested, the word 'revolution' is a little extravagant.[3] Compared with the social reforms of the Edwardian era, those of c. 1830–70 seem less fundamental.[4] It could be argued that the state continued to play a minor and essentially peripheral role until the First World War gave Britain its first taste of large-scale collectivization.[5] Public expenditure – a good index of government growth – remained a more or less steady percentage of gross national product until the early twentieth century; indeed, it actually fell during the years of Gladstone's dominance.[6] If we look before 1830, caution again seems in order. Perhaps the 1780s are a more appropriate starting-point, when attitudes to the responsibilities of government began to change in response to failure in the American war of independence.[7] We could go back still further and regard the Victorian reforms merely as a continuation of the gradual centralization of power and erosion of local privileges that had been taking place for centuries. But the long-term perspective can all too easily subject events to a levelling effect that minimizes their importance. Small-scale and tentative as the steps taken in the mid-nineteenth century might have been, they set the trend for the future. As Oliver MacDonagh has pointed out, a significant qualitative change occurred about 1830. Before then, most social reforms were the work of individual MPs; after that date governments themselves increasingly took the initiative, and legislation consequently tended to be better constructed and more effectively enforced.[8]

The main debate, however, has not been about the validity of the concept of a revolution in government, but about its causes. The primary aim of this essay is to argue the case for considering the ideas of Jeremy Bentham as an important influence. This, it must be stressed, is not to say that Benthamism alone provides a sufficient explanation. Ideally, Bentham's contribution needs to be placed in context by presenting it alongside the many other factors involved. No comprehensive account of the revolution in government could ignore the vital part played by agrarian change, industrialization, urbanization, and rapid population growth in creating the problems that much of the mid-nineteenth-century social legislation tried to solve. Nor could it omit consideration of the inability of antiquated local structures to cope with these problems;[9] developments in science and technology that made government intervention a practical possibility;[10] the example set by foreign, imperial, and, perhaps above all, by Irish practice;[11] the self-generating nature of government growth;[12] the cautious and piecemeal efforts of politicians to adapt British institutions to radically changing circumstances;[13] the desire of many in governing circles to exercise more effective social control in a time of uncertainty and perceived danger to the political system;[14] the persuasiveness of paternalistic attitudes;[15] and the influence of evangelicals like Lord Shaftesbury.[16] No such comprehensive account is, or could be, offered here.

There are other good reasons for concentrating on Bentham. Although there have been a number of important interventions in recent years, the academic battle over Bentham's role was at its height, and at its most influential, in the late 1950s and early 1960s. Since then, with the appearance of the fruits of more detailed research on Bentham and the Benthamites, and with the publication of several volumes in the new *Collected Works* edition, we are in a better position to assess Bentham's thought and its impact. A more fundamental reason, however, is the strength of the reaction against the view that Bentham and Benthamism made a significant contribution. Historians – as distinct from philosophers and social scientists – have tended recently either to discount or even totally reject Bentham's ideas as worthy of serious discussion. When we find it argued in a widely-read and much respected textbook that 'Had Bentham never lived, most of the reforms popularly ascribed to his influence would probably have come about',[17] the time is ripe for a fresh statement of the claims that can be made on his behalf.

This essay is in three sections. The first seeks to show that the core of Bentham's thought was in harmony with the general thrust of governmental developments in the middle decades of the nineteenth century, and that Bentham anticipated several of the features of those developments. The second attempts to assess the degree to which Bentham's friends and associates directly involved in the reforms can legitimately be described as followers who were applying his principles. The final section examines the possibility that other participants in the revolution in government, who were not consciously his followers, might nevertheless have been influenced by his ideas.

I

For analytical purposes, the revolution in government can be conceived as falling into two parts. The first consisted of the dismantling or destruction of old institutions and practices, mainly at the local level, which were judged to be inadequate or inefficient. The second involved the creation of new institutions and practices, usually directed or supervised by central authorities. Few would deny that Bentham's thought was consistent with the first stage of this process. Other thinkers – especially William Paley, Archdeacon of Carlisle – might have employed utilitarian arguments to explain and justify the existing dispensation, but in Bentham's hands the principle of utility, or the greatest happiness principle as he came to call it, was used to challenge traditional arrangements.[18] Bentham was more systematic and more thoroughgoing than earlier utilitarians in his insistence that the greatest happiness of the greatest number was the only proper end of all human action. He elevated the greatest happiness principle into an exacting test against which all prevailing institutions and methods could be measured.[19] Those that failed to promote the maximum of felicity stood condemned and were deemed ready for abolition or reform. As J. S. Mill noted in 1838, Bentham was 'the great questioner of things established'.[20]

Whether the destructive potential of Benthamite utilitarianism was matched by an equally strong potential for construction is a matter on which there is rather less agreement. One of the arguments used to suggest that Bentham's thought played little or no part in the revolution in government is that his general aim was to remove restrictions, not to create new ones; to reduce state interference, not to increase it.[21] This impression can certainly be gained by reading parts of Bentham's work, as we shall see, but it often seems to owe more to A. V. Dicey's immensely influential *Lectures on the Relation Between Law and Public Opinion in England in the Nineteenth Century*, which was first published in 1905. Dicey, while acknowledging a 'collectivist' element latent in Bentham's thought, was convinced that Benthamism could, broadly speaking, be equated with *laissez-faire* individualism.[22] One of Dicey's objectives – perhaps, in fact, his primary objective – was to make a political point about the 'socialistic' trend of the liberalism of his own day by comparing it unfavourably with the individualistic liberalism that, he maintained, had predominated in earlier decades.[23] Even so, the image of Bentham that Dicey presented was not one that had been specially fabricated to meet the demands of the moment. The idea that

73

Bentham and Benthamism could be categorized in such a way has much deeper historical roots. Generations of Victorians had been accustomed to see Bentham in this light.[24] He had come to be connected with the proponents of vigorous individualism. This was partly because the attacks that he and his friends made on the aristocracy naturally associated him in the public mind with other middle-class critics of the nineteenth-century political order.[25] His reputation as an advanced democrat, established with the publication and popularization of his *Plan of Parliamentary Reform* in 1817–18, no doubt contributed to this association, as did his denunciation of financial waste and advocacy of cheaper government, which led him, along with many other Radicals, to call for the ending of those invaluable props of aristocratic government: sinecure posts and pensions.[26] We should also remember the way in which he was linked with that great epic of *laissez-faire*, the battle for free trade. Bentham's followers had been involved in the foundation of the metropolitan-based Anti-Corn Law Association in 1836, and it was Charles Pelham Villiers, a member of the utilitarian circle, who can be said to have started the parliamentary campaign against the Corn Laws in 1838. In the same year, John Bowring, the editor of Bentham's *Works* helped to stimulate the creation of the Anti-Corn Law League in Manchester.[27] But it was not just the involvement of prominent Benthamites that was important; no less so was the way in which they invoked Bentham's name as if to legitimize the cause. In the heady days after repeal, Bowring described Bentham as 'one of the earliest labourers', and 'one of the most untiring', in the great struggle; adding that Bentham was responsible for his own participation in the free trade movement.[28] Similarly, Archibald Prentice, the Manchester journalist and long-standing admirer of Bentham, wrote in his monumental and triumphal history of the League – a work still cited in modern studies – that Bentham was 'the father of the practical free traders'.[29]

This was unquestionably an exaggeration. But turning from those Victorian perceptions of Bentham that continue to cast a lingering spell over some twentieth-century writers, and looking instead at his own work, we can see that he was a fairly consistent supporter of free trade, and that his writings provide ample evidence that seems to lend credence to the view that he was a non-interventionist, anxious to reduce and minimize the role of government. He read and digested Adam Smith's *Wealth of Nations*, and held its author in high esteem.[30] In the early 1790s, Bentham referred to Smith as 'a writer of great and distinguished merit', and explained that his own 'Manual of Political Economy' was in conformity with Smith's principles.[31] Bentham's *Defence of Usury*, published in 1787, was a plea for the ending of legislative interference that has been characterized as criticizing Smith from 'a more Smithian-than-Smith point of view'.[32] Bentham's arguments against an active and interventionist foreign policy also seem to attest to his *laissez-faire* leanings. In 1789, he maintained that international harmony was impossible until the peoples of the world recognized their economic interdependence, a recognition that would come only in the wake of the widespread diffusion and acceptance of the truths of political economy.[33]

With government interference evidently in mind, he advised that 'In foreign affairs, as in political economy, the great secret is to do nothing.'[34]

Yet for all this, to identify Bentham as a champion of non- intervention and minimal government would be misleading. If Dicey envisaged him as an advocate of *laissez-faire*, Joseph Chamberlain saw him as willing to use the power of the state, and accordingly cited 'the greatest happiness of the greatest number' to justify his own 'constructionist' proposals.[35] In truth, Smithian political economy was never central to Bentham's thought: it had relevance only to his consideration of certain specific subjects, such as international relations, and the means of increasing abundance.[36] Moreover, even in his own later economic writings, Bentham – much to the bewilderment of the more orthodox Ricardo and James Mill – often adopted positions substantially different from Smith's.[37] Bentham was not, in short, a dogmatic *laissez-faire*ist. He was, from first to last and above all else, a utilitarian. Actions were to be judged by their consequences, not on their intrinsic merits. Thus Bentham might characterize government as a choice of evils, and explain that coercion by government was an undeniable evil;[38] but he held that so long as such evil was employed 'for the production ... of more than equivalent good', then it was acceptable.[39] So, since the greatest happiness was the end in view, after careful consideration of the impact of government action on the elements into which utility could be decomposed – namely security, abundance, subsistence, and equality – state intervention could be recommended on some occasions, and denounced on others.[40] Without any inconsistency, Bentham could urge the temporary imposition of a ceiling on the price of grain during a shortage, and call for free trade on the grounds that protection favoured small groups of producers at the expense of much larger numbers of consumers.[41]

It would be just as distorting, then, to portray Bentham as an invariable advocate of *dirigisme*. Yet there was undoubtedly an inclination on Bentham's part to favour active and attentive government, and, correspondingly, no disposition to shy away from legislative interference when this was calculated to be the best means of promoting happiness. In a revealing passage in one of his writings, he explained that, unlike Adam Smith and his friends, he had no 'horror ... of the hand of government'.[42] So long as intervention created more happiness than it took away, he looked upon it with satisfaction – with the same degree of satisfaction as he looked upon non-intervention when it produced the same outcome. What he could never look upon with satisfaction, he added, was negligence on the part of government.[43] As he put it in another work, it was 'incumbent' on government to make sure that the community pursued courses of action conducive to 'the *maximum* of well-being'.[44]

To understand more fully Bentham's belief in the need for watchful and interested government, ready and willing to act wherever and whenever necessary, we must briefly consider his views on the nature of political society and the role of legislation. In his early writings, Bentham explained that political society could not exist without a sovereign – a governor or governors – and a set of people who obeyed the commands of that sovereign. The sovereign exercised supreme power on a fiduciary basis for the benefit of the people.[45] As society was made up of a mass of individuals all pursuing their own interests, and as the interests of different individuals often clashed, the sovereign's task was to harmonize individual interests with the general interest.[46] Legislation, in the form of punishments or prohibitions and rewards or encouragements, was the tool with which the sovereign could try to engineer this social co-operation. In his later democratic phase the ultimate power of the people was more overtly stated: 'The sovereignty is in *the people*', he wrote in *Constitutional Code*.[47] In a democracy they would possess the power to select and dismiss their rulers, and would therefore be able to ensure that the interests of the rulers were closely tied to the universal interest. But this did not alter the importance he attached to legislation as a means of creating the greatest happiness. Hence his life-long concern with 'the science of legislation'.[48] Hence, also, some of his objections to the common law and natural rights – both were rivals to the authority of the legislator or the legislative body, an authority that had to be allowed to be indefinite.[49] And hence, as a consequence of these, his hostility to all attempts to limit the field of legislation.[50] Any imposition of boundaries, any endeavour to declare, in advance, that certain areas were beyond legislative control, was a derogation of sovereign power, and therefore a limitation on the ability of the sovereign power to maximize happiness. In the present context, this point is crucial. By denying that there were limits to legislative activity, other than those imposed by utility itself, Bentham was opening the door to a very considerable degree of state intervention.

Moving from general principles to particular proposals, we can see that Bentham anticipated many of the features that were to characterize mid-nineteenth-century government. In material written in the 1780s but not published until 1802, he urged a more universal and centralized system for the registration of births, marriages, and deaths – requirements that were substantially to be met by the 1836 Registration Act.[51] In one of his early works, *An Introduction to the Principles of Morals and Legislation*, published in 1789, Bentham indicated that government might take responsibility for a wide range of matters, including education and the care of the sick and the insane.[52] In the 1790s, as part of his work on preventive policing, he urged the establishment of permanent police forces.[53] In his *magnum opus*, the *Constitutional Code*, he envisaged separate ministers of education, health, and 'indigence relief', government regulation of conditions in factories and mines, and competitive examinations for civil servants.[54] Even his idea of a 'patriotic auction', whereby candidates for official posts bid against each other to perform the required duties for a lower salary, or even offered to buy the offices in question, found expression, albeit only briefly and to a very limited extent, in the auctioning of Poor Law medical posts that took place until 1837.[55] Central inspection, which was a much more important and enduring facet of the mid-nineteenth-century reforms, was recommended in many different parts of Bentham's work: in his early writings on the Poor Law, where he suggested 'a central office of *general inspection*'; in his scheme for a river police on the Thames;[56] and in architectural form in his various applications of the Panopticon, with its centrally located overseer who could watch all the inmates.[57] The famous, or infamous, 'less eligibility principle' embodied in the Poor Law Amendment Act of 1834 – the principle that life in the workhouse should be less attractive than life as an independent labourer – was similarly foreshadowed in Bentham's writings on poor relief and the Panopticon.[58]

Now it is true that in some respects the reforms advocated by Bentham differed materially from the reforms actually carried out. He believed, at least in the 1790s, that poor relief should be organized by a joint-stock company – the National Charity Company – financed by pauper labour, which was, of course, a far cry from what came to pass.[59] Equally, certain aspects of mid-nineteenth-century government would probably have been uncongenial to Bentham. The new boards and commissions set up by the Poor Law and Public Health Acts were clearly at odds with his preference for 'single-seatedness' as a means of ensuring individual responsibility.[60] But none of this seriously detracts from the impression that, to a remarkable extent, Bentham foresaw and recommended many of the elements that made up the nineteenth-century revolution in government.

To anticipate changes is one thing; to inspire them, quite another. Despite the similarities, we cannot *assume* a relationship between Bentham's recommendations and the legislative enactments that took place after his death. There were, as I have indicated in the most summary fashion, many alternative sources of inspiration. If a connection is to be established between the principles and proposals to be found in Bentham's voluminous writings and the governmental developments of the mid-nineteenth century, it has to be shown that, in all probability, Bentham's thought influenced at least some of the participants in the revolution in government. Cautionary and qualificatory phrases like 'in all probability' are here of more than usual importance. Tracing 'influence' is a notoriously difficult and complex business; not least because the evidence available rarely allows us to pronounce with certainty. But so long as this is borne in mind, there seems to be no overwhelming reason for abandoning the endeavour, as some scholars have implied that we should do.[61] After all, historical study in general is, by its very nature, based on incomplete information about historical characters and their motives; but this does not mean that it is impossible to suggest connections that might further our understanding of the past.

The obvious place to start is by looking at the figures conventionally described as 'Benthamites'. Without aiming to give an exhaustive list, we can see that several of them played a part in the revolution in government. Joseph Hume, Bentham's old friend, advocated public health legislation and favoured government action to ensure proper ventilation in mines.[62] Another radical MP, John Arthur Roebuck, who was perhaps even more thoroughly versed in the utilitarian thought of Bentham and James Mill, was a consistent champion of a national system of education.[63] Henry Warburton, MP for Bridport and an 'avowed Benthamite', is credited with having written the parliamentary select committee report that led to the 1832 Anatomy Act, with its central inspectorate designed to regulate the use of the dead for medical research.[64] Outside parliament, Walter Coulson, Bentham's former amanuensis, served as a member of the Royal Commission that laid the foundation of the Poor Law Amendment Act; while Dr Thomas Southwood Smith, editor of Bentham's educational work *Chrestomathia*, was a noted sanitary reformer and was involved in the Royal Commissions that preceded the Factory Act of 1833 and the Mines Act of 1842. But the most well known of the mid-century reformers usually labelled as a utilitarian is Edwin Chadwick, who acted as Bentham's secretary in 1831–2. John Stuart Mill described Chadwick as 'one of the most remarkable men of our time in the practical art of Government'.[65] The extent of Chadwick's involvement justifies the accolade. He was intimately connected with the Poor Law Amendment Act, the 1833 Factory Act, and the 1839 Police Act. He also influenced the provisions of the Registration Act of 1836, and was the author of *The Sanitary Condition of the Labouring Population* (1842), the report that eventually opened the way to the public health legislation of 1848.

It could legitimately be countered that Benthamites also opposed certain of the reforms. Hume objected to the education grant of 1833 on the grounds that it was too small for a national system, 'and without such a system no grant at all ought to be made'.[66] Hume's opposition was not, of course, opposition in principle to state participation; but in other areas Benthamites resisted reforming legislation precisely because they objected to interference by government. Roebuck, Hume, and even Chadwick strongly opposed legislative regulation of the hours of adult labour, while Bowring spoke against the imposition of restrictions on the employment of coal-heavers in the port of London. Their disapproval stemmed from dislike of deviations from what Bowring called 'the sound principles of political economy'[67] – principles which, as we have seen, may sometimes have been compatible with utilitarianism, but were by no means coterminous with it.

This raises a succession of important questions. If Bowring and others could argue against some reforms on grounds that were not strictly utilitarian, is it appropriate to regard them primarily as Benthamites? Equally, were the utilitarian advocates of reform mainly motivated by other considerations? Is it, in fact, misleading to think in terms of a dedicated group of Benthamites seeking to apply Bentham's principles? William Thomas has shown that the Philosophic Radicals – he prefers the term to the more pejorative 'Benthamites' – were deeply individualistic, and the products of many influences besides Bentham's.[68] An examination of some of the members of the utilitarian circle who are not discussed in any detail in Thomas's work seems merely to confirm his conclusions. Bowring was a man of many parts – Radical MP, journalist, poet, translator, hymn-writer, free-trader, merchant, and peace campaigner as well as editor of Bentham's *Works*. He readily acknowledged that he owed as much to the Unitarian minister Lant Carpenter as he did to Bentham.[69] Southwood Smith like Bowring, was an active and enthusiastic Unitarian, and served for a time as a minister. In 1820 he published *An Appeal to the Serious and Candid Professors of Christianity*, a short tract arguing that there was no scriptural justification for the Trinity, which was frequently reprinted.[70] His religious background, together with his medical training and experience, no doubt helps to explain why he became a social reformer.[71] Chadwick's thinking was equally clearly moulded by other influences. He appealed to Christian feeling in a way that suggests that it affected his own actions, and he seems to have been especially impressed by French administrative and governmental practice.[72]

But it would be a mistake to let a proper appreciation of the multiplicity of forces at work on the Benthamites become an argument for discounting Bentham's role in shaping their ideas. Roebuck and Hume, devoted as they were to the principles of political economy, contended for state regulation of the railways in a decidedly utilitarian fashion. Interference was necessary, Hume told the House of Commons in 1846, 'for the greatest amount of benefit for the community'.[73] On another occasion, Roebuck declared that the business of government was not simply to prevent evil, but positively to promote happiness.[74] Bowring, whatever his debt to Carpenter, had no hesitation in describing Bentham as 'my venerated master' in a private letter to his son, Frederick Herman Bowring.[75] Southwood Smith was, if anything, even more lavish in his praise of Bentham, publicly referring to him as 'the foremost among the benefactors of the human race with which the world has ever yet been blessed', and, only slightly more moderately, as 'one of the most illustrious men of our country and of our age'. That Southwood Smith had absorbed and thoroughly approved utilitarian ideas is evident from his exposition of them in his lecture on Bentham delivered in 1832. Indeed, in that lecture he explicitly linked the work of medical practitioners with Bentham's philosophy. Health he described as 'the first of human enjoyments' and 'indispensable to the rest'; disease as the producer of physical and mental pain and the destroyer of pleasure.[76] His utilitarian credentials were even more obviously on display when, in 1836, he urged the establishment of an adequate inspectorate to enforce the education provisions of the 1833 Factory Act. A more effective inspectorate was needed, he argued in impeccably Benthamite style, because so many interests were ranged against acceptance of the provisions: both parents and mill-owners believed it to be against their own interests to allow the children time off for schooling.[77]

Chadwick does not fit the image of loyal follower quite so readily. He wrote of Bentham as a friend, yet in his later life went so far as to deny Bentham's influence altogether.[78] David Roberts, for one, has drawn attention to these denials, and Chadwick's assertions of independence, as evidence in favour of the argument that Bentham's influence on the nineteenth-century reforms was limited.[79] Given that Chadwick was such an important figure in the revolution in government, we should look at him a little more closely. That Chadwick took a different line from Bentham on a number issues adds colour to Chadwick's claims about Bentham's impact on his own ideas. For instance, Bentham's proposal that public posts should be auctioned held no attractions for Chadwick. Indeed, Chadwick was willing to conscript Burke, whom Bentham had attacked on this subject,[80] to support his contention that adequate pay was essential if candidates of the right quality were to be found.[81] But differences of this kind are hardly sufficient to sustain the notion that Bentham exerted no influence on Chadwick, and it would be most unwise to take Chadwick's own denials on face value. In 1841, he complained to John Hill Burton that he was constantly meeting opposition in his public work because he was regarded as 'a Benthamite & a theorist'.[82] It was from about this time that he sought publicly to distance himself from Bentham. Further disappointments, combined with a growing conviction that he had not received due recognition, added to Chadwick's determination to insist that he was his own master.

An apparently minor incident illustrates this rather well. In 1860 the third part of Henry Dunning Macleod's *Dictionary of Political Economy* briefly referred to Bentham as 'the first to conceive that immense reform of the Poor Laws, which was only effected in 1834'. In the same piece, Bentham's writings on the poor were described as 'the precursors of the Poor Law Amendment Act'.[83] Chadwick took great umbrage at these inaccurate but hardly unforgivable observations. He laboriously explained to Macleod that Bentham's pauper proposals were quite different from those adopted in 1834, and emphasized that so far as his own relationship with Bentham was concerned, 'antecedent writings before even those which he himself published, will justify the independence of my views especially in sanitary matters.'[84] The impression that this was an over-reaction is heightened by Macleod's reply. 'I never supposed', he wrote with an air of surprise, 'that Bentham actually contemplated the actual reform that was carried out, yet I see that the words there might perhaps bear that construction.'[85]

As if to make amends, the subsequently issued fifth part of Macleod's *Dictionary* stated that Chadwick could not truly be considered as a disciple of Bentham, since Chadwick entered into his enquiries in the spirit of investigation 'just as if nothing had already been settled'.[86] There was, of course, nothing in such an approach that was inconsistent with Bentham's, and it seems likely that Bentham would have encouraged Chadwick to employ these very methods. Careful collection of data, assessment of the evidence in a coolly scientific manner, and the consequent drawing-up of clear and rational proposals were as much the hallmarks of Bentham's style as they were of Chadwick's.[87] A glimpse of Chadwick's methodological debt to Bentham can be snatched in one of Chadwick's private letters recalling the preparation of the report of the Poor Law commission of enquiry. Had time allowed, Chadwick explained, he would have liked to 'arrange the facts and instances of the evils requiring remedy which Mr. Bentham would have termed explicative, & the matter which he designated as racionative and expositive as premises to the conclusions or the enactive matter.'[88] Small wonder he was accused of being 'a Benthamite & a theorist'! It would be difficult to imagine a better example of the rigorous use of Bentham-like idiom, or a more faithful reproduction of Bentham's style of presentation.

Indeed, despite his denials, there are many good reasons for believing that Chadwick owed a great deal to Bentham. It is true that Chadwick first met Bentham only in 1830, by which time Chadwick had already published his views on a number of important topics. Chadwick, as we have seen, was fond of reminding people of this as a means of proclaiming his independence. But he had been associated with members of Bentham's circle since 1824, so we should not assume that he was exposed to Bentham's ideas only from 1830. Indeed, here it might be worth noting that Chadwick's essay 'On Preventive Police', which appeared in the *London Review* in 1829, while ostensibly based on parliamentary reports and French authorities, is strikingly similar to parts of Bentham's discussion of 'indirect legislation' in Etienne Dumont's *Traités de législation civile et pénale*, published in 1802.[89] The *Traités* are not included in the extant lists of Chadwick's books,[90] but this does not necessarily mean that he was unacquainted with the work, for it was well known among Bentham's friends and followers.

At any rate, even if he knew nothing of Bentham's thought before 1830, Chadwick rapidly became familiar with it thereafter. And we can be confident that he was deeply impressed by what he read and heard. In Chadwick's papers there is a 'Table of Cases calling for Relief', docketed in Chadwick's hand: 'Poor Law. Bentham's classification of working ability and disability'.[91] Chadwick, indeed, was so taken with Bentham's ideas that, in 1832, he proposed to bring out his own selection of extracts from Bentham's works, 'with such a preparatory account of Mr. Bentham's writings as may serve to give enquirers an introductory outline of his discoveries'.[92] The scheme eventually had to be abandoned due to the pressure of his public duties, but not before he had assembled a fair amount of material.[93] At one stage, Chadwick was also to have edited the fuller version of the 'Constitutional Code' that appears in the Bowring edition of Bentham's *Works*, but again lack of time forced him to give up the task.[94] In about 1838, however, he did succeed in privately printing an edition of Bentham's critical essay on Pitt the Younger's Poor Bill. In his introduction, Chadwick suggested that Bentham's arguments were a good example of the scientific approach to legislation, adding, for good measure, that the 1834 Poor Law Amendment Act was perhaps the first piece of legislation based on such an approach.[95]

It was this, apparently, that prompted John Hill Burton to marvel at Chadwick's 'courage in infusing Benthamism so strongly into public proceedings' and to recommend that Chadwick simply gain instruction from Bentham's work without drawing attention to it.[96] Others close to him similarly observed that Chadwick bore Bentham's stamp. Alexander Bain, who worked with Chadwick as assistant secretary both to the Royal Commission on London Sanitation and to the General Board of Health, later wrote that Chadwick, although 'a man of great independence and originality of mind', was strongly influenced by James Mill and Bentham.[97] But the last and perhaps most telling word on Chadwick should be left to his daughter. 'Bentham was his ideal, his guiding star,' she recalled. 'He unconsciously copied him in his little habits of life. Even in his private letters he shaped his style on that of Bentham.' Chadwick's feelings towards Bentham, she explained, were 'as a son to a father'.[98]

III

There appear, then, to be reasonable grounds for regarding Bentham's influence as significant, even if we accept, as some say we must, that his impact was felt only through his followers.[99] But if we can go further, the case for Bentham becomes all the stronger. That many of those involved in the revolution in government were not Benthamites – either by admission or repute – scarcely needs to be said. Were some of them, however, perhaps unwitting Benthamites, applying Bentham's principles and precepts without appreciating that he was the intellectual father of those ideas? The question is, of course, impossible to answer with any degree of certainty; but for the proposition to be feasible, Bentham's thought would have had to contribute sufficiently to the general climate of opinion to be adopted almost unconsciously by those in positions of power and influence.[100] So we should turn next to the diffusion of Bentham's ideas.

The first aspect to consider is the transmission of utilitarian principles and recommendations by word of mouth or by correspondence. Bentham himself played a part here. Notwithstanding the popular image of him as a retiring eccentric – an image, incidentally, that he encouraged in order to deter distracting visitors – he was in regular contact with government ministers, MPs, and civil servants, particularly in relation to his Panopticon penitentiary scheme and his offers to codify the law.[101] Most of these public figures were either dead or out of politics by the 1830s, but some of them rose to prominence in the years after Bentham's death. Sir Robert Peel, for instance, was to reach the peak of his career in the 1840s. While Peel was Home Secretary in the 1820s, Bentham exchanged letters with him on many issues, including bodies for dissection, the subject of the 1832 Anatomy Act.[102] Bentham discovered that Peel already knew about the Panopticon – such was Bentham's reputation in governing circles – but he appears to have been pleased when the Home Secretary accepted his offer of a copy of *Pauper Management Improved*, which Peel anticipated reading 'with interest and attention'.[103] Henry Brougham, the leading Whig MP and Lord Chancellor in 1830–4, was another recipient of relevant work of Bentham's: the sections of *Constitutional Code* containing the parts relating to the examination of civil servants were sent to him in 1827, three years before their publication in the first volume of the *Code*.[104]

The personal and professional connections forged by Bentham's followers also need to be taken into account. As Professor Finer has demonstrated, their network of friends, acquaintances, and colleagues provided them with much scope for transmitting Bentham's thought.[105] In this respect, James Mill, who once described himself as more 'thoroughly of the same way of thinking' as Bentham than anyone he knew,[106] was probably particularly important. J. S. Mill later explained that his father was actively sought out, due to 'the vigour and instructiveness of his conversation', which he used very largely for didactic purposes.[107] Etienne Dumont, Bentham's Genevan editor, perhaps deserves a special mention too. He accompanied the young Lord Henry Petty on a European tour in 1801–2, and Petty, as third Marquis of Lansdowne and Lord President of the Council, was to contribute significantly to the increasing of the education grant and the establishment of the education inspectorate in 1839.[108]

But even within the confines of the closely-knit world of the nineteenth-century political classes, personal contacts could only carry Bentham's message so far. For his ideas to have been more widely disseminated, they would have had to be read in published form. Several scholars have pointed to the idiosyncrasies of Bentham's literary style as a formidable obstacle to the transmission of his thought,[109] and it has to be conceded immediately that the direct impact of Bentham's writings was, so far as we can tell, very restricted. *An Introduction to the Principles of Morals and Legislation*, Bentham's early exposition of his utilitarianism, attracted little contemporary attention.[110] Only thirteen copies of volume I of the *Constitutional Code* had been bought by the close of 1831.[111] Nor did Bowring's edition of Bentham's *Works* prove to be a best-seller. Bowring's son Lewin later confessed that the eleven volumes 'did not attain extensive popularity'.[112] Even *Benthamiana*, a short book of extracts from the Bowring edition assembled by John Hill Burton to circulate 'choice morsels of Bentham's opinions',[113] met with a disappointing reception. About three years after its publication, Burton noted sadly that 'if it pays its expenses I believe that will be all'.[114] As for Dumont's French revisions of Bentham's writings, they sold well overseas but made much less of a mark in Bentham's own country.[115]

Indirectly, on the other hand, Bentham's views almost certainly reached a much larger readership. James Mill presented utilitarian arguments in a style much more accessible than Bentham's. Many of Mill's articles in the *Encyclopaedia Britannica*, though his own work, show how much he had absorbed Bentham's thought. Frequently reprinted in the 1820s, they are believed to have made a considerable impression on contemporary Cambridge undergraduates.[116] Excerpts from Bentham's writings, or summaries of them, appeared in leading periodicals and newspapers from the early years of the century; particularly in the *Edinburgh Review*, the *Examiner*, the *Spectator*, the *Morning Chronicle*, and, above all, the *Westminster Review*, which was launched in 1824 with financial backing from Bentham himself.[117] William Tait, the publisher of the Bowring edition, was as enthusiastic about Bentham as anyone on the staff of the *Westminster Review*, and he ensured that essays on the writings of 'our great master' were included in *Tait's Edinburgh Magazine*, for a time the most popular Scottish periodical.[118] Indeed, Tait told Chadwick in February 1832 that he hoped his magazine would become 'the means of Spreading a knowledge of Mr

Bentham's principles. My principal writers here', he added, 'are studying his works once more, with that view.'[119]

By 1840 Bowring was able to recall with some regret that 'many writers had drawn upon Bentham without acknowledging whence they had derived their inspirations'.[120] He had no real cause for complaint, however; partly because he was a guilty as anyone else – he even slipped Benthamism into his didactic work for juveniles[121] – but mainly because this was an essential part of the process by which ideas are disseminated and become accepted as common property. Seven years later, Roebuck could write of a 'silent revolution' that had been accomplished by the diffusion of Bentham's principles to writers who for the most part had no conception of their origin.[122] Perhaps in this sense the *Westminster Review* was correct when it claimed in September 1844 that 'We live in an age of Benthamites.'[123] Even in 1833, the year after Bentham's death, Edward Lytton Bulwer, by no means an uncritical commentator, stated that Bentham was 'the most celebrated and influential teacher of the age – a master ... from whom thousands have, mediately and unconsciously, imbibed their opinions'. Bentham's thought, Bulwer explained, first influenced the minds of 'a minute fraction of the men who think', then spread from them '(their source unknown)' to become 'familiar and successful'.[124] If these and other contemporary assessments have any value – and I can see no reason for dismissing them as totally unreliable – Bentham can safely be said to have exerted an influence far beyond the narrow group that either knew and revered him, or read his work at first hand.

Notes

1 For a contemporary perception, see 'Mines and Collieries', *Westminster Review*, XXXVIII (1842), p. 86.
2 See, especially, Oliver MacDonagh, 'The Nineteenth-century Revolution in Government: a Reappraisal', *Historical Journal*, I (1958), pp. 52–67; and idem, *Early Victorian Government 1830–1870* (London, 1977), p. 1.
3 Valerie Cromwell, 'Interpretations of Nineteenth-century Administration: an Analysis', *Victorian Studies*, IX (1965–6), p. 246.
4 A. J. Taylor, *Laissez-faire and State Intervention in Nineteenth-century Britain* (London, 1972), p. 56; E. T. Stokes, 'Bureaucracy and Ideology: Britain and India in the Nineteenth Century', *Transactions of the Royal Historical Society*, 5th series, XXX (1980), p. 139.
5 See K. O. Morgan, *Consensus and Disunity: The Lloyd George Coalition Government 1918–1922* (Oxford, 1979), pp. 13–25.
6 Stokes, 'Bureaucracy and ideology', p. 137; W. H. Greenleaf, *The British Political Tradition*, vol. I, *The Rise of Collectivism* (London, 1983), table I, p. 33; H. C. G. Matthew, *Gladstone 1809–1874* (Oxford, 1986), p. 115 n.
7 Norman Baker, 'Changing Attitudes Towards Government in Eighteenth-century Britain', in Anne Whiteman et al. (eds), *Statesmen, Scholars and Merchants* (Oxford, 1973), pp. 202–19.
8 MacDonagh, *Early Victorian Government*, p. 23. For a contemporary view, see Lord John Russell's remarks of 1840 in Sir Llewellyn Woodward, *The Age of Reform*

1815–1870, (Oxford, 1962, 2nd edition), p. 447.

9 See, for instance, David Roberts, *The Victorian Origins of the Welfare State* (New Haven, Conn., 1960), p. 316.

10 See R. J. Lambert, 'A Victorian National Health Service: State Vaccination, 1855–71', *Historical Journal*, V (1962), pp. 1–18; R. M. Macleod, 'The Alkali Acts Administration, 1863–84', *Victorian Studies*, IX (1965–6), pp. 85–112.

11 See Edward Hughes, 'Civil Service Reform 1853–5', *History*, new series, XXVII (1942), p. 77; MacDonagh, *Early Victorian Government*, pp. 51, 168–9; L. J. Hume, *Bentham and Bureaucracy* (Cambridge, 1981), p. 53.

12 MacDonagh, 'The Nineteenth-century Revolution in Government', esp. p. 53. For support, see R. J. Lambert, *Sir John Simon 1816–1904 and English Social Administration* (London, 1963), pp. 168–9.

13 W. C. Lubenow, *The Politics of Government Growth* (Newton Abbot, 1971), esp. pp. 183–8.

14 Jennifer Hart, 'Reform of the Borough Police, 1835–56', *English Historical Review*, LXX (1955), pp. 426–7; Anthony Brundage, 'The Landed Interest and the New Poor Law', ibid., LXXXVII (1972), pp. 27–48; idem, *The Making of the New Poor Law 1832–39* (London, 1978), esp. pp. 182–3; Alan Heesom, 'The Coal Mines Act 1842, Social Reform, and Social Control', *Historical Journal*, XXIV (1981), pp. 69–88.

15 David Roberts, 'Tory Paternalism and Social Reform in early Victorian England', *American Historical Review*, LXIII (1958), pp. 323–7; idem, *Paternalism in Early Victorian England* (Rutgers, N. J., 1979), passim; Peter Mandler, 'Cain and Abel: Two Aristocrats and the early-Victorian Factory Acts', *Historical Journal*, XXVII (1984), pp. 83–109.

16 G. F. A. Best, *Shaftesbury* (London, 1964), chs 4–5; Georgina Battiscombe, *Shaftesbury: A Biography* (London, 1974), chs 6, 10, 14, and 15.

17 Norman Gash, *Aristocracy and People: Britain 1815–65* (London, 1979), p. 46. For a more positive assessment, based on study of one particular area, see Peter Dunkley, 'Emigration and the State, 1803–1842', *Historical Journal*, XXIII (1980), pp. 353–80.

18 See T. P. Schofield, 'A Comparison of the Moral Theories of William Paley and Jeremy Bentham', *The Bentham Newsletter*, XI (1987), pp. 4–22.

19 This was clearly understood in relation to law reform by Sir Henry Maine. See his *Ancient Law* (London, 1906, 10th edition), pp. 83–4. See also Jennifer Hart's emphasis on utility as a standard, 'Nineteenth-century Social Reform: a Tory Interpretation of History', *Past and Present*, XXXI (1965), p. 46.

20 *Essays on Ethics, Religion and Society*, ed. J. M. Robson (Toronto, 1969), p. 78. See also Edward Lytton Bulwer, *England and the English*, ed. Standish Meacham (Chicago and London, 1970), p. 319.

21 MacDonagh, 'The Nineteenth-century Revolution in Government', p. 66; David Roberts, 'Jeremy Bentham and the Victorian Administrative State', *Victorian Studies*, II (1959), pp. 194, 199.

22 Dicey entitled one of his lectures 'The period of Benthamism or Individualism', *Law and Opinion*, pp. 125–209.

23 See Henry Parris, 'The Nineteenth-century Revolution in Government: a Reappraisal Reappraised', *Historical Journal*, III (1960), p. 18; Harold Perkin, 'Individualism versus Collectivism in Nineteenth-century Britain: a False Antithesis', *Journal of British Studies*, XVII (1977–8), pp. 117–18.

24 See Stefan Collini, *Liberalism and Sociology* (Cambridge, 1979), pp. 44, 45 n. Significantly, Leslie Stephen had already described Bentham as a *laissez-faire* economist. See his *The English Utilitarians*, 3 vols (London, 1900), I, p. 310.

25 W. H. Coates, 'Benthamism, *laissez-faire*, and collectivism', *Journal of the History of Ideas*, XI (1950), p. 363.

26 In Bentham's model 'Legislator's Inaugural Declaration', the legislator pledges to keep the establishment 'clear of all needless offices, of all useless offices, of all overpay of overpaid offices, of all dutiless offices'. See *Constitutional Code*, vol. I, ed. F. Rosen and J. H. Burns (Oxford, 1983), p. 138.

27 Bowring was always keen to stress this. See Bowring to Edwin Chadwick, 17 May 1865, Bentham MSS UC clv. 100, University College London; Bowring to Revd R. L. Carpenter, 8 February 1860, Carpenter Papers, Manchester College, Oxford.

28 'Free Trade Recollections. No. VII – Jeremy Bentham', *Howitt's Journal of Literature and Popular Progress*, II (1847), pp. 123–4.

29 Archibald Prentice, *History of the Anti-Corn Law League*, 2 vols (London, 1853), I, p. 47. For Prentice's contact with Bentham, see Prentice's *Some Recollections of Jeremy Bentham* (Manchester, 1837); Bentham to Prentice, 11 April 1831, Bentham Papers, British Library Additional MSS 33,546, fos 498–501; Bentham to Francis Place, 23, 24 April 1831, Place Papers, BL Add. MSS 35, 149, fos 71, 73–4.

30 See Bentham MSS UC xcix. 181–3 for an analysis of and observations on *Wealth of Nations*.

31 W. Stark (ed.), *Jeremy Bentham's Economic Writings*, 3 vols (London, 1952–4), I, 223.

32 T. W. Hutchinson, 'Bentham as an Economist', *Economic Journal*, LXVI (1956), p. 292.

33 Bentham MSS UC xxv. 133.

34 Ibid., 110.

35 Richard Jay, *Joseph Chamberlain: A Political Study* (Oxford, 1981), p. 332. Beatrice Webb described Bentham as her husband's 'intellectual godfather', but, while accepting that 'human action must be judged by its results in bringing about certain defined ends', she rejected the greatest happiness as too vague. See *The Diary of Beatrice Webb*, ed. N. and J. Mackenzie, 4 vols (London, 1982–5), II, p. 200. See also, Mary P. Mack, 'The Fabians and Utilitarianism', *Journal of the History of Ideas*, XVI (1955), pp. 76–88.

36 Hume, *Bentham and Bureaucracy*, p. 93; Stephen Conway, 'Bentham versus Pitt: Jeremy Bentham and British Foreign Policy 1789', *Historical Journal*, XXX (1987), pp. 791–809.

37 Jacob Viner, 'Bentham and J. S. Mill: the Utilitarian Background', *American Economic Review*, XXXIX (1949), p. 369; Hutchinson, 'Bentham as an Economist', pp. 295–300.

38 Bentham to Governor Simon Snyder, 14 July 1814, *The Correspondence of Jeremy Bentham*, vol. VIII, ed. Stephen Conway (Oxford, 1988), p. 398.

39 *Constitutional Code*, vol. I, pp. 19–20. See also *Codification Proposal Addressed by Jeremy Bentham to all Nations Professing Liberal Opinions* (London, 1822), p. 13; 'Institute of Political Economy' (1801–4), in *Jeremy Bentham's Economic Writings*. III, p. 341.

40 This has been recognized by a number of scholars. See Parris, 'The Nineteenth-century Revolution in Government', p. 35; Hart, 'Nineteenth-century Social Reform', p. 47; L. J. Hume, 'Jeremy Bentham and the Nineteenth-century Revolution in Government', *Historical Journal*, X (1967), pp. 361–75; idem, *Bentham and Bureaucracy*, pp. 93–4.

41 See 'Defence of a Maximum' (1801), in *Jeremy Bentham's Economic Writings*, III, pp. 247–302; *Observations on the Restrictive and Prohibitory Commercial System*, ed. J. Bowring (London, 1821), p. 36 (in *Jeremy Bentham's Economic Writings*, III, p. 409); P. E. L. Dumont (ed.), *Théorie des peines et des récompenses*, 2 vols (London, 1811), II, 145, in J. Bowring (ed.), *The Works of Jeremy Bentham*, 11 vols (Edinburgh, 1843), II, pp. 227–8.

42 'Defence of a Maximum', *Jeremy Bentham's Economic Writings*, III, pp. 257–8.

43 Ibid., p. 258.

44 'Institute of Political Economy', *Jeremy Bentham's Economic Writings*, III, p. 310.

45 See, for instance, *An Introduction to the Principles of Morals and Legislation*, ed. J. H. Burns and H. L. A. Hart (London, 1970), p. 263.

46 Ibid., pp. 12, 282–3.

47 *Constitutional Code*, vol. I, p. 25.

48 See, for example, Bentham to Samuel Bentham, 22 September 1804, *The Correspondence of Jeremy Bentham*, vol. III, ed. J. R. Dinwiddy (Oxford, 1988), p. 279.

49 *An Introduction to the Principles*, pp. 8, 301–2; *A Fragment on Government and A Comment on the Commentaries*, ed. J. H. Burns (London, 1977), p. 484

50 For example, *An Introduction to the Principles*, pp. 308–9.

51 'Des moyens indirects de prévenir les délits', in P. E. L. Dumont (ed.), *Traités de législation civile et pénale*, 2 vols (Paris, 1802), III, pp. 85–6, in Bowring, *Works*, I, p. 553.

52 *An Introduction to the Principles*, p. 262.

53 Hume, *Bentham and Bureaucracy*, p. 123.

54 *Constitutional Code*, vol. I, pp. 171–2, 316. For the supervision of mines and factories by the Health Minister, see 'Constitutional Code', ch. XI, in Bowring, *Works*, IX, p. 445.

55 Ursula Henriques, 'Jeremy Bentham and the Machinery of Social Reform', in H. Hearder and H. R. Loyn (eds), *British Government and Administration* (Cardiff, 1974), p. 186.

56 Hume, *Bentham and Bureaucracy*, pp. 123, 151.

57 This point is taken up by M. Foucault, *Discipline and Punish*, trans. A. Sheridan (London, 1977), pp. 195–228.

58 J. R. Poynter, *Society and Pauperism: English Ideas on Poor Relief, 1795–1834*, (London, 1969), p. 327; S. E. Finer, *The Life and Times of Sir Edwin Chadwick* (London, 1952), pp. 74–5.

59 He was, however, willing to acknowledge that a time might come when government itself would be fit to run the administration of poor relief. See Hume, *Bentham and Bureaucracy*, p. 138.

60 Sir Norman Chester, *The English Administrative System 1780–1870* (Oxford, 1981), p. 253 makes this point and argues that the reforms did not follow Bentham's design. See also Roberts, 'Jeremy Bentham and the Victorian Administrative State', p. 210.

61 See William Thomas, *The Philosophic Radicals* (Oxford, 1979), pp. 10–11.

62 Ronald K. Huch and Paul R. Ziegler, *Joseph Hume: The People's MP* (Philadelphia, 1985), pp. 135–6; Oliver MacDonagh, 'Coal Mines Regulation', in Robert Robson (ed.), *Ideas and Institutions of Victorian Britain* (London, 1967), p. 67.

63 See, for instance, *Parliamentary Debates*, 3rd series, XXIV, 128 (3 June 1834). For Hume's occasional doubts about utilitarianism, see Huch and Ziegler, *Joseph Hume*, p. 15.

64 Ruth Richardson, 'Bentham and "Bodies for Dissection"', *The Bentham Newsletter*, X (1986), p. 23.

65 Mill to John Pringle Nichol, 17 January 1834, *The Earlier Letters of John Stuart Mill*, ed. F. Mineka, 2 vols (Toronto, 1963), II, p. 211.

66 *Parliamentary Debates*, 3rd series, XX, 733 (17 August 1833).

67 David Roberts, 'The Utilitarian Conscience', in P. Marsh (ed.), *The Conscience of the Victorian State* (Hassocks, 1979), pp. 58, 62.

68 Thomas, *The Philosophic Radicals*, passim.

69 Sir John Bowring, *Autobiographical Recollections* (London, 1877), pp. 42, 337;

Bowring to Revd Lant Carpenter, 15 April 1837, Carpenter Papers. For Bowring's Unitarian background, see Allan Brockett, *Nonconformity in Exeter 1650–1875*, (Manchester, 1962), pp. 177, 187.

70 Southwood Smith also published *Illustrations of the Divine Government* (Glasgow, 1816).

71 See G. Kitson Clark, *The Making of Victorian England* (London, 1962), pp. 98–100 on the traditional involvement of medical men in social investigation and reform.

72 Finer, *Life of Chadwick*, pp. 17–18; and the curious paper, partly in Chadwick's hand, entitled 'Practical Christianity versus Professing Christianity but Practical Infidelity', Bentham MSS UC clv. 9–16.

73 Roberts, 'The Utilitarian Conscience', p. 62.

74 Ibid., p. 65.

75 Bowring to F. H. Bowring, 19 November 1844, Bowring Papers, Eng MS 1229/130, John Rylands University of Manchester Library.

76 Thomas Southwood Smith, *A Lecture Delivered over the Remains of Jeremy Bentham* (London, 1832), pp. 3, 7–8, 64.

77 'The Factories', *Westminster Review*, XXVI (1836), pp. 200–1, 206. This piece is attributed to Smith, in Walter E. Houghton, *The Wellesley Index to Victorian Periodicals 1824–1900*, 3 vols (Toronto, 1966–79), III, p. 588.

78 For Chadwick's description of Bentham as a friend, see Chadwick to Edward Gulson, July 1837 (draft), Chadwick MSS, University College London; 'A Short Sketch of E. C.'s career'[n.d.], Chadwick MSS 128. For Chadwick's denials see, for instance, his *On the Evils of Disunity in Central and Local Administration* (London, 1885), p. 2 n.

79 Roberts, 'Jeremy Bentham and the Victorian Administrative State', pp. 200–1. See also idem, 'The Utilitarian Conscience', p. 43.

80 See Bentham's 'Defence of Economy against the late Mr. Burke', *The Pamphleteer*, IX (1817), pp. 1–47 (in Bowring, *Works*, V, pp. 282–301).

81 Henriques, 'Jeremy Bentham and the Machinery of Social Reform', p. 186.

82 Chadwick to Burton, 2 January 1841, John Hill Burton Papers, MS 9406, fo. 96, National Library of Scotland, Edinburgh.

83 H. D. Macleod, *A Dictionary of Political Economy*, Part III (London, 1860), pp. 262–3.

84 Chadwick to Macleod, 19 January 1860 (draft), Chadwick MSS.

85 Macleod to Chadwick, 23 January 1860, Chadwick MSS.

86 Macleod, *Dictionary*, Part V (London, 1860), p. 398.

87 See Frederick Rosen, *Jeremy Bentham and Representative Democracy* (Oxford, 1983), p. 11.

88 Chadwick to Burton, 18 June 1844, John Hill Burton Papers, MS 9406, fo. 158.

89 *Traités de législation*, III, pp. 1–199, in Bowring, *Works*, I, pp. 533–80.

90 Chadwick MSS 130, Parts I and II.

91 Chadwick MSS 18. The 'Fable' is taken from Bentham's essays on 'The situation and relief of the poor', *Annals of Agriculture*, 1797–8; reprinted as *Pauper Management Improved*, 1812.

92 Chadwick to William Tait [n.d.], (draft), Bentham MSS UC clv. 58. Tait's reply (ibid., p. 59) is dated 28 January 1832.

93 See Bentham MSS UC clv. 9–22; and Chadwick MSS 138.

94 For correspondence on this, see Burton to Chadwick, 31 October, 5 December 1839, Chadwick MSS; Bowring to Burton, 22 August 1838, 2 February, 25 November 1839, 22, 28 January 1840, John Hill Burton Papers MS 9404, fos 6, 15, 30, 40, 41.

95 *Bentham's Observations on the Poor Bill. Introduced by the Right Honourable William Pitt. Written February, 1797* (London, 1838?), pp. i–ii.

96 Burton to Chadwick, 25 January 1841, Chadwick MSS.
97 Alexander Bain, *Autobiography* (London, 1904), pp. 196, 200; idem, *James Mill: A Biography* (London, 1882), p. 256.
98 Finer, *Life of Chadwick*, p. 514.
99 MacDonagh, 'The Nineteenth-century Revolution in Government', p. 65; Roberts, 'Jeremy Bentham and the Victorian Administrative State', pp. 208–9.
100 See Hart, 'Nineteenth-century Social Reform', p. 45; and Parris, 'The Nineteenth-century Revolution in Government', pp. 28–9.
101 See, for instance, his letters to Lord Sidmouth, then Home Secretary, in 1812: *Correspondence of Jeremy Bentham*, VIII, pp. 246–51, 263–82.
102 Richardson, 'Bentham and "Bodies for Dissection"', pp. 24–7. For Bentham's correspondence with Peel on *Constitutional Code*, see Bentham to Peel, 7 April 1827, Peel Papers, BL Add. MSS 40, 393, fos 148–9.
103 Bentham to Peel, 28 March 1830, Peel papers, BL Add. MSS 40,400, fos 134–7; Peel to Bentham, 1 April 1830, Bentham MSS UC xiv. 360; Bentham to Peel, 2 April 1830, Peel Papers, BL Add. MSS 40,400, fo. 151.
104 *Constitutional Code*, vol. I, p. xl.
105 S. E. Finer, 'The Transmission of Benthamite ideas 1820–50', in G. Sutherland (ed.), *Studies in the Growth of Nineteenth-century Government* (London, 1972), pp. 11–32.
106 Mill to Bentham, 19 September 1814, *Correspondence of Jeremy Bentham*, VIII, p. 417.
107 J. S. Mill, *Autobiography and Literary Essays*, ed. J. M. Robson and J. Stillenger (Toronto, 1981), p. 104.
108 For Dumont's accompanying Petty, see *The Correspondence of Jeremy Bentham*, vol. VI, ed. J. R. Dinwiddy (Oxford, 1984), pp. 439, 450, 457.
109 See Thomas, *The Philosophic Radicals*, pp. 28–9; J. R. Dinwiddy, 'Bentham and the Early Nineteenth Century', *The Bentham Newsletter*, VIII (1984), pp. 17–18; idem, 'Early Nineteenth-Century Reactions to Benthamism', *Transactions of the Royal Historical Society*, 5th series, XXXIV (1984), pp. 49–51.
110 Dinwiddy, 'Bentham and the Early Nineteenth Century', p. 16.
111 *Constitutional Code*, vol. I, p. xlii.
112 'A Brief Memoir of Sir John Bowring', in Bowring, *Autobiographical Recollections*, p. 14.
113 Burton to Chadwick, 16 December 1843, Chadwick MSS.
114 Burton to Chadwick, 1 April 1846, ibid.
115 For Bentham's own estimates of the circulation of the *Traités*, see Bentham to Sir Frederick Morton Eden, 4 September 1802, Bentham to Revd Samuel Parr, 16 September 1803, *Correspondence of Jeremy Bentham*, VII, pp. 124, 243.
116 J. S. Mill, *Autobiography and Literary Essays*, p. 105; W. H. Burston, *James Mill on Philosophy and Education* (London, 1973), p. 49. Significantly, perhaps, at least six utilitarian MPs attended Cambridge. See Roberts, 'The Utilitarian Conscience', p. 42.
117 On this subject generally, see J. W. Flood, 'The Benthamites and their Use of the Press 1810–40', University of London PhD thesis, 1974.
118 *Tait's Edinburgh Magazine*, II (1832), pp. 49–56; ibid., new series, III (1836), pp. 606–7; ibid., V (1838), pp. 12–20, 328–31. Parts of Bowrings 'Memoirs of Bentham', published in vols X and XI of his edition of the *Works*, first appeared in *Tait's Edinburgh Magazine* from VII (1840) to IX (1842).
119 Tait to Chadwick, 29 February 1832, Bentham MSS UC clv. 61.
120 Bowring to F. H. Bowring, 19 November 1840, Bowring papers, Eng MS 1229/130.
121 See Bowring's *Minor Morals for Young People*, 3 parts (London, 1834–9).

122 R. E. Leader (ed.), *The Life and Letters of John Arthur Roebuck* (London, 1897), p. 217.
123 Quoted in Roberts, 'The Utilitarian Conscience', p. 64.
124 Bulwer, *England and the English*, pp. 317–18. For an earlier expression of the same view see Richard Lovell Edgeworth 33/II, fo. 66, Bibliothèque Publique et Universitaire, Geneva.

Chapter six

J. S. Mill, liberalism, and progress

John Gibbins

Introduction

Few British philosophers in the Victorian age were as aware as John Stuart Mill of their own place and that of their society in the course of history.

To understand Mill on any issue we need to know, among other things, how he contextualized the subject in his whole theory, his notion of the spirit of the age, his view of the epoch's place in the history of mankind and how he saw his own ideas, prescriptions, and actions as contributing to human development.[1] This essay explores and attempts a verdict upon both Mill's allegiance to and conception of liberalism and liberal democracy, making use of these insights.

My own approach eschews, as far as possible, close textual and analytic arguments and works rather at two levels: the level of historical and biographical development; and a more synoptic level, concentrating on Mill's vision of his age and his view of history. I shall argue in support of several propositions. First, that within the primary source material on Mill's life there is evidence to support many of the available interpretations of Mill's political theory; that, indeed, sound arguments in support of Mill the Old and New Liberal, the conservative, the co-operative socialist, the democrat, the elitist, the libertine, and the authoritarian are not only possible, but were invited by Mill. Second, that there were some unresolved tensions, incoherences, inconsistencies, and even contradictions within Mill's corpus that recent 'defences' of Mill have failed to remove. Mill's own efforts towards blending 'manysidedness' with 'eclectic synchrony' were not always successful. Harmony and complementarity were not always forged anew as a result of Mill's intellectual promiscuity. But thirdly, we can still trace several linking threads, even a coherence, throughout Mill's work on liberty and democracy once we contextualize each of Mill's works and assign it a place in his overall history of ideas, his notion of his own place in intellectual history and the progress of civilization. Finally, Mill's liberalism is transitional in character. While his arguments retain a commitment to individualism and a *laissez-faire* approach, his exposure to alien ideas and his growing awareness of history brought him to a new view of individuals and of society as progressive beings. He believed that government could, in his revised theory, act to encourage progress by creating the appropriate fertile conditions. While not arguing with Green and others who came later that the state should act positively, his vision of the perfectible human self, reached by 1861, made positive liberalism an attractive possibility.

History and progress

At the centre of Mill's philosophy were three related theories, a commitment to historicism, to utilitarianism, and an optimistic and developmental theory of human nature, all of which embodied a teleology of progress. Through an examination of these elements I hope to explain Mill's fluctuating allegiances, and his apparently qualified defences of liberalism and democracy.

A fundamental part of the education provided by James Mill and Bentham for the young Mill was in history. Throughout his life Mill studied the works of the great historians, and he wrote many critical reviews and commentaries on them. This was not a minor exercise, since Mill regarded history as being the laboratory in which both sociological laws and political practices were to be tested for their validity. The study of contemporary trends and recent history under the micro-scopes of utility, laws of ethology, and the principles of liberty and progress, were to provide evidence that could lead to the verification, rejection, or modification of laws, empirical generalizations, and principles.[2]

In his *History of British India*, John Mill's father had produced a philosophical history in which Indian society was to be judged on a 'scale of civilization', or a 'moral ladder', in Thomas's words.[3] The graduations of this scale were to be judged entirely by utility; the further a society had progressed towards utility the higher it appeared on the scale of civilization. The criteria of advance towards civilization were a matter of dispute between father and son, but as John Mill developed his thought, so the now familiar criteria of the fully developed moral self emerged: independent not dependent, educated not ignorant, open-minded not dogmatic, rational not prejudiced, virtuous (seeking higher pleasures) not animal, eccentric not respectable, radical not conservative, progressive not reactionary. Individuals or societies which stressed the former were defined as 'advanced' or 'civilized', those that exhibited the latter were 'backward' or 'barbarian'.

James Mill had developed these ideas from his acquaintance with the Scottish historians Hume, Smith, Robertson, and Millar, and the pioneering French sociologist Montesquieu.[4] When John Mill became acquainted with the work of George Grote, Saint Simon, de Tocqueville, and Auguste Comte, he was able to modify his father's theory into a thoroughgoing philosophical history, most clearly exhibited in the early essay *The Spirit of the Age*.[5] Here John Mill combined the lessons of Comte's three-stage theory and Saint Simon's staircase of civilization by which ascent or progress is marked by alternate periods of stability (organic) and change (transitional). In an organic or natural period society was permanent or stable. Power and wealth were usually in the hands of men intellectually able to perform those functions necessary for well-being. By and large, there was a consensus among the ruling class that permeated to all lower classes as authoritative. In the transitional or critical ages, when society was characterized by change or progress, centres of power and wealth came under attack, fell into disrepute and their influence was transferred to the hands of new elites better equipped to promote the public good. Consensus, the tyranny of common or elite opinion, broke down, and revolutionary ideas were contested and debated until the new truth and a new consensus arose.

From Comte, Mill learned that a third and final stage in historical progress was coming into existence in modern Europe – the Positivist Age. The earlier theological and metaphysical stages of development, characteristic of backward societies whose modes of thought were dominated by either 'supernatural agencies' or 'metaphysical abstractions' such as natural rights, were being left behind. Mill believed the positivist revolution had first taken place in the natural sciences, but was now permeating history, sociology, political science, and philosophy. By the 1840s, Mill had evolved an optimistic and developmental version of historicism, within which societies and individuals advanced in proportion to the form of knowledge and level of development of the speculative faculties they possessed.[6]

If George Grote taught Mill that, in addition to speculative development, liberty of discussion and democracy were the key agents of advance, de Tocqueville had warned that a tyranny of customary opinion, accompanying an otherwise progress-enhancing egalitarianism, could hold up development. From the French historian Michelet, Mill learned that 'diversity' of culture, even within a society, produced progress, and from others that radical breaks were counter-productive. But Mill attested that it was Wilhelm von Humboldt who had confirmed in him the key theme of his mature social and political thought: 'the absolute importance of human development in its richest diversity', for not only are the cultivation of 'freedom, and variety of situations', of 'individual vigour and manifold diversity', causes of human progress, but also its ideal or goal. Self-development is the engine and goal of human history.[7]

Mill was not content to rest with this philosophy of history, he needed 'a science of history' to complete both the historical maturation of that subject, and to provide a set of tools for diagnosing and prescribing for the progress of mankind. In 1844 he wrote that, in this science,

> All history is conceived as a progressive chain of causes and effect: or [by an apter metaphor] as a gradually unfolding web .... To find on what principles, derived from the nature of man and the laws of the outward world, each state of society and of the human mind produced that which came after it; and whether there can be traced any order of production sufficiently definite, to show what future states of society may be expected to emanate from the circumstances which exist at present – is the aim of historical philosophy in its third stage.[8]

By the time of Mill's fruitful period of political theorizing in the 1860s, he had come, with varying degrees of confidence, to believe that a successful sociology could provide a science of history, politics, and morals which allowed both deductions from the laws of mind and inductions from the historical and contemporary social facts.[9] In practice, help would come most from appeal to the *axiomata media* not the ultimate principle, and the most useful middle principles were concerned with the rules for creating progress, the rules of social dynamics, by which one state of society advances into the next, improved state.[10]

This Inverse Deductive Method, as he called it, would only be perfected in the social sciences when the law of progress generalized from history as an empirical law could be converted 'into a scientific theorem by deducing it *a priori* from the principles of human nature, as the laws of ethology must ultimately be deduced from laws of mind.[11] But he was confident that for practical purposes his theory of social and self-development would suffice.

The laws of mind were not to be confused with the moral ideals of 'what is ultimately desirable' in Mill's account. The scale or criteria for judging progress was an *a priori* moral conviction or intuition (for which there was some ready, but inconclusive, inductive empirical evidence). This was the principle of utility, the happiness principle.[12] Utilitarianism provided Mill not only with a single criterion of progress but a teleological goal that made his social science meaningful and operable. But, while happiness was the ideal end-state, approximation to happiness or progress was the operational criterion for making moral and political judgements. History and sociology could provide *axiomata media*, principles, and rules of and for progress.[13] Once these were accepted, it was the job of the practical politician

> to surround any given society with the greatest possible number of circumstances of which the tendencies are beneficial and to remove or counteract, as far as practicable, those of which the tendencies are injurious.[14]

Contrary to the view of Eldon Eisenach,[15] Mill did have an ethology, but it was embedded in his whole political theory and practice, and especially his policies towards liberalism, democracy, and socialism, and not just in his narrative account of his own life. This ethology stated that all societies and individuals could progress towards the mature development of their potential, that this depended in part on removing internal and external constraints, and in part on creating the internal and external conditions for self-development. In this process education, and especially the acquisition of self-mastery, were axial. Yet we must not conclude with Geoffrey Smith that it is Mill's optimistic theory of human nature and his metaphysics of free will alone which explain this conclusion, for both are circumscribed by an optimistic theory of historical development.[16]

The role Mill had reserved for himself in the narrative of modern history was that of philosophical statesman. With his knowledge of the ultimate ideal, the theory and empirical laws of social progress, and a practical desire to see an advance in human well-being towards happiness, he could negotiate between warring theoretical and practical factions and advise the government, and indeed the world, on the most judicious strategy for achieving the agreed end.[17] By so doing, he perhaps realized his prediction that a 'great man' will arise who can advise on what is best, even when 'knowledge insufficient for prediction' was unavailable. The statesman must be involved,

> not only in looking far forward into the future history of the human race, but in determining what artificial means may be used, and to what extent, to accelerate the natural progress in so far as it is beneficial, to compensate for whatever may be its inherent inconveniences or disadvantages, and to guard against the dangers or accidents to which our species is exposed from the necessary incidents of its progression.[18]

Progress, according to Mill, was the link between the secondary ends, principles, and rules and the *summum bonum* of utility. It was the intermediate and operational principle in politics. Only on the grounds that a rule, principle, or ideal was consistent with improvement or development towards the realization of the greatest happiness (in the widest and highest sense) of the greatest number, could it be given moral and political approval.[19] As Alexander Brady writes of the liberty principle in Mill, 'Progress for all depends on liberty for each.'[20] Where liberty and freedom of discussion would not ensure progress as self-development, then its provision must either be withheld, prepared for, or enforced. Hence liberty and democracy for children and the mentally handicapped should be withheld until they have been educated to meet the obligation and use the opportunities bestowed properly. Similar considerations applied to dependent barbarians abroad and the dependent and uneducated members of the working classes at home.[21] Exactly the same restrictions cover the applicability of the democratic principle to advanced and backward individuals and societies.[22] For overall 'Conduciveness to Progress, thus understood, includes the whole excellence of government.'[23]

Utility, liberty, and democracy

John Stuart Mill's reputation as a liberal, a democrat, and a promoter of other causes, such as female suffrage and co-operative socialism, and the textual evidence and arguments in their support is well established. However, Mill's commitment to an historically-based social science of dynamics and contingency made the support of absolute rules, principles, methods, practices, and institutions, except utilitarianism, illogical. Mill neither sought nor achieved unconditional or absolutist axioms in politics and morality but rather stressed the conditional and the relative.

Mill's ideas and prescriptions for liberty and democracy altered as his mental development progressed through the various phases of his life, his friendships, his acquaintances with new schools of thought, and his practical acquaintance with history and politics. Adopting the strategy of 'practical eclecticism' following his mental crisis, Mill sought out intellectual controversy and according to his 'law of improvement' and the aim of diminishing disagreement, he trimmed and amended his views where needed.[24] As we shall see, each part of his philosophy needed modification as some new discovery was made elsewhere in the whole, as when Mill decided to widen his account of happiness. Above all else, Mill recognized that diagnosis and prescription depended upon 'states of society' and 'individuals', their 'stage of development', and their potential for 'reform' and 'advance'.

Utility

Mill was a utilitarian, but he was also a revisionist. He not only challenged the old utilitarianism of Bentham, he altered and modified his own views on several occasions to meet internal incoherences and external criticisms.[25] The key modifications lay in widening the definition of happiness to include several new components and to allow for differences in quality and quantity. These changes involved providing a new account of the moral motives, including sociability, sympathy, and universal altruism; a revision of his attitude to moral rules which now treats them as practical precepts of applied utilitarian philosophy; and a new theory of justice involving impartiality as a key theme. In a variety of essays, but especially those on Bentham, the essays on Sedgwick, Whewell, and eventually *Utilitarianism* itself, Mill applied his practical eclecticism to his central moral convictions. Defenders of Mill have argued for consistency within the later essay, but few expand that to cover all Mill's writing on the subject. By 1861 Mill's account of utilitarianism was ideal and idealistic. Happiness was an ideal end-state, the perfection of human nature that ought to be promoted, and not the sum total of rather immediate, actually desired, wanted, and quantifiable pleasures. In addition, his account of what constituted happiness had become teleological. The ideal happiness was that experienced by individuals who had fully developed their faculties, who had complete mastery of their wants, especially their animal desires, and who could recognize and realize their individual and collective interests.

One contemporary critic, John Grote, complained that Mill's aim in *Utilitarianism* appeared to be 'to save appearances by accumulating cycle on epicycle where the fault is in the original supposition'.[26] He argued that Mill's 'neo-utilitarianism' in effect contained so many profound modifications and additions that not only is the new system incoherent, it is heterodox in regard to old utilitarianism.[27] Within the context of Mill's eclectic strategy, the axial importance of the principle of utility, his philosophy of history, and his self-selected statesmanly ambitions, Mill's equivocation on and within utilitarianism was both understandable and even predictable.

Liberalism

The strengths of Mill's theory of liberalism lay both in its apparent singularity, simplicity, and absoluteness and in its inherent plurality, complexity, and relativity. At the heart of his liberalism appeared to be the 'simple' liberty principle, but on examination this was a very supple tree that could bend to the historical and contingent wind to produce shapes not originally perceived as viable. What Mill produced was an apparently single and absolute principle which in reality applied only to one state of society and which allowed, and even recommended, different principles for alternative historical situations. This was most clearly evident in the original juxtaposing of the absolute principle and the immediate disqualification of its appropriateness to backward individuals and societies in *On Liberty*. Here Mill stated his object to be to 'assert one very simple principle to govern absolutely the dealings of society with the individual in the way of compulsion and control ...'

> That principle is, that the sole end for which mankind are warranted, individually or collectively, in interfering with the liberty of action of any of their numbers, is self protection. That the only purpose for which power can be rightfully exercised over any member of a civilised community, against his will, is to prevent harm to others.[28]

This paragraph is immediately followed by the qualifying condition: 'It is, perhaps, hardly necessary to say that this doctrine is meant to apply only to human beings in the maturity of their faculties.' To Mill this specifically excluded children, invalids, the mentally handicapped, and barbarian societies in which the race itself may be considered as in its 'nonage'. Where individuals or society were neither educated for liberty nor were capable of being improved by free and equal discussion or persuasion, liberty was to be withheld. It is probable that Mill considered excluding not only the majority of the peoples of the globe who then lived in backward societies from liberty and liberalism, but that at times he also had in mind those backward individuals and groups within existing advanced societies, the uneducated, prejudiced, and somewhat authoritarian segment of the working classes. Either way, in such conditions listed above,

> a ruler full of the spirit of improvement is warranted in the use of any expedients that will attain an end, perhaps otherwise unattainable. Despotism is a legitimate mode of government in dealing with barbarians, provided the end be their improvement, and the means justified by actually effecting that end. Liberty, as a principle, has no application to any state of things anterior to the time when mankind have become capable of being improved by free and equal discussion.[29]

For dependent individuals one alternative to despotism that Mill allowed was paternalism. The conditions for and applications of paternalism were severely restrictive. According to M. E. Waithe, they included:

First, the prospective paternalized person must be morally nonresponsible for his actions in the specific situation in which paternalism is being contemplated. Second, the prospective paternalized person must be causing, or about to cause, wrongful harm to those of his interests which can be considered his 'rights'. Third, it must be the case that paternalizing him will enhance his capacity to develop (or to be restored to) the capacity to be self-governing, or that paternalizing him will prevent further deterioration of his capacity to be self governing. Finally, the way in which we paternalize him must be the least restrictive alternative conducive to preventing the wrongful harm to his interests and to developing or restoring his capacity for self-government.[30]

In reality, Mill considered paternalizing children, barbarians, those considering the option of slavery and an irrevocable marriage contract, the mentally impaired, and those inadvertently embarking upon such dangerous pursuits as crossing flimsy bridges. But such a strategy was an extreme expedient, to be used only in cases where the normal and most effective methods for bringing individuals to a capacity for freedom, namely education and training in independence, were inapplicable.

Other important qualifications based on contingent states of society or of individuals appeared elsewhere in Mill's writings, and reveal the ebb and flow of his commitment to liberty as a general principle. At times, Mill suggested that liberty was desirable primarily in transitional or critical ages when it could further progress towards a new organic or natural age.[31] He equivocated on its applicability in the latter periods. In past organic periods the key to success had been the coincidence of wisdom, virtue, religious and worldly power in a single class, with the subordinate society held in sway by 'received doctrines' and 'inherited opinions', with little or no opportunity or encouragement to free thought or action .[32] Looking forward, as he did in 1831, to an imminent move from a contemporary critical age to a 'healthier' organic state, Mill argued that the old ruling classes, should be 'divested of the monopoly of worldly power, when the most virtuous and best instructed of the nation will acquire that ascendancy over the opinion and feeling of the rest, by which England can emerge from this crisis of transition, and enter once again into a natural state of society.'[33] The future 'natural state' pictured at various times, envisaged a new liberal consensus, with a new class of leaders, sometimes called the 'clerisy', and a new rational authority to which deference would be given voluntarily.[34] Once achieved, this coincidence of wisdom, virtue, reason, and worldly powers would need to be defended in the normal ways by education, law, and the cultivation of supportive circumstances. While never advocating imposed uniformity, compulsion, or the abandonment of tolerance, Mill encountered a paradox of modern liberalism captured, perhaps, in the notion of 'repressive tolerance' – namely, that to protect and promote liberalism as the established doctrine and practice of an age, a state elite cannot be neutral, that there will be limits to tolerance (i.e. tolerating the intolerant and the collectivist), and that the freely and democratically chosen opinions and preferences of the mass would not always hold sway.[35]

While in principle allowing government interference in acts that harm the interest of others, Mill often found good utilitarian reasons for disallowing such action. Hence with almost the entire management of the economy, where the interests of all are affected, and intervention was justified on the liberty principle, Mill still argued that society was the greater gainer by allowing each individual to act as they thought fit.[36] Legitimate government interference was considered counter- productive because where governments did interfere, they usually did so badly. Mill considered centralized power generally to be retrogressive. Individuals benefited from independence, they were educated when making private choices, and they then worked more effectively.[37] However, Mill did allow some fairly draconian sanctions in those areas where legal intervention was not applicable. We could persuade, educate, condemn, and use an array of other social sanctions, including public reprobation, against those whose views or actions we found unpleasant or distasteful.[38] While Mill felt that intervention should generally be restricted to cases where harm to the interests of others was proved, he recognized that it was not always possible to do so. In such circumstances governments should be biased in favour of interference.[39] Finally, Mill suggested to his readers that while liberty should be spread as widely as possible throughout an advanced society, in practice the masses should defer to the advice and authority of a more wise and gifted few.[40]

No reader of Mill's *Logic* should be surprised at these positions. There Mill argued for 'the law of the successive transformation of human opinion', in which the level of the 'progression in the intellectual convictions of mankind' determined human progress. Liberty was a principle designed to develop human intellects, but where counteracting causes suggested qualification the practice had to be modified.[41] Again, we find in Book VI, ch. II the famous commitment to the idea that while circumstance determines character and character our actions and will, persons with a strong enough will to posses self-mastery could break the chain of determination by placing themselves 'under the influence of other circumstances'.[42] Similarly, policies which aimed to bring barbarians, children, and mature citizens habituated to dependence to independence by altering circumstances, were justified as preconditions for the exercise of free will itself.

We can now throw some light on the major debate over consistency between the liberty and utility principles. Textual and analytic studies have brought us to a point where the most popular argument in Mill's defence rejects the need to choose between the dependent and independent value of the liberty principle, and indeed the principles of individuality, self-development, virtue and justice. According to Gray, Mill believed liberty and individuality were desired as vital interests or preconditions for the achievement of happiness, defending as they do the other vital interests of autonomy and security.[43] Liberty was a fundamental precondition for a worthy human life. Both the liberty and happiness principles had absolute deontic status because without the former the latter was implausible.

Peter Berger and Harry Clor take the alternative route of making liberty, individuality, and self-development constitute parts of happiness, though whether this is an absolute identity, or whether they only became so by an act of association, is not at all clear.[44] Bernard Semmel is even more adamant on this point. He treats the virtuous life as synonymous with Mill's idea of happiness.[45] C. L. Ten has made Mill a consistent liberal, not by reconstructing Mill's utilitarian principle but by rendering it subservient to and inconsistent with the liberty principle. Mill is a liberal because he consistently believed in 'freedom of choice' as a good in itself. Ten treats Mill's famous statement aligning liberty to utility as a rhetorical gesture.[46]

All of these interpretations run into intricate analytic, conceptual, and historical problems that are too many and complex to discuss here. These analyses understate Mill's fundamental and optimistic assumption about the developmental potential of human nature and the progressive potential of history. Clor, Semmel, and more recently Geoffrey Smith have noticed the importance of self-development and improvement in John Mill. By considering the higher pleasures as the true goals of self-development, the ideal object of self-regarding activities, and the true constituents of happiness in the widest sense, Mill was able to find a proper place for government and unite the liberty and utility principles. Fully free individuals, adept at self-mastery, would invariably choose the superior of any range of optional pleasures. Therefore, in virtuous conduct they realize their liberty. Without these optimistic assumptions the liberty principle is incomprehensible and Mill's utilitarianism a mystery.

But in addition, we can see that many of the principles and prescriptions in *On Liberty* were little more than empirical generalizations from history and hypothetical ethological laws. The key law was that of progress, but there were subordinate rules governing the retrogressive effects of paternalism, despotism, custom, and the tyranny of opinion as well. The liberty principle was Mill's attempt at a middle principle, the *axiomata media* that linked these lower-level empirical generalizations to the higher law of progress and the ultimate laws of mind. This principle asserted that 'Mankind are the greatest gainers by suffering each other to live as seems good to themselves, than by compelling each to live as seems good to the rest.'[47] Mill aimed, then, to defend his long-standing preferences for liberty and liberalism within the context of his historical and teleological system, with special reference to the final end of utility. He defended liberty because of its developmental potential, arguing that only in a society providing liberty and diversity would there be a chance for both social and self-development. But because the true goal of self-development was the realization of the higher pleasures, then such imposed and educative practices as state intervention in education, the workhouse, redistributions of land, and the legitimation of trade unions were considered desirable and compatible with liberty. Thus, as Richard Bellamy argues, 'Mill neatly resolved the conflict between liberty and utility by asserting that our true freedom inhered in our maximizing utility'[48] Mill's defence of liberty was at least consistent with his theory of history, his preoccupation with improvement and his theory of the perfectible self.

Economy and state

Classical economic theory, into which Mill had been inducted by Bentham and Ricardo, recommended the general policy of non-intervention by the state in private economic affairs on utilitarian grounds. As a general rule, they believed that the majority in a society were the gainers by leaving individuals to make, implement, and bear the consequences of whatever economic choices they made. State intervention should usually be limited to the provision of a legal framework for making and enforcing contracts, and to defending the liberty, rights, and life of persons and property. Yet on occasions Mill deviated from this theory and advocated some 'optional' areas for interference. Such circumstances included the revolution in Europe in the 1840s, the Irish famine, and the early efforts of working men's organizations to improve their wages, conditions, and power in the 1870s.

For some commentators there was a pattern to these deviations. George Holyoake, the late Victorian Radical considered Mill to be a socialist at his death, a view shared this century by the economist Lionel Robbins.[49] Others see the change as being personal not political and consider F. D. Maurice and later Harriet Taylor as having influenced his views. However, when placed within the context of Mill's historical theory of progress and self-development, his practical eclecticism and his utilitarian ethic, a new account of Mill on the economy and the state emerges.

A few examples will illustrate this point. Mill argued that in Ireland during the Victorian period the traditional agrarian economy regularly failed to provide for the subsistence of the peasantry. The resulting famines were calamitous in the cost of lives, depopulation of the countryside, and in emigration. Mill recognized the problem as long-term and found its origins in the inefficient system of hereditary ownership and the absentee landlord farming system. In order to remedy this situation, Mill proposed the curtailment of the normal right of inheritance and the compulsory redistribution of the large holdings of absentee landlords to the local peasantry, who Mill considered to be those best equipped to cultivate the land efficiently. In this way the state would encourage the independence and self-development of the peasant farmers, competitiveness, and efficiency.[50] In a similar spirit Mill also advocated compulsory elementary education for this would allow the otherwise ignorant and dependent to become wise, competent, and independent judges.[51]

Another circumstance where state intervention would best guarantee progress was in those fields where the market failed to offer goods or services at all, or to a standard considered acceptable. Mill's list of examples of what a government may legitimately facilitate if it considered the market product to be unsatisfactory covers almost the entire outputs of twentieth-century welfare states, including 'roads, docks, harbours, canals, works of irrigation, hospitals, schools, colleges, printing presses'.[52] Market or voluntary provision was, of course, preferable; but in the absence of both, state provision was justified to further progress and utility. Interference with the market in the form of government tribunals might also be necessary to protect the interests of those who have placed them in the hands of others, such as the directors of joint-stock companies or the guardians of charitable institutions.[53] More controversially, as Martin Hollis argues, Mill allowed interference in the market, 'where the force of law is needed, not to overrule the judgement of individuals but to give effect to it'.[54] In the cases of wage-bargaining and colonization, Mill argued that few individuals could realize their individual interests unless a common rule was made and enforced by law on all parties.[55] To allow individuals with a trade or profession to undercut wage rates or to exceed standard work hours would reduce the freedom of the majority and the interests of all.

Finally, Mill was aware of some imperfections in the logic of the market deriving from differences between its theory and practice. Not only were many individuals not educated to compete, but others through poverty, inequities, and enforced dependency were inhibited from doing so. This was true of large proportions of the labouring classes in Victorian Britain, and especially women, who by custom, class, gender barriers, and the law were prevented from becoming independent, entrepreneurial, and innovatory. One response was to advocate experiments that would extend access to an entrepreneurial society to previously excluded groups, so under the influence of the ideas of Owen, Maurice, Harriet Taylor, and others, Mill began to encourage experiments in socialism alongside those in the market. Market and socialist systems should be allowed to flourish and compete in terms of product, efficiency, conditions for workers, wages, and profit, so that the true benefits of competition and co-operation could be assessed.[56]

In his optimistic moments Mill conceived of a society of free, equal, independent, powerful, and virtuous citizens, where all laboured and contributed to the common good and received fair rewards for effort. He also considered the hereditary class system to be doomed as it created inefficiency and other obstacles to progress arising from the 'theory of dependence' exposed by and practised by the landed and capitalist classes. Hence Mill's socialism was libertarian and involved neither collectivism, planning, nor communism. Its logic and aim was to make the working classes and women into self-developing individuals, enslaved neither to hereditary landlords nor capitalist employers. As he puts it:

The aim of improvement should be not solely to place human beings in a condition of which they will be able to do without one another, but to enable them to work with or for one another in relations not involving dependence.[57]

The policy objective was hence to make every worker into a self-employed private owner or a joint-owner in a partnership or co-operative. Each worker should become the master of his own destiny and have every opportunity to develop and employ the virtues of freedom, prudence, temperance, and self-control.

All experiments in paternalistic forms of socialism, such as communism, state socialism, and revolution, were rejected by Mill firmly as anti-progressive, although he did allow experiments in what Marx called 'utopian socialism', providing they were of a variety and on a scale to facilitate empirical evaluation of their effects. Support was given to local workers co-operatives, to retail co-operatives, to schemes sharing profits between workers and managers, to workers saving, investment, and insurance schemes. On balance, Mill expected them to fail for several reasons, some because they attempted 'to dispense with the inducements of private interest in social affairs, while no substitute for them has been or can be provided', others because the 'uncultivated herd who now composes the labouring masses' and many managers were not sufficiently educated or lacked the moral virtue to manage a co-operative, and others because the products were not competitive in quality or price.[58]

Mill, then, remained an unrepentant defender of the *laissez-faire* system of the economy and a radical libertarian in his efforts to extend its practice and benefits from capitalist employers and the self-employed to all peasant and industrial workers. He advocated experiments in socialism where they made up for the defects of the market or led to its better and wider operation in the long run. Utopian and experimental though they were, Mill felt that the experience of failure would be educative:[59]

> In the meantime we may, without attempting to limit the ultimate capabilities of human nature, affirm, that the political economist, for a considerable time to come, will be chiefly concerned with the conditions of existence and progress belonging to a society founded on private property and individual competition; and the object to be principally avoided in the present stage of human development, is not the subversion of the system of individual property, but the improvement of it, and the full participation of every member of the community in its benefits.[60]

Democracy

In his essay of 1861, Mill argued that representative democracy was the only form of government conducive to permanent progress.[61] The grounds provided consisted of a series of sociological generalizations governing the connection between circumstances and their happiness-giving effects. First, democracy allowed citizens to develop and use the highest powers of human beings; it allowed for and promoted virtue, excellence, and intelligence.[62] Second, representative government was an agent of education for the people and provided

103

an efficient forum for 'conducting the collective affairs of the community'.[63] Third, the clashes or 'intercourse' between men that democracy allowed increased the chances that the best and wisest leaders would arise, and that truth would emerge from the arguments between them. Representative government, or true democracy was judged by how far it 'promotes the good management of the affairs of a society by means of the existing faculties moral, intellectual, and active, of its various members and by "improving" those faculties.'[64]

However, Mill also mounted a considerable array of qualifying conditions against representative government. First, such a government was suitable only where the character of citizens was appropriate, namely where they have 'an active, self-helping character'. Passivity and dependency were excluding characteristics, and it must be remembered that these were found not only among most people in backward states of society but among some people in advanced societies.[65] Next, Mill insisted that the candidate society for democracy must reveal that the people should be willing to receive it; that they should be willing and able to do what is necessary for its preservation; and that they should be willing and able to fulfil the duties and discharge the functions which it imposes on them.[66] Prior to the 'advanced stage' of society, few of the necessary conditions were considered to be present. In particular, in backward states, citizens exhibited two disqualifying inclinations, 'one is, the desire to exercise power over others; the other is disinclination to have power exercised over themselves.'[67]

The most revealing evidence of Mill's conditional, restricted, and relativistic theory of democracy occurred in the central prescriptive chapter of his most mature work on suffrage reform, Chapter VII of the *Considerations on Representative Government*. Here Mill exhibited the statesman's skills, qualifying the democratic ideal under the influence of the empirical historical law that if the numerical majority in a democracy were composed of only one class, and that not highly cultivated, then not only would progress not occur, but it could be reversed. This lesson, drawn from de Tocqueville's thesis of the tyranny of the majority, confirmed Mill in other beliefs about the unequal qualities, potentialities, and hence the unequal rights and powers of dependent and independent persons. In addition, Mill prescribed a liberal democracy which limited the powers of legally elected majorities by enshrining and protecting the rights of individuals from the majority. Here we have a case of Mill's paternalism, for he advocates the use of constitutional law to prohibit a properly elected majority government from doing what it wants on the grounds that this will protect the interest of the minority and promote the long-term interests of the majority itself. Just as a wife may not enter into a marriage contract that would reduce her long-term freedom and capacity for self-development, no majority should be allowed to legislate in a way that would prevent existing mature individuals from partaking in 'experiments in living' and the possibility that they too may wish at a later date to be able to do so. So qualified by individual liberty,

Mill sought to moderate the numerical power of the majority in a democracy by adjusting the franchise.

Despite his call in 1859 for universal adult enfranchisement, Mill wrote in 1861: 'I regard it as wholly inadmissible that any person should participate in the suffrage without being able to read, write, and I will add, perform the operations of arithmetic.'[68] Registration tests would be set up to check performance; and to facilitate high pass rates Mill prescribed compulsory universal education for all children. If the uneducated were not to vote, the better educated were to have a plurality of votes. Reflecting deep-seated Victorian prejudices, he could write: 'No one but a fool, and only a fool of a peculiar description, feels offended by the acknowledgement that there are others whose opinion, and even whose wish, is entitled to a greater amount of consideration than his.'[69]

Three categories of the dependant were also recommended for disqualification. First, all those who were not contributing to local rates.[70] For those who were unwilling or unable to pay, there should be a total exclusion, voting was to be 'exclusively by those who pay something towards the taxes imposed'. Next, persons who had been dependent upon public welfare were to be excluded for five years from the last day of receipt. In true melodramatic style, Mill justified a wide range of sanctions for dependency: 'By becoming dependent on the remaining members of the community for actual subsistence, he abdicates his claim to equal rights with them in other respects.'[71] The third category of dependants to be excluded were legal bankrupts and other moral deviants such as habitual drunkards. Finally, Mill advocated equal voting for all people independent of sex and colour. Two considerations should temper our judgement on Mill's radicalism in this regard. First, in 1861, while many women would have gained the vote under his proposals, most women, those in the working class, like working-class men, would have remained disenfranchised. Aware of the limited educational status of that class, aware that few women and working-class men paid direct taxes, and aware of the large numbers of women and the poor who fell into destitution, Mill was prescribing a most limited suffrage that gave only the appearance of equal rights to all. Second, Mill considered that only the independent, not the dependent, should be enfranchised. Women, like working-class males, must be liberated from dependence, paternalism, and reliance upon others in any form before the suffrage was extended to them. Equal voting, universal suffrage, unqualified democracy, like liberty and equal rights then, were not absolutes. As he writes of the former:

> I do not look upon equal voting as among the things which are good in themselves, provided they can be guarded against inconveniences. I look upon it as only relatively good, less objectionable than inequality of privilege ...[72]

Democracy, like liberty, was a conditional good. Voting rights, like much else, were only to be given to those who had already cultivated the appropriate characteristics of self-direction and self-control and who had the ability and interest to invest them in promoting the public good. The political policy for government in franchise reform should be 'To make a participation in political rights the reward of mental improvement'.[73] This policy is just one more illustration of a more general idea, for 'the most important point of excellence which any form of government can possess is to promote the virtue and intelligence of the people themselves'.[74]

Conclusion

As he grew older Mill developed a deep antipathy for absolutes, for unconditional allegiances, and unqualified prescriptions. Even his attachment to utilitarianism, liberty, and democracy became subject to distrust and even disillusionment as his optimism waxed and waned on progress and the possibility that human nature could be perfected. From the study of logic Mill concluded that the social sciences could provide only a few absolute laws. The laws of mind were primarily dynamic, dealing with the progress of human development. The laws of psychology and history were generally contingent empirical generalizations, and the laws of ethology were developmental and relativistic. Both the essays *On Liberty* and *Representative Government* were consistent with the above, with Mill's historical *Weltanschauung* and with his view of the spirit of the age. Mill could not give unqualified approval to complete *laissez-faire* liberalism or radical democracy, for both were to be judged against the historical mission of the progressive development of mankind. What is more, his beliefs and theories about them were always in the process of revision, and towards the end of his life he began to entertain some ideas consistent with the 'New Liberalism'.

The presence of tensions, even inconsistencies, in and between the various works that make up Mill's philosophy should not come as a surprise then. Mill's thought was always in a state of flux. His deepest convictions recognized contingency and progress in the world, in history, and in knowledge. Mill's method and strategies encouraged and embraced contradiction. However, we can still detect a consistent imperative in his corpus: to promote the greatest happiness, in the widest sense, of the greatest number, by the expediency of discovering the aids and obstacles to human progress and advising on the artificial devices that may allow social and self-development.

This objective led Mill to reject a pure form of negative liberalism which simply drew a circle around each individual and prevented interference from outside. By the 1860s Mill was seriously considering the use of law to overcome those obstacles, both internal and external, such as ignorance and customs that constrain individuals both possessing and exercising freedom. Finally, in a more authoritarian mode, when preventing women and men from entering into binding contracts of marriage and slavery, in forcing parents to send their children to school, in supporting the 1834 Poor Law Amendments Act, and in making the right to vote contingent on literacy, moral self-mastery, and economic independence, Mill was using the law to guide individuals and culture along the path of independence and personal responsibility and away from dependence and the culture of dependency. In the language of Michael Oakeshott, the state was to be an enterprise association, nevertheless committed to the intellectual, moral, and cultural perfection of its subjects. The state was not to be neutral in terms of its view of the good life but actively committed. Qualified liberalism and democracy, an extended and invigorated market society with socialist experiments, what we today call liberal democracy, Mill concluded, was the most likely source of social progress towards well-being in the advanced states of society in the nineteenth century world.

The liberal democratic theory Mill had come to by the end of his life differed considerably from that inherited from his father and Bentham. The effect of his historical theory and his belief in progress, with the practice of eclecticism, had brought him to see happiness as a full development and use of higher human potential: liberty and democracy were considered good because they encouraged and capitalized upon such development.

Mill, we may conclude, was a transitional thinker between old and new, *laissez-faire* and collectivist forms of liberalism, who imposed a perfectionist teleology of progress upon liberalism. He not only made the negative demand that the state respect the existing capacities of 'autonomy, reason and agency' among its citizens, he maintained that it should do what it could, more positively, to encourage their attainment. True liberty, to Mill, was concerned with the full development of the self and society, the cultivation of man 'as a progressive being'. Hence the state's encouragement and even legal enforcement of independence, self-development, and self-control. It may have been left to Green and Hobhouse to add to the list of actions government could take to create the social conditions for self-realization, but Mill had prepared the way.

Notes

1 The most coherent defence of this approach to Mill is by Eldon J. Eisenach, 'Mill's Autobiography as Political Theory', *History of Political Thought*, VIII, I (1987), pp. 111–29.
2 J. H. Burns, 'The Light of Reason: Philosophical History in the Two Mills', in J. M. Robson and M. Laine (eds), *James and John Stuart Mill: Papers of the Centenary Conference* (Toronto, 1976), p.12.
3 Eric Stokes, *The English Utilitarians in India* (Oxford, 1959), p. 53; W. Thomas, *The Philosophical Radicals* (Oxford, 1979), pp. 105–19, 176–7; W. Thomas, *Mill* (Oxford, 1985), pp. 67–8, 97–8.
4 Thomas, *The Philosophical Radicals*, pp. 98–9.
5 J. S. Mill, 'The Spirit of the Age', in J. B. Schneewind (ed.), *Mill's Essays on Literature and Society* (London, 1965), pp. 14–16, 27–78.
6 J. S. Mill, *The System of Logic* (London, 1966), pp. 604–5.
7 J. S. Mill, *Utilitarianism, On Liberty, Representative Government*, ed. A. D. Lindsay (London, 1964), pp. 62, 115–16.
8 J. S. Mill, *A Selection of his Works*, ed. J. M. Robson (London, 1966), pp. 436–7.
9 The key sources on this are L. S. Feuer, 'J. S. Mill as a Sociologist: *The Unwritten Ethology*', in Robson and Laine, *James and John Stuart Mill*; and Robert Brown, *The Nature of Social Laws: Machiavelli to Mill* (Cambridge, 1984). The best brief survey

is in G. L. William's Introduction to John Stuart Mill, *On Politics and Society* (London, 1976). On Mill, see Mill, *Logic*, VI, 5, 1–6, pp. 562–71.

10 J. S. Mill, *Logic* VI, 10, 2; Brown, *The Nature of Social Laws*, p. 192.

11 J. S. Mill, *Logic*, VI, 10, 7, p. 605; VI, 5, p. 567.

12 Ibid., X, 12, 7, p. 621.

13 Ibid., X, 10, 6, pp. 603, 612.

14 Ibid., p. 586.

15 Elden J. Eisenach, 'Mill's Autobiography as Political Theory', p. 128.

16 G. W. Smith, 'J. S. Mill on Freedom', in Z. Pelczynski and J. Gray (eds), *Conceptions of Liberty in Political Philosophy*, (London, 1984), pp. 188–200.

17 Mill, *Logic*, pp. 610–15.

18 Ibid., p. 607.

19 J. M. Robson, *The Improvement of Mankind* (London, 1968), p. ix.

20 A. Brady 'Introduction', in Mill, *Collected Works* (Toronto and London, 1963–), XVIII, p. lii.

21 Mill, *Utilitarianism, On Liberty, Representative Government*, pp. 73–4, 124–5, 160, 164–6.

22 Ibid., pp. 185–99, 207–18, 218–27, 276–92. For more detail on the equivocations Mill makes on democracy, see J. H. Burns, 'J. S. Mill and Democracy, 1829–61', *Political Studies*, (1957); reproduced in J. B. Schneewind (ed.), *Mill* (London, 1968), pp. 280–328.

23 J. S. Mill 'Coleridge', in J. B. Schneewind (ed.), *Mill's Essays on Literature and Society* (London, 1965) p. 298; Mill, *On Liberty*, pp. 96–103; R. J. Halliday, *John Stuart Mill* (London, 1976), pp. 25–33, 60–4; Thomas, *The Philosophical Radicals*, pp. 175–8; *Mill*, pp. 35–7.

24 Mill, *Utilitarianism, On Liberty, Representative Government*, p. 190.

25 J. B. Schneewind, *Sidgwick's Ethics and Victorian Moral Philosophy* (Oxford, 1977), p. 166.

26 J. Grote, *An Examination of the Utilitarian Philosophy* (Cambridge, 1870), p. 151.

27 J. Grote, *An Examination of the Utilitarian Philosophy*, pp. 15–17; J. R. Gibbins, *John Grote, Cambridge University and the Development of Victorian Ideas*, PhD Thesis, University of Newcastle upon Tyne, 1987, ch. VIII; J. Plamenatz, *The English Utilitarians* (Oxford, 1958), p. 144 echoes this view.

28 J. S. Mill, *On Liberty*, p. 73.

29 Ibid.

30 M. E. Waithe, 'Why Mill was for Paternalism', *International Journal of Law and Psychiatry*, 6 (1983), pp. 102–3.

31 J. S. Mill, *On Liberty*, p. 73; idem, 'The Spirit of the Age'; idem, *On Liberty*, p. 114.

32 Mill, 'The Spirit of the Age', p. 61.

33 Ibid., p. 77. See also *On Liberty*, pp. 105, 114–15; Mill, *Collected Works* (Toronto and London, 1963–), xii, p. 77.

34 Halliday, *John Stuart Mill*, pp. 69–92; M. Cowling, 'Mill and Liberalism', in Schneewind, *Mill*, pp. 329–53; R. B. Friedman, 'An Introduction to Mill's Theory of Authority', in Schneewind, *Mill*, pp. 379–425.

35 H. Marcuse, R. P. Wolff, and Barrington Moore Jr, *A Critique of Pure Tolerance* (Boston, 1967); Marcuse, 'Repressive Tolerance', in P. Connerton (ed.), *Critical Sociology* (Harmondsworth, 1976); G. Duncan and J. Street, 'Liberalism, Marxism and Tolerance', in S. Mendus (ed.), *Justifying Tolerance, Conceptual and Historical Perspectives* (Cambridge, 1988), pp. 223–36.

36 J. S. Mill, *On Liberty*, pp. 74, 150–1.

37 Ibid., p. 75–6, 164–7.

38 Ibid., p. 135.

39 Ibid., pp. 80–1.
40 Ibid., pp. 123–4; Thomas, *Mill*, pp. 44–50.
41 Mill, *Logic*, pp. 605, 612–13.
42 Ibid., p. 550.
43 John Gray, 'John Stuart Mill on Liberty, Utility and Rights', *Nomos* (1981), p. 95; *Mill on Liberty: A Defence* (London, 1983).
44 Peter Berger, *Happiness, Justice and Freedom* (London, 1984), p. 14; H. M. Clor, 'Mill and Millians on Liberty and Moral Character', *Review of Politics* 47 (1985), pp. 3–26.
45 B. Semmel, *John Stuart Mill and the Pursuit of Virtue* (New York and London, 1984).
46 C. L. Ten, *Mill on Liberty* (Oxford, 1980), p. 148; Mill, *On Liberty*, p. 74.
47 Mill, *On Liberty*, p. 75.
48 R. Bellamy, 'T. H. Green, J. S. Mill and Isaiah Berlin on the Nature of Liberty', unpublished paper of the P.S.A. Conference, Nottingham, 1986; *Liberalism and the Modern Social Order* (Cambridge, forthcoming), ch. 2.
49 G. Holyoake, *John Stuart Mill: As Some of the Working Classes Know Him* (London, 1873); L. Robbins, *The Theory of Economic Policy in English Classical Political Economy* (London, 1952), p. 143.
50 J. S. Mill, *Principles of Political Economy* (London, 6th edition, 1902), II, ii, 6, pp. 141–5; IX–X, pp. 193–207; see also *Dissertations and Discussions*, Vol. V (New York, 1875).
51 Mill, *Principles*, V, XI, 16, pp. 575–7.
52 Ibid., V, XI, 16, pp. 590–1.
53 Ibid., V, XI, 11, pp. 579–81.
54 M. Hollis, 'The Social Liberty Game', in A. Phillips Griffiths (ed.), *Of Liberty* (Cambridge, 1982), p. 35.
55 Mill, *Principles*, V, XI, 12–14, pp. 581–9; M. Hollis, 'The Social Liberty Game', pp. 34, 37–8.
56 J. S. Mill, *Socialism*, ed. W. D. P. Bliss (New York, 1891).
57 Mill, *Principles*, IV, VII, 4, pp. 460–1.
58 Mill, *Autobiography* (London, 1963), p. 198; *Principles*, pp. 25–133.
59 Mill, *Autobiography*, p. 198.
60 Mill, *Principles*, II, i, 4, p. 133.
61 Mill, *On Representative Government*, p. 217.
62 Ibid., pp.193–5.
63 Ibid., p. 196.
64 Ibid., p. 208.
65 Ibid., pp. 214, 220–4.
66 Ibid., p. 218.
67 Ibid., p. 226.
68 Ibid., p. 280.
69 Ibid., pp. 284, 286.
70 Ibid., pp. 281–2.
71 Ibid., p. 282.
72 Ibid., p. 288.
73 J. S. Mill, 'Thoughts on Parliamentary Reform', *Dissertations and Discussions* (London, 1867), III, p. 26.
74 J. S. Mill, *On Representative Government*, p. 193.

Chapter seven

Herbert Spencer's liberalism – from social statics to social dynamics

Tim Gray

The content of Herbert Spencer's liberalism underwent remarkably little change during the sixty years in which he articulated it. With the exception of his views on landownership and the franchise, Spencer enunciated in 1902 virtually the same views that he had expressed in 1842. What had changed, however, and markedly so, was his mode of justification for those liberal ideas. In his earlier writings he adopted a mode of argument based exclusively upon the concept of the natural right to equal freedom (the centre-piece of liberal theory, according to many commentators). In his later writings, however, Spencer added an evolutionary element to his argument, in order to show how the triumph of liberalism was assured.

In this essay I wish to trace this transition from 'social statics' to 'social dynamics', explaining its causes and its consequences for the coherence of Spencer's defence of liberalism. I shall show that the main cause of the change was Spencer's need to make explicit what was implicit in his earlier work – namely, the mechanism by which a society of autonomous individuals would be created. In *Social Statics* Spencer merely asserted that adherence to the principle of equal freedom was the condition of a liberal society of self-developed agents. In his later writings his discovery of evolutionary theory enabled Spencer to explain precisely how that liberal society would come about. I shall argue that, far from remedying a deficiency in his earlier theory, Spencer's adoption of evolutionary ideas created more problems than it solved, and led him into a blind alley, while the more pressing deficiencies of his liberalism – the lack of a deep theory of human autonomy, and the consequent failure to distinguish between self-determination and self-development – were ignored.

The Law of Equal Freedom (LEF) – social statics

In his early writings, especially in *Social Statics* (1851), Spencer derived his liberal doctrines solely from the 'law of equal freedom' (henceforth LEF), which he expressed thus: 'Every man has freedom to do all that he wills, provided he infringes not the equal freedom of any other man...'[1] From the LEF Spencer deduced a panoply of individual rights, some of which went far beyond those traditionally associated with Victorian liberalism, and formed the basis of a radical libertarianism. The derived rights included: the rights of *life and liberty* ('For he who is killed or enslaved is obviously no longer equally free with his killer or enslaver');[2] the right to the *use of the land* ('no one ... may use the earth in such a way as to prevent the rest from similarly using it, seeing that to do this is to assume greater freedom than the rest, and consequently to break the law');[3] the right of *physical, intellectual and reputational property*;[4] the right of *exchange* ('The two parties in a trade transaction ... are not assuming more liberty than they leave to others');[5] the right of *free speech*;[6] *equal rights of women* ('Equity knows no difference of sex. ... The law of equal freedom manifestly applies to the whole race – female as well as male');[7] the right *to ignore the state* ('He cannot be coerced into political combination without a breach of the law of equal freedom; he *can* withdraw from it without committing any such breach; and he has therefore a right so to withdraw');[8] and the right of everyone to *vote*.[9]

Spencer argued that protection of these rights was the sole function of government, and that if it strayed beyond this role, the state necessarily violated the LEF and committed injustice. For example, if the state endowed an established church from taxpayers' money, it infringed individual property rights: 'For ... by diminishing a subject's liberty of action more than is needful for securing the remainder, the civil power becomes an aggressor instead of a protector.'[10] Similarly, if the state provided relief for the poor it was in breach of the LEF:

> In demanding from a citizen contributions for the mitigation of distress – contributions not needed for the due administration of men's rights – the state is ... reversing its function, and diminishing that liberty to exercise the faculties which it was instituted to maintain.[11]

For the same reasons, the government had no responsibility for the health of its citizens, beyond protecting them from mutual injury.[12] Finally, a national education system was forbidden, since 'inasmuch as the taking away of his property to educate his own or other people's children is not needful for the maintaining of his rights; the taking away of his property for such a purpose is wrong.'[13]

The formal and negative concept of liberty involved in Spencer's LEF was made explicit in his discussion of education: the child had no right to be *educated*, only a right to be *free*; and education was not a *sine qua non* of freedom:

> that only can be called an infringement of rights which ... cuts off a previously existing power to pursue objects of desire ... Omitting instruction in no way takes from a child's freedom to do whatsoever it wills in the best way it can.[14]

Breaches of the LEF were active aggressions, not passive omissions. A parent's failure to educate a child was not a breach of justice, but of beneficence.

Given that he took no notice of the differential worth or effectiveness to different people of their equal portions of liberty, Spencer's deduction of the various individual rights and of the circumscribed range of governmental duty was straightforward enough, even impressive. But what was his justification for the LEF itself? There is some controversy on this matter between Spencer's interpreters. John Gray sees it as a teleological principle of indirect utilitarianism;[15] while Hillel Steiner regards it as a deontological principle of intrinsic rectitude.[16] My own view is that while it is true that Spencer did tie the LEF to the greatest happiness principle, he did so in such an indirect way as effectively to render it independent of utility. Of course, the LEF would promote the greatest happiness in the long term, but we must apply the LEF as a principle of justice, and ignore all considerations of expediency. The *right* was prior to the *good*. Steiner's deontological interpretation of Spencer's LEF is therefore the more convincing. But Spencer did not merely *stipulate* the LEF as a basic moral axiom as Steiner implies. Spencer attempted to *justify* the LEF as a principle of right by deriving it from two sources – God and the Moral Sense. God willed that we obey the LEF:

> For what does a man really mean by saying of a thing that it is 'theoretically just', or 'true in principle', or 'abstractedly right'? Simply that it accords with what he, in some way or other, perceives to be the established arrangements of Divine rule.[17]

And from the intuitions of the Moral Sense, we possessed '*an instinct of personal rights ... a sense* of what is fair'.[18] Neither of these arguments is convincing. The appeal to divine rule and the assertion of the Moral Sense both suffer from arbitrariness: who is to tell whether Spencer's interpretation of either God's intentions or human moral instincts was reliable?

There was, however, an 'unofficial' justificatory argument for the LEF alluded to by Spencer towards the end of *Social Statics*. This was the argument of individuality. Spencer had a vision of a perfect society of self-developed individual agents, all abiding by the LEF:

> That condition of things dictated by the law of equal freedom – that condition in which the individuality of each may be unfolded without limit, save the like individualities of others – that condition towards which ... mankind are progressing ...[19]

It could be argued that this end-state of a society of fulfilled individuals was Spencer's real justification for the LEF. 'To be that which he naturally is – to do just what he would spontaneously do – is essential to the full happiness of each, and therefore to the greatest happiness of all.'[20] But instead of making this explicit, and instead of showing convincingly *why* individuality was such an important human good, and how one person's individuality was compatible with another's, Spencer allowed himself to be diverted to another issue – that of the mechanism by which individuality was to be attained. This was the sphere of social dynamics:

Social philosophy may be aptly divided ... into statics and dynamics; the first treating of the equilibrium of a perfect society, the second of the forces by which society is advanced towards perfection. To determine what laws we must obey for the obtainment of complete happiness is the object of the one, whilst that of the other is to analyze the influences which are making us competent to obey these laws. Hitherto we have concerned ourselves chiefly with the statics. ... Now however, the dynamics claim special attention.[21]

Spencer's remarks in *Social Statics* on the issue of the mechanism of social progress were vague and perfunctory. He merely offered the prediction that eventually the Moral Sense would have grown strong enough to make men obey the LEF without external coercion,[22] and that the appropriate social arrangements would then emerge. 'That same modification of man's nature which produces fitness for higher social forms, itself generates the belief that these forms are right, and by doing this brings them into existence.'[23] But as to *how* human character was to become capable of keeping to the LEF, Spencer was silent.

Accordingly, there were two deficiencies in Spencer's early theory of liberalism: the first was a failure adequately to justify the notion of individuality as a moral and distributional principle – a deficiency which he never attempted to rectify. Why did Spencer fail to explain adequately why individuality was such an important good? Partly because he was not interested in theories of autonomy – he found Kant's ideas unintelligible; partly because he took it for granted that his readership would accept the value of individuality without deep philosophical analysis. From his own family and social circle, Spencer imbued the spirit of radical individualism connected with a strong sense of personal moral responsibility, and he assumed that such notions were widely shared among the progressive middle classes – not least because they reflected a growing consensus in the economic sphere which endorsed the value of entrepreneurial initiative and self-improvement. Indeed, Spencer's image of the perfect society of self-developed individuals abiding by the LEF bears more than a passing resemblance to the model of the private partnership, the prevailing economic unit in mid-nineteenth-century England. The second deficiency was a failure to make clear precisely how the good society would be achieved – a deficiency which he did set out to rectify, by means of his theory of social evolution, where social dynamics became the central focus of attention.

Before examining Spencer's evolutionary theory, however, there was one non-evolutionary explanation for the attainment of the good society which most liberals enunciate, and which Spencer himself appeared on occasion to adopt. This was the view that a society of self-developed individuals could be created simply by persuading citizens to obey the LEF. In a sense, this was precisely what Spencer sought to do by writing *Social Statics* – to recommend the LEF to the faint-hearted as a rule of life which alone could bring fulfilment. Even more obviously, in his involvement with various political pressure movements, Spencer appeared to be attempting to persuade the public. Let us pause for a moment to consider this question of Spencer's political involvement.

Although it was principally through his writings that Spencer sought to influence events, he did become actively engaged in politics in an attempt to mobilize public opinion. He did so not through the formal political channels, but by involving himself with pressure groups. It is worth noting that pressure group activity was the main form of middle-class political involvement in England before the 1867 Reform Act. It reflected a belief that the only sure and permanent route to social progress lay in improving the character of the population, rather than in influencing the government. In his early days Spencer was involved in the 'Anti-Church State Association' (on whose behalf he drafted an address to the nonconformists of England) and in the 'Complete Suffrage Movement' (in 1842 he became honorary secretary of its Derby branch). However, it was in his later years that Spencer's political activism took on a more leading role. Although he declined invitations from Derby and Leicester to stand for parliament, on the grounds that 'Far too high an estimate is, I think, made of the influence possessed in our day by a member of Parliament ... those who form public opinion are those who really exercise power ...'[24], Spencer played a major role in various public agitation movements. In particular, he took an active part in the 'Anti-Aggression League', a campaign established to erode the militaristic sentiments in England in order to reduce the incidence of international conflict. Peace between nations was, for Spencer, the single most important key to all social progress. In a letter of 1879 he explained his reasons for his involvement with the League:

> I have been so strongly impressed with the re-barbarization that is going on in consequence of the return to militant activities, that I have come to the conclusion that it is worth while to try to do something toward organizing an antagonistic agitation. We have, lying diffused throughout English society, various bodies and classes very decidedly opposed to it, which I think merely want bringing together to produce a powerful agency, which may do eventually a good deal in a civilizing direction. ... I have talked to several about the matter – Rathbone, member for Liverpool, Harrison, Morley and others – and I am about to take further steps. There is a decided sympathy felt by all I have named; and I think that it is important to move.[25]

In other words, Spencer regarded his role as that of catalyst, galvanizing and mobilizing incipient strands of opposition to militarism.[26] He solicited support from a wide variety of influential persons, including Gladstone[27] and Bright, and he tried to persuade the poets Swinburne and Buchanan to write satirical pieces denouncing the 'miserable hypocrisy' of Christian imperialists.[28] He also approached the 'International Arbitration Cooperative Society' and the 'Workman's Peace Association'. One of Spencer's main objectives was to impress upon the public the crucial difference between non-aggression and pacifism.[29] The 'Anti- Aggression League' was not, however, successful; it made little headway against the extreme jingoism provoked by the persistence of belligerence on the continent.[30]

In more parochial matters, Spencer was a founder member in 1891 of the 'London Ratepayers League', established to curb local government extravagance. He prepared a short paper for the League on 'County Council Tyranny', exposing the shortcomings of the LCC in carrying out the Public Health Act.[31]

But it was principally by his writings rather than by his active involvement in pressure groups that Spencer hoped to have influence in turning public opinion away from what he regarded as illiberal policy. To that end, some of his writings were expressly pitched at a popular level. For example, of *The Man versus The State* – one of his most trenchant and polemical works – Spencer wrote that he hoped it would 'eventually form a new departure in politics ... presently to give a positive creed for an advanced party in politics'.[32] In addressing public opinion so directly, Spencer adopted a style which appealed less to reason than to emotion. He had become disillusioned about the effectiveness of persuading people by rigorously reasoned arguments. Let me explain this disillusion.

At first, Spencer's approach was highly cerebral, following the conclusions of reason wherever they led. If such conclusions were at variance with practice, it was practice that was at fault, not reason. For example, on the issue of enfranchisement of children – a proposal which he endorsed somewhat equivocally – Spencer remarked that 'the alleged absurdity is traceable to the present evil constitution of society, and not to some defect in our conclusion.'[33] If passions or feelings were in conflict with reason, they were denounced as perversions. Spencer looked forward to a time when reason would finally triumph over the passions. 'The long acknowledged rationality of man and the obvious corollary that he is to be guided by his reason rather than by his feelings, is at length obtaining a practical recognition.'[34] However, Spencer later abandoned this faith in reason, as he became progressively more impressed by the role of feelings in forming people's ideas. Indeed he denied that human beings were rational creatures at all:

> Men are not rational beings as commonly supposed. A man is a bundle of instincts, feelings, sentiments, which severally seek their gratification, and those which are in power get hold of the reason and use it to their own ends, and exclude all other sentiments and feelings from power.[35]

Accordingly, Spencer argued that social progress would never be brought about by abstract theoretical disquisitions, but only by appeals to popular emotions, since the 'chief component of mind is feeling'.[36] He held that 'behaviour is not determined by knowledge, but by emotion ... change in the actions of these passive spectators is not to be effected by making their cognitions clearer, but by making their higher feelings stronger.'[37] The fact was that 'Men care nothing about a principle, even if they understand it, unless they have emotions responding to it.'[38] It was naive to assume that 'when men are taught what is right, they will do what is right – that a proposition intellectually accepted will be morally imperative.'[39] On the contrary, 'the operativeness of a moral code depends much more on the emotions called forth by its injunctions than on the consciousness of the utility of obeying such injunctions.'[40]

It might appear that this shift of emphasis from reason to emotion was simply the result of Spencer's gradual disillusionment with human nature[41] due to the shift in the political climate in England from individualism to collectivism. 'My confidence in the rationality of mankind was much greater then [1859] than it is now [1894].'[42] But in fact, Spencer portrayed his later position in very positive terms: the sensations were a better guide to progress than was reason because the sensations were the guides given to us by Nature herself. This was an evolutionary doctrine:

> for bodily welfare the sensations are the most trustworthy guides ... this guiding principle ... is a corollary from a general biological truth – the truth that among all lower forms of life, uncontrolled by commands, traditions or creeds, there has been no other prompter to right physical actions than obedience to the sensations.[43]

It was 'a law of the individual that the strongest desires correspond to the most needful actions'.[44] So the shift of confidence from reason to feeling in Spencer's theory was not merely a negative reaction to political disappointment, but a positive reflection of his increasing commitment to the evolutionary creed.

However, the fact remains that Spencer did not seriously believe that appealing either to people's reason or to their feelings, whether at public meetings or by the written word, would do much to advance the attainment of the good society of self-determining individuals. What was needed was a change in people's character. This was a view Spencer shared with other liberals including J. S. Mill, for whom the idea of a minimal state and a co-operative social order presupposed a fundamental transformation of human nature. In *Social Statics* Spencer had pointed out that national character was formed not by persuasion but by long experience.[45] Changes in people's opinions were the *result*, not the *cause*, of changes in their character. Modification of character through experience came first, then came modification of opinions, and lastly modification of institutions;

> That same modification of man's nature which produces fitness for higher social forms, itself generates the belief that those forms are right and by doing this brings them into existence. And as opinion, being the product of character, must necessarily be in harmony with character, institutions which are in harmony with opinion, must be in harmony with character also ... opinion is the agency through which character adapts external arrangements to itself ...[46]

And character modification was a slow process. 'it is impossible for popular character to undergo a great change all at once ...'[47]

In order to show how Spencer sought an explanation for the necessary change in national character to produce the perfect society of self-developed individuals, we must turn to his theory of evolution.

The Normal Relation of Conduct and Consequence (NRCC) – social dynamics

There were some embryonic evolutionary ideas in *Social Statics* (1851) and even in *The Proper Sphere of Government* (1843),[48] but they remained notions incidental to Spencer's theory until his essays on 'The Development Hypothesis' (1852) and 'Progress, its Law and Cause' (1857) pointed him in a new and exciting direction. These essays contained a vision of a world process in which Spencer could found his theory of the perfect society on a more secure basis than moral philosophy – a basis in natural science. Instead of being *sui generis*, the moral sphere was seen to be part of a universal pattern.

This discovery of the evolutionary basis of the universe so exhilarated Spencer that it transformed his existence: he devoted the rest of his life, literally, to the enunciation and elaboration of evolutionary theory, at the expense of both his health (he suffered from a nervous disorder brought on by overwork) and normal family life (he was never able to afford to get married, or so he claimed). His resolve was 'to set forth a general theory of Evolution exhibited throughout all orders of existences'.[49] His 'Synthetic Philosophy' was the result.[50]

Spencer claimed to have detected in every aspect of Nature a progressive development from a condition of homogeneity, simplicity, incoherence, and uniformity, to a condition of heterogeneity, complexity, coherence, and variety. He traced this progress in *geology* (the earth's surface over a period of millions of years had changed from a homogeneous molten mass to a highly differentiated crust); in *meteorology* (climatic patterns, once uniform, now varied enormously over time and place); in *botany* and *zoology* (plants and animals had become increasingly complex in structure); and in *human biology* (the organization of the human body was now much more intricate). And he claimed that a similar process was at work in society – social evolution was of a piece with natural evolution – indeed, the one was simply an aspect of the other.[51] Early societies, termed by Spencer the 'militant' type of society, were homogeneous and simple, in which most members performed identical functions. Later societies, termed by Spencer the 'industrial' type of society, were progressively more diversified, as the division of labour developed to differentiate political from religious functionaries and to perform specialized economic roles.[52]

Everything that Spencer subsequently wrote on social affairs reflected this universality of evolution. For example, when commissioned to write an article on music for *Fraser's Magazine*, Spencer remarked that 'As usual, the leading thought was evolutionary. ... How has music naturally originated?'[53] Similarly, of his essay on the moral discipline of children, Spencer wrote that 'the subject was certain to be treated by me from the point of view now reached. Consciously or unconsciously the theory of evolution furnished guidance.'[54] Referring to 'my intellectual leaning towards belief in natural causation everywhere operating',[55] he admitted that 'Many examples have made it clear that nearly everything I wrote had a bearing, direct or indirect, on the doctrine of evolution.'[56] In short, it is no exaggeration to say that Spencer had become obsessed with evolution: for him it promised a solution to all problems. In particular, it provided an answer to the question left unanswered in *Social Statics* – that of how society will progress to the perfect society of self-developed individuals.

Before examining Spencer's theory of *social* evolution, a brief word must be said about his theory of *organic* evolution. Writing before the publication of Darwin's *Origin of Species* (1859), Spencer adopted the theory of organic evolution associated with Lamarck – the theory of the inheritance of functionally produced modifications. According to this theory, improvements in the structure of animals took the form of the inheritance by offspring of some modified characteristic acquired by a parent as a result of some environmental circumstance faced by that parent. In 1852, Spencer wrote that evolutionists 'can show that any existing species – animal or vegetable – when placed under conditions different from its previous ones, *immediately begins to undergo certain changes fitting it for the new conditions.*'[57] After the publication of Darwin's *Origin of Species*, however, Spencer acknowledged that natural selection explained most of the facts of organic evolution more convincingly than did Lamarckianism. The theory of natural selection postulated that the species which survived were the ones that were better suited to their environment. There was no suggestion that any species changed its structure in order to survive; the process of natural selection was random, and those species which happened to have the appropriate structure tended to survive.

However, Spencer's position on *social* evolution was much less clear. He claimed at one point that Lamarckianism was the chief factor explaining social evolution, natural selection being more confined to the plant world and to the lower animals.[58] Lamarckianism certainly fitted in better than did Darwinianism with the prevailing Victorian ideas about the self-improvement of a person's character and the transmission of that improvement to offspring, thereby contributing to the improvement of the national character. It also tied in closely with Victorian notions of personal moral responsibility, which the random nature of Darwinian natural selection appeared to undermine. Nevertheless, Spencer welcomed Darwin's theory of natural selection, because of the huge fillip it gave to evolutionary theory in general,[59] and he made extensive use of the notion of natural selection in analysing social development. The resulting ambiguous mixture of Lamarckianism and Darwinianism in Spencer's system made him vulnerable to attack from both sides. For example, defending himself against Huxley's charge that he condoned a Darwinian 'devil take the hindmost' approach to social problems, Spencer found himself attacked by Ritchie for failing to see the need for more extensive governmental intervention in order to create the Lamarckian conditions for social progress.

It was Spencer who, in 1864, coined the phrase 'the survival of the fittest' as a synonym for 'natural selection'[60] to avoid the teleological impression of selection *by* Nature, or of 'favoured' races.[61] We must now turn to an analysis of the principal mechanism devised by Spencer to ensure the survival of the fittest within and between societies – the 'normal relation between conduct and consequence' (henceforth NRCC).[62] This 'relation' is the key to social progress – the essence of Spencer's explanation of the way society will become a community of fully-developed agents.

As with the LEF, Spencer characterized the 'normal relation between conduct and consequence' (NRCC) in terms of justice: 'Justice, then, as here to be understood, means preservation of the normal connections between acts and results – the obtainment by each of as much benefit as his efforts are equivalent to – no more and no less.'[63] But they were very different conceptions of justice. Whereas the LEF was a static conception of the rights of individuals, the relation between conduct and consequence was defined by Spencer in terms which clearly revealed it as a dynamic conception of the mechanism of social change:

a fundamental law, by conformity to which life has evolved from its lowest up to its highest forms, that each adult individual shall take the consequences of its own nature and actions: survival of the fittest being the result.[64]

The NRCC explicitly sought to favour the survival of an individual endowed with a particular set of characteristics and values, in order that the goal could be achieved of the preservation of certain species, nations and individuals. The 'superior' must not be deprived of the advantage of their superiority: 'superiority must be allowed to bring to its possessor all the naturally-resulting benefits, and inferiority the naturally-resulting evils.'[65]

Sometimes Spencer presented the NRCC in ethical terms: 'each adult gets benefit in proportion to merit – reward in proportion to desert.'[66] But he then interpreted the words 'merit' and 'desert' naturalistically, as elements of evolutionary progress: 'merit and desert ... being understood as ability to fulfil all the requirements of life – to get food, to secure shelter, to escape enemies'.[67] At other times, Spencer appealed to everyday perceptions of morality to verify the NRCC:

Sayings...daily heard imply a perception that conduct and consequence ought not to be dissociated...the comment on one whose misjudgement or misbehaviour has entailed evil upon him, that 'he has made his own bed, and now he must lie on it', has behind it the conviction that this connexion between cause and effect is proper.[68]

But again he interpreted such ethical perceptions in evolutionary terms; they helped to mould people into conformity with the conditions of the perfect society, by exposing them to the proper stimuli. Hence equal liberty was no longer automatically a right in itself, but an instrument for purifying the race by ensuring that the superior were not prevented from benefiting from their superiority. Accordingly, where a particular right – such as the right to vote – stood in the way of this purification process, then it must be restricted. This is why Spencer's deduction of universal suffrage from the LEF in *Social Statics* was subsequently withdrawn. The vote was no longer regarded as an entitlement, but as a means to the end of advancing the perfect society. Since its extension to the working classes and to women would prejudice that end by fuelling the demand for a more interventionist state to provide benefits to persons who had not made efforts to obtain them, then the working classes and women must be denied the vote.[69] Nothing must stand in the way of the mechanism of evolutionary progress to 'a higher form of social life'.[70]

> when it is seen that all perfection, bodily and mental, has been achieved through this process, and that suspension of it must cause cessation of progress while reversal of it would bring universal decay ... there comes a conviction that social policy must be conformed to [these truths] ... and that to ignore them is madness.[71]

Governments must make 'the connexion between cause and consequence more definite and certain' by refraining from 'measures which give to individual citizens benefits which their individual efforts have given them no claims to', and by implementing 'measures which ensure to them the full advantages due to their efforts'.[72]

This, then, was Spencer's explanation of the mechanism of social change. By enforcing the NRCC, the government would ensure that those people who were incapable of living an autonomous life would gradually be weeded out, and a community composed entirely of self-governing agents would emerge. Failure to enforce the NRCC necessarily increased the proportion of dependent people, and postponed indefinitely the dawn of the perfect society.

> For if the unworthy are helped to increase, by shielding them from that mortality which their unworthiness would naturally entail, the effect is to produce, generation after generation, a greater unworthiness. From diminished use of self-conserving faculties already deficient, there must result, in posterity, still smaller amounts of self-conserving faculties.[73]

Before examining the serious flaws in Spencer's theory of social change, there is an important preliminary issue to be discussed, that of the general relationship between Spencer's ideal of the perfect society and his liberalism. At first, in *Social Statics*, that relationship was assumed to be harmonious, in that the perfect society was one in which everyone obeyed the LEF. But later, when Spencer introduced the NRCC as a means of explaining the mechanism whereby that perfect society would be brought about, the image of the perfect society altered its shape in Spencer's mind, and took on the character of a community of superior individuals. It was this new element in Spencer's picture of the perfect society that appeared to be in conflict with his earlier interpretation of liberal principles. For the new perfectionism seemed to be asserting what his previous definition of liberalism had denied: that one person, and/or one life-style, was better than another. If Spencer's perfectionism required policies which imposed restrictions on individuals, not to safeguard their mutual rights to equal freedom, but to bring about a state of affairs in which an improved citizenship would be created, then there is serious doubt as to whether it could remain within the framework of liberalism as defined in *Social Statics*. Spencer's response to this criticism might have been to say that this new element of perfectionism was not a good to be sought by government independently of guaranteeing everyone equal freedom, but an end which would be attained automatically if equal liberty were secured. But this would be a disingenuous reply, since, as we shall see, there were several disjunctions between the LEF and the NRCC. (We have already seen one such disjunction, on the issue of the suffrage.) It is simply not true, therefore, that enforcement of the LEF was a necessary and sufficient condition for the implementation of the NRCC. In any case, the whole point of Spencer's social evolutionary doctrine was to explain how the perfect society would be brought about – i.e. how general adherence to the LEF would eventually be secured by the operation of the NRCC. Therefore Spencer could not, without circularity, argue that the LEF was a prior condition of the NRCC. The truth is that what began as a means (NRCC being introduced as a means to the LEF) became an end in itself, and considerably altered his earlier understanding of the liberal ethos. The result was an emasculation of the more libertarian elements in Spencer's theory – a blunting of his earlier radical cutting-edge.

This brings me to the central problem surrounding the NRCC, namely that whether as a means or an end, it is not at all clear what the NRCC implied, and how it was to be implemented. This problem arises out of the doubts which Spencer himself expressed concerning the effectiveness of the NRCC in guaranteeing the survival and increased proportion of the better type of person in society. Spencer acknowledged that the better type of person was often *not* favoured by the NRCC, and he sharply criticized people who failed to recognize this.[74] Indeed, he somewhat plaintively claimed that his own life exemplified the disjunction between worthy conduct and good consequences ('right-doing often brings heavy penalties') since in return for his lifetime's devotion to the public weal, 'the total result is a feeling the reverse of pleasurable'.[75] In fact, the scientific truth was that natural processes were not only *often* immoral, they were *nearly always* immoral. 'For 99/hundredths of the time life has existed on the Earth (or one might say 999/thousandths) the success has been confined to those beings which, from a human point of view, would be called criminal.'[76] This was the reason why Spencer subsequently distinguished between 'fittest' and 'best': those who were fittest to survive were not necessarily the most worthy:

> The law is the survival of the *fittest* ... the law is not the survival of the 'better' or the 'stronger', if we give to those words anything like their ordinary meanings. It is the survival of those which are constitutionally fittest to thrive under the conditions under which they are placed; and very often that which, humanly speaking, is inferiority, causes the survival. ... When it is remembered ... that there are more species of parasites than there are species of all other animals put together – it will be seen that the expression 'survivorship of the better' is wholly inappropriate.[77]

It was also the reason why Spencer regretted using the word 'progress' in his

1857 article – 'I had not then recognized the need for a word which has no teleological implications.'[78]

But if the word 'fittest' was merely a figure of speech; if it simply meant 'most suited', and as such had no evaluative connotation whatever;[79] if the survival of the fittest implied no moral superiority or greater self-reliance in the fittest – then two conclusions immediately suggest themselves. First, Spencer's evolutionary doctrine is reduced to the truism that those who survived were the fittest because they survived. At one point Spencer seemed deliberately to enunciate just this truism: 'survival of the fittest is inevitable – is just as certain a truth as a mathematical axiom – which we accept because the negation of it is inconceivable.'[80] Second, any moral imperative to observe the NRCC has been eliminated. If the fittest were simply those who were best equipped to survive, not those who deserved to survive or who were better or more autonomous persons, then why must we adhere to rules which favoured them? Why was the survival of the fittest to survive of any moral significance whatsoever? Surely the truly moral position, as T. H. Huxley argued against Spencer, was that of resistance to evolutionary pressures whenever they were clearly malign?[81]

There was another way in which Spencer eroded the status of his evolutionary principle of the natural relation between conduct and consequences. As if in recognition of the above difficulties, he considerably qualified the application of the NRCC. But these restrictions simply compounded the problem. For example, Spencer distinguished between the ethics of the family and the ethics of the state. In the family, he said, we could not possibly apply the NRCC, because that would have endangered the survival of children. If benefits were apportioned in accordance with ability or effort, then babies, who are incapable of making any productive contribution, would be denied nutrition:

> The law for the undeveloped is that there shall be most aid where there is least merit. ... Import into the family the law of the society, and let children from infancy upwards have life-sustaining supplies proportioned to their life-sustaining labours, and the society disappears forthwith by death of all its young.[82]

Hence there was a 'cardinal distinction between the ethics of the family and the ethics of the state'.[83] While the ethics of the state demanded the application of the NRCC, the ethics of the family demanded its suspension.[84] Indeed there was *conflict* between family and state ethics: 'essentially at variance as are the ethics of the family and the ethics of the State ... the ... welfare of the species requires the maintenance of two antagonistic principles ...'[85]

Apart from the fact that it seems odd for Spencer to require two mutually antagonistic principles to be operating simultaneously in society (which one had priority when they clashed?), the question arises as to why, if infants were immune from the NRCC on grounds that they were incapable of making any productive contribution, other groups who were similarly incapable, such as the elderly and the disabled, were nevertheless subject to the NRCC? Spencer partially answered this question, but only by further weakening the significance of the NRCC. He said that private charity, if kept within bounds, was acceptable: 'I regard voluntary beneficence as adequate to achieve all those mitigations that are proper and needful.'[86] Addressing himself to the issue of 'How far the mentally-superior may, with a balance of benefit to society, shield the mentally-inferior from the evil results of their inferiority', Spencer remarked that 'Doubtless, in many cases the reactive influence of this sympathetic care which the better take of the worse, is morally beneficial, and in a degree compensates by good in one direction for evil in another.'[87] It seemed that, provided charity was private, limited in scope, and discriminately distributed (favouring the more deserving of the disadvantaged) it could be beneficial.[88] But private charity quite clearly breached the NRCC, in that it distributed goods to people which they had not earned by their own efforts. If the NRCC could be 'beneficially' breached by limited and discriminating *private* charity, why could it not be beneficially breached by limited and discriminating *public* charity? Why, for instance, could not the government legitimately interfere with the operation of the NRCC in order to assist the deserving poor?

A further restriction imposed by Spencer upon the operation of the NRCC was the interdict laid down by him on the use of force by physically superior individuals. This restriction raised many difficulties for Spencer's evolutionary theory. Despite the fact that the doctrine of 'the survival of the fittest' explicitly identified physical superiority as one of the qualities of the fittest which helped to ensure their survival, Spencer refused to sanction a policy of allowing strong people to coerce weak people. The use of force might have been inevitable in the early stages of social evolution – 'abject submission of the weak to the strong, however unscrupulously enforced, has in some times and places been necessary'[89] – but it was no longer justifiable. Hence Spencer deplored colonialist exploitation of indigenous native populations – 'of all the feelings I entertain concerning social affairs, my detestation of the barbarous conduct of strong peoples to weak people is the most intense ...'[90] And he insisted that property-owners were not to be dispossessed of their holdings by the physically stronger property-less members of the population.

It was true that Spencer presented this latter restriction in terms of *enforcing* the NRCC:

> recognition of the right of property is originally recognition of the relation between effort and benefit ... many in our days are seeking to override this right. They think it was wrong that each man should receive benefits proportionate to his efforts – deny that he may properly keep possession of all which his labour has produced, leaving the less capable in possession of all which their labours have produced.[91]

But the restriction could equally be interpreted as a *breach* of the NRCC. Spencer was here selecting one aspect of human superiority – the capacity for effort – to justify investing a right of property in the product of that effort. But it would be equally consistent with the NRCC to select an alternative aspect of human superiority – the capacity of physical strength – to justify the expropriation of effete property-owners by robust non-owners. The notion of 'superiority' was in fact used by Spencer to mean quite different things at different times. The most common characterizations appeared in terms of 'labour', 'work', and 'effort', but he frequently referred to 'nature', 'capacity', and 'power', as well as using more anodyne terms such as 'conduct', and 'actions.[92] In his defence of private property rights, therefore, Spencer was affirming that one form of superiority (capacity for effort) must take precedence over another kind of capacity (capacity for force).[93] But such an affirmation was, of course, arbitrary from the point of view of evolution: what was it in the theory of the survival of the fittest that required us to favour the superiority of effort over the superiority of force? What was it in the NRCC that demanded that consequences naturally attendant upon certain kinds of lack of ability (such as the inability to make an effort) were to be suffered, but that consequences attendant upon other kinds of lack of ability (such as the inability to withstand physical force) were not to be suffered? Was not Spencer merely defending those evolutionary factors of which he personally approved, and attacking those evolutionary factors of which he personally disapproved?

Spencer did, however, have a reply to this criticism – namely, that it overlooked the role of human intervention in the process of social evolution. That is to say, the theory of evolution must take into account the civilizing contribution that human beings could make to evolutionary progress. This civilizing contribution included helping to bring about one kind of evolutionary outcome rather than another. Hence when human beings intervened with the cosmic struggle, for example to prevent the use of force by the physically superior individuals, they were furthering, not obstructing the evolutionary process. Spencer criticized Huxley for failing to grasp this point.

> The position he takes, that we have to struggle against or correct the cosmic process, involves the assumption that there exists something in us which is not a product of the cosmic process, and is practically going back to the old theological notion, which put Man and Nature in antithesis. Any rational, comprehensive view of evolution involves that, in the course of social evolution, the human mind is disciplined into that form which itself puts a check upon that part of the cosmic process which consists in the unqualified struggle for existence.[94]

This ingenious argument however, is quite unsatisfactory. For one thing, it deprived social evolution of any determinate content, in that it implied that every human action that occurred was consistent with it; in other words, that everything that humans did, individually or collectively, could be interpreted as bringing about one evolutionary outcome rather than another. How, then, could Spencer criticize governments for reversing evolutionary processes? How was it *possible* for human beings to resist the forces of social evolution? How could there ever be retrogression?[95] For another thing, it once more deprived social evolution of any recommendatory thrust, in that it implied that any outcome was equally acceptable. If it was possible for human intervention to influence the course of social evolution, in what direction should it attempt to do so? The theory of social evolution in itself could not supply an answer to this question. Spencer merely stipulated his own preferences – that property-owners should be protected, for example – but he provided no argument of an evolutionary kind capable of substantiating this preference. There was, therefore, considerable incoherence, arbitrariness, and indeterminacy in Spencer's explanation of the mechanism of social change. It was not at all clear that enforcement of the NRCC would produce the perfect society of autonomous agents, and indeed, Spencer's own doubts on the matter led him so severely to qualify its operation that its very meaning was obscured.

These problems were compounded by Spencer's unconvincing application of Lamarckian and Darwinian concepts to social development. For example, Spencer used the Lamarckian theory to claim that human beliefs concerning the NRCC could be functionally produced and then passed on by inheritance:

> If functionally-induced modifications are inheritable, then the mental associations habitually produced in individuals by experiences of the relations between actions and their consequences, pleasurable or painful, may in the succession of individuals, generate innate tendencies to like or dislike such actions.[96]

Hence if a poor person suffered the consequences of her inability or folly, then that lesson would genetically impress any children she subsequently bore. Indeed, Spencer claimed more than this – that a whole nation's beliefs could be changed by a Lamarckian process, and much quicker than by any natural selection process.[97] But Spencer produced little or no evidence to support these claims. And at face value they do seem implausible. How could *beliefs* be inherited? Beliefs may of course be transmitted *socially*, but surely not *genetically*, from one generation to the next.

Spencer's attempt to apply Darwinian ideas of natural selection to society has, however, attracted more sustained criticism. (Darwin himself confined his conclusions to organic phenomenon – no doubt wisely.) The central difficulty lay in Spencer's inconsistency on the question of the inevitability of social progress. In tracing the transition between the 'militant' and the 'industrial' types of society, Spencer oscillated between determinism and voluntarism.

The *militant* type of society was typically that form of organization required when a society was in a state of warfare with other societies. In order to survive, the society was obliged to impose a military pattern upon all its inhabitants,[98] and this entailed a completely autocratic system of rule in which the whole was prior to the parts. Clearly such a society was the antithesis of the liberal state.

By contrast, the *industrial* type of society, which presupposed international peace, allowed individuals a high degree of freedom to go about their business in their own way. Government's only purpose was 'to keep private action within due bounds'.[99] The regime of contract replaced the regime of status, and rewards were determined, not by authority, but by the forces of supply and demand, ensuring that there was preserved the normal relation between conduct and consequences (NRCC). In short, it was a genuinely free market society.

Spencer maintained that as international hostilities had lessened, there had been a gradual transition from the militant to the industrial type of society in accordance with the general law of evolution – from the homogeneous and simple to the heterogeneous and complex. The scientific presumption was that this evolutionary process would continue until it culminated in the establishment of pure industrial types of society throughout the world. Spencer was confident in 'inferring from the changes that civilization has thus far wrought out, that at some time, more or less distant, the industrial type will become permanently established ...'[100]

But this presumption was far from consistently maintained by Spencer. He admitted that in many societies no such developmental path had occurred – they might never escape the militant stage. Spencer even found examples of the militant society in some present-day regimes which were not obviously threatened by international hostilities: there was nothing automatic about peaceful societies choosing to enforce the NRCC. Moreover, Spencer never satisfactorily explained just how international peace came about. As we have seen, the militant type of society could not disappear while international conflict was rife.[101] If, after a period of peace and the consequent establishment of the industrial type of society, international conflict recurred, then evolutionary regression took place, with the consequent return of the militant type of society.[102] Since, clearly, the maintenance of international peace was critical to Spencer's scientific theory of social evolution, we might have expected him to have carefully analysed its cause. But Spencer's explanation of international peace was anything but rigorous. At times, he seemed to regard it as a purely contingent factor, random and unpredictable in its incidence, and therefore not susceptible to scientific analysis.[103] At other times, he subsumed it under a notion of endless oscillation between the two social types, exemplifying a rhythmical pattern which he claimed to be at work in the universe as a whole,[104] and which suggested that the industrial type of society would never be *permanently* established.[105]

> On recognising the universality of rhythm, it becomes clear that it was absurd to suppose that the great relaxation of restraints – political, social, commercial – which culminated in free-trade, would continue. A re-imposition of restraints, if not of the same kind then of other kinds, was inevitable ...[106]

On yet other occasions, however, Spencer dismissed these considerations, and declared that there was an underlying tendency towards social progress which transcended any temporary retrogressions.[107] Civilization would eventually triumph over barbarism: there was a final position of permanent equilibrium –

'equilibration': 'the changes which Evolution presents cannot end until equilibrium is reached, and ... equilibrium must at last be reached.'[108] But Spencer had misgivings about this conclusion, especially when Tyndall pointed out to him that, scientifically speaking, 'equilibration' meant 'death'.[109]

Finally, Spencer sometimes adopted a voluntarist explanation – that international peace (like the civilized interdict upon the use of force by the physically superior noted above) depended upon human efforts devoted to bringing it about. Rejecting the fatalist doctrine that 'societies ... passively evolve apart from any conscious agency', Spencer denied that 'it is needless for individuals to have any care about progress, since progress will take care of itself.' Just as it was absurd to expect 'that organic evolution would continue if the instincts and appetites of individuals of each species were wholly or even partially suspended', so it was absurd to expect 'that social evolution will go on apart from the normal activities, bodily and mental, of the component individuals – apart from their desires and sentiments, and those actions which they prompt.'[110] Indeed, people's beliefs and behaviour were vital factors in influencing social progress:

> the thoughts and actions of individuals, being natural factors that arise in the course of evolution itself, and aid in further advancing it, cannot be dispensed with, but must be severally valued as increments of the aggregate force producing change.[111]

But of course, this was to assert what Spencer had rejected elsewhere – that opinions could bring about social improvement. Hence Spencer quickly qualified that assertion; beliefs cannot independently advance social evolution, though they may retard it:

> For though the process of social evolution is in its general character so far pre-determined, that its successive stages cannot be ante-dated, and that hence no teaching or policy can advance it beyond a certain normal rate, which is limited by the rate of organic modification in human beings, yet it is quite possible to perturb, to retard, or to disorder the process.[112]

In the end, therefore, we are left with an unsatisfactory account of the process of social development. Far from explaining how the arrival of the industrial type of society was a scientific certainty, Spencer seemed to lose his nerve when faced by the range of objections to his theory of social evolution.

Conclusion

It seems that Spencer's foray into the field of evolutionary theory did not succeed in remedying one of the deficiencies of *Social Statics* – that of explaining how a liberal society would be brought about. But why did Spencer embark on this task in the first place? Why did he deem it important, not only to explain what liberalism was and why it was a coherent theory and a justified creed, but how it would be achieved? Most contemporary liberal philosophers do not regard it as necessary to address these sociological questions, but are content to restrict themselves to the conceptual and moral planes of identifying and defending liberalism. Spencer's obsession with evolutionary theory led him down a false trail – he would have been better advised to have concentrated upon developing a more substantial and effective philosophical justification for his conception of the perfect society. That is to say, instead of addressing himself to the question *how* will the perfect society be brought about?, Spencer would have been more profitably employed in demonstrating more convincingly *why* the perfect society is perfect – Why must individuals be self-determining? Why does self-determination promote self-development? How is one person's self-determination compatible with another's?

The reason why Spencer turned to the question of how a liberal society would be achieved was that, after 1860, he became more pessimistic about the popularity of individualistic principles and sought a means of demonstrating that a free market society was not only desirable but inevitable. In 1851 it had looked as though the ideal society of perfected individuals was within reach in England, but only ten years later its prospects seemed to have receded with increasingly belligerent foreign policies and collectivist and authoritarian domestic policies. But the qualifications and inconsistencies in his evolutionary theory were symptoms of Spencer's failure to comprehend these retrogressive forces, and, ironically for one who prided himself on his Radicalism, he eventually found himself in the camp of conservatism, opposing the collectivist social changes that were taking place in the final quarter of the nineteenth century.

Notes

1 Herbert Spencer, *Social Statics* (London, Chapman, 1851), p. 172.
2 Ibid., p. 112.
3 Ibid., p. 114
4 Ibid., pp. 135, 145
5 Ibid., p. 146.
6 Ibid., p. 149.
7 Ibid., p. 155.
8 Ibid., p. 206.
9 Ibid., p. 217.
10 Ibid., p. 305.
11 Ibid., p. 311.
12 Ibid., pp. 372–4.
13 Ibid., p. 330.
14 Ibid., pp. 330–1.
15 John N. Gray, 'Spencer on the Ethics of Liberty and the Limits of State Interference', *History of Political Thought*, III (1982), pp. 465–81.
16 Hillel Steiner, 'Land, Liberty and the Early Herbert Spencer', *History of Political Thought*, III (1982), pp. 515–33.
17 Spencer, *Social Statics*, pp. 49–50.
18 Ibid., pp. 93, 26.

19 Ibid., p. 436.
20 Ibid., p. 434.
21 Ibid., p. 409.
22 Ibid., pp. 427–8.
23 Ibid., p. 474.
24 David Duncan, *The Life and Letters of Herbert Spencer* (London, Methuen, 1908), p. 240.
25 Spencer, *An Autobiography* (London, Williams and Norgate, 1904), II, pp. 329–30.
26 Ibid., p. 376.
27 Duncan, *Life and Letters*, p. 224.
28 Ibid., pp. 220, 307–8.
29 Ibid., p. 221.
30 Spencer, *Autobiography*, II, pp. 377–8.
31 Duncan, *Life and Letters*, p. 313.
32 Ibid., p. 243.
33 Spencer, *Social Statics*, p. 191.
34 Duncan, *Life and Letters*, p. 46.
35 Ibid., pp. 366–7.
36 Spencer, *Facts and Comments* (London, Williams and Norgate, 1902), p. 25.
37 Spencer, *The Study of Sociology* (Michigan, Ann Arbor, 1961), p. 329.
38 Duncan, *Life and Letters*, p. 355.
39 Spencer, *Facts and Comments*, p. 29.
40 Spencer, *Study of Sociology*, pp. 280–1.
41 Duncan, *Life and Letters*, pp. 201–2.
42 Spencer, *Autobiography*, II, p. 50.
43 Ibid., p. 20.
44 Spencer, *Essays: Scientific, Political and Speculative* (London, Williams and Norgate, 2nd edition, 1901), III, pp. 263–4.
45 Spencer, *Social Statics*, pp. 432–3.
46 Ibid., p. 474.
47 Ibid., p. 473.
48 Spencer, *The Proper Sphere of Government* (London, W. Brittain, 1843).
49 Spencer, *Autobiography*, II, p. 103.
50 Spencer, *Various Fragments* (London, Williams and Norgate, 1907), p. 183.
51 Spencer, *Essays*, I, pp. 9–10; Spencer, *First Principles* (London, Williams and Norgatge, 6th edition, 1911), pp. 438–9.
52 Spencer, *Essays*, I, pp. 19–23.
53 Spencer, *Autobiography*, I, p. 507.
54 Ibid., II, p. 18.
55 Ibid., p. 6.
56 Ibid., p. 29.
57 Spencer, *Essays*, I, p. 3 (Spencer's emphasis).
58 Ibid., p. 462.
59 Spencer, *Autobiography*, II, p. 50.
60 Spencer, *Principles of Biology* (London, Williams and Norgate, 2nd edition, 1898), I, p. 530.
61 Ibid., p. 609.
62 Spencer, *Principles of Ethics* (London, Williams and Norgate, 1904), II, p. 19.
63 Spencer, *Principles of Sociology* (London, Williams and Norgate, 3rd edition, 1893), II, p. 610.
64 Spencer, *Principles of Ethics,* II, p. 60.
65 Duncan, *Life and Letters*, p. 408.

66 Spencer, *The Man versus The State* (London, Watts, 1940), p. 79.
67 Ibid.
68 Spencer, *Principles of Ethics*, II, p. 18.
69 Ibid., p. 177.
70 Spencer, *Principles of Sociology*, II, p. 666.
71 Spencer, *Study of Sociology*, pp. 322–3.
72 Ibid., pp. 382, 386.
73 Ibid., p. 313.
74 Spencer, *Autobiography*, I, pp. 324–5.
75 Ibid., II, pp. 381, 382.
76 Duncan, *Life and Letters*, p. 280.
77 Spencer, *Essays*, I, pp. 379–80; cf. Spencer, *Principles of Biology*, I, pp. 427ff.
78 Spencer, *Autobiography*, I, p. 500.
79 Spencer, *Essays*, I, p. 430.
80 Ibid., p. 493.
81 T. H. Huxley, 'Evolution and Ethics', Romanes Lecture 1893, repr. T. H. Huxley and Julian Huxley, *Evolution and Ethics 1893–1943* (London, 1947).
82 Spencer, *Principles of Sociology*, I, pp. 708, 709.
83 Spencer, *Principles of Ethics*, II, p. 42.
84 Ibid., p. 84.
85 Ibid., p. 170.
86 Duncan, *Life and Letters*, p. 366.
87 Spencer, *Study of Sociology*, p. 315.
88 Ibid., Spencer, *Principles of Sociology*, III, p. 571; Spencer, *Principles of Biology*, II, p. 533.
89 Spencer, *Principles of Sociology*, II, p. 232.
90 Duncan, *Life and Letters*, p. 399.
91 Spencer, *Principles of Ethics*, II, pp. 99, 100.
92 See, T. S. Gray, 'Herbert Spencer's Theory of Social Justice – Desert or Entitlement?', *History of Political Thought*, II (1981), pp. 161–86.
93 Spencer, *Study of Sociology*, p. 320.
94 Duncan, *Life and Letters*, p. 336.
95 Indeed, evolutionary arguments could very easily be employed to justify state interference with property rights, as Ritchie and Hobhouse demonstrated. See chapter 10, in this volume, on the New Liberals.
96 Spencer, *Essays*, I, p. 464.
97 Ibid., pp. 464–5.
98 Spencer, *Principles of Sociology*, II, pp. 569–70.
99 Ibid., p. 607.
100 Ibid., p. 648.
101 Ibid., pp. 663–4.
102 Ibid., I, p. 567.
103 Ibid., II, p. 648.
104 Spencer, *First Principles*, pp. 202ff.
105 Spencer, *Principles of Sociology*, III, pp. 596–7.
106 Spencer, *Autobiography*, II, p. 369.
107 Spencer, *Principles of Sociology*, II, p. 660.
108 Spencer, *First Principles*, pp. 413–14.
109 Duncan, *Life and Letters*, p. 104.
110 Spencer, *Various Fragments*, p. 120.
111 Spencer, *Study of Sociology*, p. 35.
112 Ibid., pp. 365–6.

Chapter eight

T. H. Green and the morality of Victorian liberalism*

Richard Bellamy

Historians of political thought have traditionally credited T. H. Green with the reinterpretation of liberal ideas in a less individualistic, even corporatist manner, thereby creating a bridge between the 'classical' liberalism of the Manchester School and the 'new' variety associated with Hobhouse, Hobson, and others at the turn of the century.[1] While recent research has modified this picture in various ways, his transitional status still forms the centre of scholarly attention. If older studies tended 'Whiggishly' to incorporate him into a story of social and political progress held to culminate in the welfare state, current work has regarded his mediating role more critically and has noted a tension between the logic of his ideas and the liberal ideology he espoused which inhibited his making the passage to a more progressive liberalism.

These later commentators have offered three contrasting interpretations of this conflict. Melvin Richter's pathbreaking book argued that, politically, Green had never gone beyond the mid-Victorian liberalism of Bright, but that the drift of his Idealist philosophy could lead to more collectivist conclusions than he intended.[2] Indeed, Richter endorsed Isaiah Berlin's famous judgement that in shifting the general understanding of liberty from a 'negative' to a 'positive' sense, Green may have acted from the motives of a 'genuine liberal: but many a tyrant could use [his ideas] to justify his worst acts of oppression.'[3] At the other end of the political spectrum, C. B. Macpherson and his followers have offered an alternative account of the source of Green's inconsistencies. They approve of the general philosophical shift within his work away from the 'bourgeois' picture of the individual as a self-interested consumer and towards a more Marxian conception of the person as a self-developer. However, they believe that Green's continued adherence to certain liberal institutions, notably his extolling of the market as the expression of freedom, vitiated his analysis of the political consequences of adopting this new view. As a result, his theory contained numerous unresolved antinomies. For the liberal practices Green endorsed belonged to the older model of 'possessive individualism' and frustrate the development of those other individual capacities Green's new notion of personality aimed to promote.[4] Finally, a third school blames the conservative tendency of Idealism simply to endorse current practices for Green's reluctance to follow his ideas through to their 'new' liberal conclusions.[5]

This paper interprets the relationship between Green's political theory and the practice of Victorian liberalism in a way which reverses the perspective adopted by these studies. Rather than seeing Green's philosophy as attempting to generate liberal conclusions from certain abstract premises, I regard it as a self-conscious attempt to express the public language of contemporary political discourse in philosophical terms.[6] If Green gained a certain critical distance from the practices of his time, his judgements remained limited by his Victorian standpoint – not least contemporary assumptions about the nature of certain social processes. Although he can be exonerated from the charge of inconsistency, therefore, he may also appear a somewhat dubious guide to solving the problems of industrial societies for those unwilling to return to the Victorian age.[7]

I

It has become commonplace to associate Green's view of liberalism with that of Gladstone and Bright. However, this ideological affiliation is best understood less as an attachment to a particular set of political policies than as an espousal of the peculiar ethos animating them. Gladstone's central achievement had been to transform the Liberal Party into a vehicle of political moralism. Gladstone had utilized the 'creed of reform', preached with such evangelical zeal by Bright and other nonconformists in the provinces, to harness a disparate set of issues and interests – not all by any means having his personal support – to the parliamentary party. Behind the various causes of liberal pressure groups, such as the Corn Law Repeal, disestablishment, land reform, the extension of the franchise etc., lay a central unifying theme – the 'assault' on the 'wall of privilege' erected by the 'selfish' interest of the 'upper ten thousand' who formed the landed aristocracy, and the opening up of opportunities to talented and hardworking individuals from amongst 'the middle and industrious classes'.[8]

This project should not be interpreted as the championing of Macpherson's 'bourgeois' individualism, the pursuit of a narrowly conceived self-interest summed up in the right to maximize the consumption and acquisition of material goods. The Victorian self-made man possessed the rather different attributes attached to the notion of 'character'. Far from being a licence for the unrestricted satisfaction of one's wants and desires, character consisted in the ability to rise above sensual, animal instincts and passions through the force of will. A variety of conventional Victorian middle-class virtues clustered around this key concept, such as sobriety, self-help, frugality, industry, duty, and independence, which taught thrift and effort as the means to worldly success rather than luck and an eye to the main chance.[9] Underwriting this liberal outlook was a fundamental faith in the goodness and rationality of humankind and the belief that individual moral improvement would lead to social progress. They expected the conflict of a 'feudal' and militaristic age to give way to a spirit of co-operation and industriousness between individuals and nations alike. Self-help was best exhibited in the small businesses, friendly societies, and savings banks that proliferated in this period. Such voluntary organizations showed, as Smiles reminded his readers, that 'the duty of helping one's self in the highest sense involves the helping of one's neighbours.'[10]

It was an ideal to which the nonconformist Protestant conscience proved particularly susceptible, possessing as it did the classic Weberian 'elective affinity' to their concern with the individual's responsibility for his or her own redemption through the overcoming of sin. Moreover, this attitude drew sustenance from a view of English history, taking as its focus the Civil War as the triumph of the righteous over the damned, of an 'almost Judaic narrowness'.[11] As a result, it had wider implications than the rise of the industrial classes. It represented the victory of a whole new political culture, which because of its religious and historical roots, was capable of spreading beyond the manufacturing centres. Gladstonian Liberalism, which gained much of its tone and support from nonconformity, had this Manichaean ethic at its core. In Sidney Webb's words '[a] Liberal reform is never simply a social means to a social end but a struggle of good against evil.'[12] Much of Green's success resided in his appeal to the religious quality of this 'Muscular Liberalism', as Collini has appositely dubbed it. Richter noted how his doctrine of social service, the construction of heaven on earth, provided a rational foundation for Christianity that was congenial to the troubled minds of his contemporaries, assailed by doubts stemming from science and historical scholarship.[13] Yet he could hardly have gained acceptance of his secular religion had the political language of his day not already been permeated with theological concepts as a result of the evangelical background he shared with so many of his fellow liberals.

Although active in local politics on the Oxford town council, and a leading member of various temperance and educational movements, he belonged to the new type of professional academic emerging in the reformed universities. Nevertheless, he conceived his teaching at Oxford, where he became Whyte's Professor of Moral Philosophy in 1878, as a civic duty. A movement of ideals and principles more than policies, liberalism accorded an importance to intellectuals that was unusual in Britain. In spite of the impenetrability of his style, Green attained an influence of almost Parisian dimensions. His achievement – if it can be called that – consisted in translating the political and emotional beliefs associated with the liberal conscience into the non-doctrinal terms of philosophical Idealism.

Green's moralism has often been ascribed to his reliance on German metaphysics and contrasted with the sound common sense of the English empiricist tradition. Yet this attitude clearly belonged to the prevailing spirit of the age and was prominent in thinkers holding very different epistemological positions. Spencer and Mill, no less than Green, Gladstone, and Bright, all gave character pride of place among the citizenly virtues as (to quote Spencer) 'the end which the statesman should keep in view above all other ends'.[14] They shared the belief that the possession of character entailed an overcoming of sin – usually defined as animal pleasure, notably sexual lust – the mark of one, following Mill's definition, 'whose desires and impulses are his own – are the expression of his own nature, as it has been developed and modified by his own culture'.[15] Indeed, Mill asserted that '[c]ivilization in every one of its aspects is a struggle against the animal instincts',[16] so that in his view 'the laws of national character' became 'by far the most important of sociological laws', character being 'the power by which all those of the circumstances of society which are artificial, laws and customs for instance, are altogether moulded'.[17] It was this tendency among Victorian political theorists to conflate individual and social morality which created such a fertile ground for the reception of Green's ideas.

Green criticized the dominant empiricist strand in British philosophy, and utilitarianism and evolutionism in particular, because he believed a moral theory based on these foundations was incapable of providing an adequate account of why the individual should act in the manner Victorian liberals prescribed.[18] He reasoned that the will to strive for self-betterment, in the character-building sense, could not arise naturalistically.[19] Such theories treated actions as evolving partly from natural impulses and wants, partly from experienced pleasures and pains. Human development was a natural sequence of events in which reason, acting on the basis of antecedent pleasures and pains, sought ever more complex forms of happiness by satisfying *de facto* desires. Green, however, noted that human desire differed in quality from animal impulse or appetite. We have the ability to change our wants and needs according to the aspirations and values we hold, people are willing to die for a cause, being capable of renouncing life itself for a higher goal (*PE*, 7). Green's main target was utilitarianism, the 'Philosophic Radicals' having provided the main intellectual support for early nineteenth-century liberal reforms. He contended that 'the modern English utilitarian is generally better than his logic', since 'he distinguishes higher and lower pleasures by some other criterion than that of quantity.'[20] Mill in particular had disavowed much of his earlier associationist thinking, going so far as to state that 'a habit of willing' or 'purpose' could be differentiated from the anticipation of pleasure and pain, and hence that '[i]t is only when our purposes have become independent of the feelings of pain or pleasure from which they originally took their rise that we are said to have a confirmed character'[21] (*PE*, 166–7).

Green regarded this capacity for self-evaluation, and hence for moral action by choosing to do what is good, as essential for self-development of even the most minimal kind and the mark of the truly free person. The resulting linkage of morality and freedom is often cited as the chief source of error in his doctrine, the means whereby he changed the nature of English liberalism by shifting the meaning of liberty from a 'negative' to a 'positive' sense.[22] These critics argue, in terms borrowed from Berlin's seminal article, that rather than viewing liberty as freedom from constraints imposed by direct human agency, Green equated it with the performance of certain actions that realize a person's 'genuine' moral self.

This criticism has a number of problems. First, Green explicitly denied that 'it is the business of the state ... directly to promote moral goodness, for that, from the very nature of moral goodness, it cannot do, but to maintain the conditions without which a free exercise of the human faculties is impossible.'[23] The freedom required for moral action was thus of a negative kind in 'the primary or juristic sense, [of] power to act according to choice or preference', without internal or external constraints. Green never implied that the good person alone was free, merely that only such individuals valued their liberty.[24]

Second, the negative/positive liberty distinction itself is notoriously elusive. Recent discussions have tended to emphasize that divergent interpretations arise less from different ideas of the formal conceptual structure of freedom than from alternative evaluations of the variables involved. The description of freedom as the liberty to make an autonomous choice, that is to say without the hindrance of removable internal or external constraints resulting from intentional human actions, forms a relatively standard common core.[25] Debate usually hinges on the degree to which particular human practices can be held to inhibit an individual's liberty, an issue which often shades into a discussion of our moral obligations towards others.[26] For example, advocates of the market as an unplanned catalaxy dispute the socialist view that those disadvantaged by market fluctuations have been denied any liberty by those seeking a profit. Similarly, while most commentators agree that the idea of freedom implies a weakly normative condition about an agent's ability to make a reasonable choice, disagreements arise about the degree to which social conditioning can induce 'false consciousness' and inhibit an individual's selection of his or her own way of life. Self-consciousness in these respects can no doubt only be pushed so far if it is not to be disabling and generate undue paranoia. But the limits will be those of conventional wisdom rather than of logic.

Victorian discussions of freedom were largely conditioned by the ideal of character in this respect.[27] It set the limits of what kind of obstacle individuals could reasonably surmount themselves and what duties they owed not to inhibit others. Mill, frequently held up as the champion of 'negative' liberty, believed no less vehemently than Green that only 'a person of confirmed virtue is completely free',[28] because the virtuous alone has the stamina and conviction to resist the debilitating effects of industrial society. Their differences reflected contrasting judgements of how and when this moral determination arose. In many respects, Green belonged to a more optimistic generation than Mill's. The prosperity of the late 1860s and early 1870s combined with the election of the first Liberal administration under Gladstone in 1868, rendered the times propitious for liberalism with its faith in social and moral progress. Once free from the shadow of Ricardian economics and the fear of the impending stagnation of capitalism in the 'stationary state', the hedonistic presuppositions of classical political economy were amended to take into account the expected evolution of human sentiments from self-interest to altruism. For Alfred Marshall, the Malthusian trap only existed for 'the more ignorant and phlegmatic of races and individuals', '[e]ducation, and the raising of our moral and religious ideals, and the growth of the printing press and the telegraph have so changed English human nature that many things which economists rightly considered impossible thirty years ago are possible now.'[29] What Gladstone called the 'magnificent moral spectacle' of the Lancashire cotton workers' self-sacrificing support for the North in the American civil war, became the touchstone of the improved morality of the British 'labour aristocracy',[30] and was appropriately rewarded by the Second Reform Bill. The lynchpin of Green's philosophy was a corresponding conception of history as the progressive acceptance of a 'theory of universal human fellowship' based on reason and morality, and obstructed only 'by those private interests which have made it inconvenient for powerful men and classes to act upon it' (*PE*, 209). The coherence of Green's argument only began to break down when events and social trends revealed this historicist faith to be misplaced.

II

Green's politics cannot be separated from his ethics and metaphysics. He originally delivered the *Lectures on the Principles of Political Obligation* sandwiched between those later published as the *Prolegomena to Ethics*, and the two formed part of an integral course. Green argued, in Kantian manner, that the view of the world, essential to science, as a related series of objects and events, was not a product but a presupposition of knowledge (*PE*, 8). But he went beyond Kant to regard these relations not simply 'as fictions of our combining intelligence', but as explicable only on the assumption of the existence of a divine consciousness present both in mind and nature and guaranteeing their ultimate unity (*PE*, 33). Adopting a parallel argument, he maintained that morality consisted of similar synthetic *a priori* judgements by which the eternal consciousness reproduced itself in people's lives (*PE*, 125). Humankind's striving after self-realization formed the operative force behind the transform-ation and development of human societies, the product of the progressive unfolding of the divine principle within the consciousness of individuals.[31] However, Green wished to avoid the suggestion that history was thus the product of a spiritual demiurge rationally ordering human affairs in a benign manner. Only individual effort could bring about this gradual moralization of social relations. Moreover, the divine unity upon which it was premised remained beyond both time and space and hence only imperfectly realized within existing institutions, which could regress from it no less than advancing towards its fulfilment (*PE*, 186–9). Thus he used the development of character as both a hermeneutic principle for studying past societies and as a critical standard whereby they could be judged.

According to Green, we can only realize ourselves within the context of society (*PE*, 190). Personal identity derived not from a number of pre-social biological or psychological determinants, but through the medium of social roles and relationships. '[J]ust as language of some sort is necessary to the real existence of thought', (*PO*, 114) so a community consisting of a number of shared ways of experiencing and interpreting the world enabled the individual to form his or her tastes and goals. Even when isolated from society we necessarily retained part of this cultural baggage when performing actions from other than pure biological necessity or arbitrary impulse: Robinson Crusoe remained an eighteenth-century gentleman on his island. As Green put it: '[t]he individual's conscience is reason in him as informed by the work of reason without him in the structure and controlling sentiments of society' (*PE*, 216). Green denied that this thesis reduced the individual to a cypher of society, or of some other supra-individual entity such as the nation or spirit. If the content of our conception of self was constrained by the available social opportunities, 'the ultimate standard' remained 'an ideal of personal worth'. The social framework made personal development possible but did not direct how we acted any more than grammar and vocabulary dictated what we said; '[t]o speak of any progress or improvement or development of a nation or society or mankind, except as relative to some greater worth of persons, is to use words without meaning' (*PE*, 184).

Green's theory of self-realization had three components. First, there was the conception of a fully perfected self present within everyone's consciousness as a divine ideal to strive for, but never actually attain. Second, it contained the partial social embodiment of this ideal within the customs and practices of a given community. Finally, Green regarded the individual's search for self-development as involving the modification of his or her own impulses in relation to each of the first two elements. For it was through the striving after the ideal that social arrangements necessary to that end came to be extended and changed (*PE*, 232).

The above reasoning provided Green with his definition of the common good. This concept that did not refer to a number of particular goods individuals commonly desired, but rather to the common pursuit of self-realization by the members of a given society. Green insisted that personal development entailed this becoming the goal of society as a whole. It coincided with what Joseph Raz terms an 'inherent public good', namely, a good whose advantages only the potential beneficiary can control, and which by its very nature no single agency can distribute or restrict.[32] Raz gives the example of tolerance. Where this is valued, only intolerance on our part elicits tolerance from others. Friendship and love provide counter-examples, for individuals can withhold them no matter how deserving potential recipients may be. Such goods are intrinsically rather than instrumentally beneficial, because their existence constitutes the quality of life of the community for all concerned. Otherwise we could adopt intolerant attitudes to gain a personal advantage, as when racialists claim that expelling coloured immigrants increases job opportunities.

For Green, character had similar properties. One cannot impose it on others because '[n]o one can convey a good character to another. Everyone must make his character for himself. All that one can do to make another better is to remove obstacles and supply conditions favourable to the formation of a good character'

(*PE*, 332). Green's main departure from traditional liberalism arose from his insistence that we have an obligation to provide these conditions.

Victorian liberals agreed on the importance of autonomy as indicating a capacity for character. However, they tended to argue that this could be obtained be securing an individual's right to non-interference by others. Unviolated rights guaranteed an autonomous existence; the possession of character depended on what you made of it. Green, while sharing much of this sentiment, believed self-realization was possible only when certain broader preconditions obtained. Some of these, such as the ability for rational thought, related to the person concerned; others to the prevailing social circumstances. These consisted of the available range of options from which the individual could choose, for the character of one's life depended on the choices one made. Character could not be achieved simply by accepting whatever came your way, or by acting from fear of coercive threats, or from the struggle to survive the perils of starvation or disease, but only through selecting from among a variety of significant and desirable possibilities (*PO*, 25). The degree to which these criteria were met depended upon the availability of certain openings within a given society.

Green contended that these preconditions for the attainment of character formed part of the common good, for they were constitutive of self-realization. Against individualist rights theorists, he denied that you could separate the rules governing self-regarding actions from those dealing with our transactions with others. A general injunction to respect other people's interests was too vague, since it could pose implausible standards of forbearance. You could not identify the limits upon your own actions without a consciousness of your obligations towards your fellow citizens, nor understand either in ignorance of what gives value to life, both personally and in general (*PE*, 183, 190; *PO*, 113). The 'general fabric of rights' depended upon respect for the intrinsic value for the common good as a source both of personal development and of our obligations towards the rest of the community (*PO*, 114). He maintained that this awareness grew out of striving after self-realization in its triadic form as outlined above:

> Under these influences there has arisen ... on the one hand an ever widening conception of the range of persons between whom the good is common, on the other a conception of the nature of the common good itself, consistent with its being the object of a universal society co-extensive with mankind. (*PE*, 286)

Green believed the common good had a value independent of its worth to the collectivity. For this reason, utilitarian justifications of public goods proved unsatisfactory. He accepted that, up to a certain point, the prerequisites 'favourable to the formation of character' such as 'healthy houses and food, sound elementary education, the removal of temptations to drink ... tend also to make life more pleasant on the whole' (*PE*, 332). But while we might often have a personal interest in the common good, the two could often conflict – notably when the temptation to 'free-ride' occurred. As Sidgwick acknowledged, the abnegation exercised by individuals pursuing their own happiness and the injunction to cultivate the greatest happiness of the greatest number were logically independent; while the move from the first to the second was difficult to derive from the psychological premises of utilitarianism (*PE*, 365; *PO*, 121). Like many liberals, Green was influenced by Mazzinian democratic nationalism to make the nation the focus of the individual's attachment to the common good. Mazzini had conceived nationality in ethical rather than racial, geographic, or linguistic terms. The citizen owed a duty to the nation greater than self-interest, because it provided the environment within which each person fashioned his or her identity. Self-determination formed a vital part of Mazzinian nationalism, because this common sense of obligation only came about through each citizen participating in the creation of the laws which expressed this national spirit. Green, following his usual method, simply took up this liberal platitude – so essential to Gladstone's foreign policy, his commitment to Irish Home Rule and his trust in the extension of democracy to the British people[33] – and gave it a Kantian gloss.[34] Whereas the 'loyal subject' recognized the rights of others merely because the state compelled him to, the 'intelligent patriot's'

> judgement of what he owes to the state is quickened by a feeling of which the *patria* ... is the natural object and of which the state becomes the object only in so far as it is an organisation of a people to whom the individual feels bound by ties ... derived from a common dwelling place with its associations, from common memories, traditions and customs, and from the common ways of feeling and thinking which a common language and still more a common literature embodies. (*PO*, 123)

He rejected what he regarded as the Fichtean or Hegelian view, which treated this national spirit as somehow superior to the personal character of the individuals who contributed to its formation (*PE*, 184). Indeed, only if the individual had a share 'in making and maintaining the laws which he obeys ... will he learn to regard the work of the state as a whole'(*PO*, 122). This patriotism did not display itself in war, but in so organizing society 'that everyone's capacities have free scope for their development' (*PO*, 171).

To a large extent, he hoped that the new society would be created by the will of its members as a result of human moral progress, rather than through the force of the bureaucratic state. A democratic nation could reasonably legislate to provide certain public services such as education and housing, or restrict certain practices, such as unhealthy factory conditions or drinking, without violating the voluntary principle. Alan Milne remarked some years ago that this thesis 'assumed that self-realization and rational moral conduct were one and the same thing, that to the extent that a man was a rational moral agent he achieved genuine selfhood.'[35] In fact, the two can conflict, since moral action may well involve some sacrifice of personal well-being. Green maintained that the possibilities for autonomous action required everyone acting morally as well, putting a regard for the common good above their own immediate gain. But he underestimated the degree of self-sacrifice this called for because the doctrine of character tended to conflate self-discipline with self-determination. Victorian liberals generally shared a hostility to licence and appetite, to simply doing as you liked, which made only self-improvement true freedom. Similarly for Green,

> Moral freedom is not the same thing as a control over the outward circumstances and appliances of life. It is the end to which such control is a generally necessary means, and which gives it its value. (*PO*, 219)

Green thought that as individuals increasingly appreciated the worth of freedom as a moral ideal, clashes between divergent personal goals would diminish. This hypothesis rested upon the belief that morality and rationality ultimately coincided, a supposition linked to his metaphysical claim concerning the existence of an 'eternal consciousness' forging the relations between objects. Green's theory can be absolved from the charge of having an inherent tendency to totalitarianism, the imposition of a prescribed way of life upon a society in the name of a dubious freedom. He denied that morality could be enforced, and asserted that the perfect life could never be totally achieved, or its outlines more than imperfectly known. Theoretically his thesis appeared to justify a liberal pluralism, allowing everyone to follow the path to moral freedom best suited to their particular capacities. But its coherence rested upon a putative harmony between all such attempts which must be regarded as over-optimistic and which hence vitiated the workability of his ideas.

Green believed that competition between individuals arose from the pursuit of material goods alone. When people aimed solely to achieve moral goodness, their different abilities proved complementary. For the desire to be good consisted 'in the settled disposition on each man's part to make the most and best of humanity in his own person and the person of others' (*PE*, 244). To use Green's example, when we treated education as an end in itself, we both added to our own self-culture and augmented the knowledge and skills available to the community at large. When we pursued learning merely to enhance our own standing and power, however, it became a 'positional' good, to employ Hirsch's term.[36] Green's argument assumed that in aiming at higher goods, we divested ourselves of the animal passion of self-interest. Moreover, it was of the nature of such goods that they benefited society in proportion to the effort and success of the individuals engaged in their pursuit. An orchestra perhaps offers the best illustration of the sort of collaborative and self-realizing endeavour Green had in mind. However, it remains highly doubtful that all, or even many, of the manufacturing processes of modern industrial societies could be assimilated to this model. More important, even Green appreciated that the commercial ethos seemed to be positively working against it, for 'in the stream of unrelenting competition ... the weaker has not a chance'. While they were admitted to the 'negative rights' of citizenship, 'the good things to which the pursuits of society are in fact directed turn out to be no good things to them'. In Green's opinion, the difficulty arose 'because the good is being sought in objects which admit of being competed for', so that the 'success of some in attaining them is incompatible with the success of others':

Until the object generally sought as good comes to be a state of mind or character of which the attainment, or the approach to attainment, by each is itself a contribution to its attainment by everyone else, social life must continue to be one of war ... (*PE*, 245)

Green hoped that once everyone valued the 'higher' goods for themselves, then the market would be transformed from a competition in which each person sought to beggar his or her neighbour into one in which everyone strove to outdo each other in moral virtue. Reviewing the *Prolegomena*, Sidgwick rightly questioned whether a personal appreciation of such 'higher' pleasures entailed conceding to everyone an equal right to their enjoyment:

The thoughtful trader knows that wealth will enable him to provide himself and those he loves with books, pictures, prolonged education, varied travel, opportunities of intellectual life: and knowing this, he allows himself to adopt methods of dealing which sometimes, perhaps, are hardly compatible with Green's ideal of justice ... In short, Green seems to me to have unconsciously tried to get the advantages of two distinct and incompatible conceptions of the human good: the one liberally comprehensive, but palpably admitting competition, the other non competitive but stoically or puritanically narrow.[37]

As the optimism which greeted Gladstone's first government waned with electoral defeat, economic decline, and a new awareness of the 'social problem', these tensions came to the fore. In attempting to justify the more 'constructive' policies of Gladstone's second term, Green revealed the ambiguities not just of his own theory but of an entire ethos.

III

According to Green, the role of the state was to secure sufficient personal freedom for citizens to act as rational moral agents. He regarded the growing complexity of modern societies as going hand in hand with a gradual diffusion of reason among their members; a process reflected in the development of a regular system of laws protecting the complex of rights and upheld by conventional morality. This testified to the increasingly self-conscious awareness of a shared morality among humankind, itself the product of an eternal divine principle of self-realization immanent in all their actions. Since Green condemned attempts 'to enforce acts as virtuous which lose their virtue when done under fear of legal penalties' (*PO*, 17), the liberal presumption against excessive state intervention was entrenched within his philosophy at a fundamental level. However, Green's definition of the role of government as 'the removal of obstacles' to the moral life was not exhausted by merely securing the individual from external interference. As we saw, it also included the attack on restrictive practices which reduced the availability of aspects of social life important for autonomy. In spite of the apparently wider sphere of state action permitted by this theory, he continued to portray the new reforms which followed from it as part of 'the same old cause of social good against class interests, for which, under altered names liberals are fighting now as they were fifty years ago.'[38] To a considerable degree, Green remained true to the traditional Radical belief that once aristocratic privileges were removed, the people would no longer have any incentive or desire to enact policies which conflicted with the common good. His principal aim was to reinforce the desirable character traits which were essential to Victorian self-help and voluntary schemes, he did not seek to substitute for them by the direct provision of welfare services or redistribution by the state.

Green's anti-paternalist strictures seem to epitomize Victorian moralism. He listed three instances when 'laws have been made which check the development of the moral disposition'. The first cited the attempts of the established church to set legal requirements on religious observance – a reference to the Thirty-nine Articles, which Green had been obliged to endorse on taking up his Balliol fellowship. The second, more vaguely, referred to 'prohibitions and restraints, unnecessary, or which have ceased to be necessary, for maintaining the social conditions of the moral life, and which interfere with the growth of self-reliance, with the formation of a manly conscience and sense of moral dignity – in short with moral autonomy which is the condition of the highest goodness.' Finally, he offered the example of 'legal institutions which take away the occasion for the exercise of certain moral virtues (e.g. the Poor Law, which takes away the occasion for the exercise of parental forethought, filial reverence, and neighbourly kindness' (*PO*, 17).

All of these criteria were conventional enough, but Green also backed causes supported by only a minority of liberals which might seem to contravene them. His promotion of temperance reform appears to conflict with the second argument, for example.[39] The Oxford Liberal MP, Harcourt, made just this observation. For him '[w]hat really makes sobriety valuable is the voluntary self-control – the deliberate self-denial which resists temptation and leads a man, for the sake of himself and others, to abstain from vicious indulgence.'[40] Indeed, Green seemed condemned out of his own mouth, for he too criticized '"paternal government"' for 'narrowing the room for the self-imposition of duties and for the play of disinterested motives' (*PO*, 18). Initially, he got around the problem by supporting the so-called 'local option', which proposed giving ratepayers the possibility for voluntarily decreasing and even abolishing local licences, a measure Harcourt himself eventually adopted.[41] However, Green came to advocate compulsory prohibition because he believed that significant numbers of poor people had become trapped into a cycle of deprivation which reduced their willpower to overcome their dependence, making 'the drink curse ... altogether too big a problem to be dealt with by individual effort only'.[42] Green did not doubt the contention of his fellow liberals that given sufficient character, people could leave the poverty trap and fashion their own lives. However, a 'drunken population naturally perpetuates and increases itself' because they lacked the incentive to self-improvement offered by a favourable environment.[43] Their condition was already so low that escape through alcohol provided as valid an option as any other. Green countered the charge of paternalism, because he denied that a person enthralled to drink had a moral capacity to lose. Of course, he did not think the entire population needed compulsorily drying out, but those already dry were not constrained by a law they accepted anyway. Finally, he justified the compulsion of moderate drinkers and the sellers of liquor on grounds stemming from the common good. The existence of the gin-shops and beer houses created an obstacle to the moral autonomy of drunkards which government had an obligation to remove, especially as it caused 'such a very slight inconvenience as it must be for those who take such a little drop'.[44] Green looked upon the liquor trade as a vested interest of the Conservatives to hinder the progress of the labouring classes, a view reinforced by the Liberal electoral defeat of 1874, despite the reformed franchise, and given extra weight by the successful tactics of the Tory Oxford brewer Hall, who exploited the unpopularity of the temperance issue in a later by-election.[45]

Green's arguments were fully consistent with his general belief that the state should merely impede hindrances to self-development which could not be reasonably removed by either individuals themselves or with the aid of the benevolent support of others. Its intolerant aspects arose not from the formal nature of the theory so much as the underlying Victorian assumption that full autonomy meant overcoming such bestial pleasures as drink, so that no civilized community lost by its suppression – an opinion which would certainly have astonished the poets and philosophers of antiquity! Indeed, by emphasizing the iniquities of drink to such a degree, Green reinforced rather than challenged the Victorian liberal belief that we have sole responsibility for our lives. The improvement of the material conditions of the poor was not his concern *per se*, merely their stature as moral agents: securing the second would bring the first in its wake.

If the voluntary principle had been kept intact, albeit only by a certain ingenuity, his argument still appeared to attack another fundamental liberal position, classically expressed by Mill, which regarded such interferences with personal morality as unjustifiable except when such lapses had harmful consequences for others. Experience and public opprobrium would discipline those capable of surmounting the perils of base pleasures, and one should neglect the failures *'pour encourager les autres'*.[46] Green attempted to circumvent this objection by contentiously claiming that 'however decently carried on, the extensive drinking of one man means an injury to others in health, purse and capability, to which no limits can be placed' – presumably because we are so interdependent that everyone would gain by the removal of this 'social evil'. Moreover, a law passed by a democracy did not entail the paternalistic or self-interested imposition of a particular form of behaviour by one class upon another, which had made such legislation so iniquitous in the past. It was an act of collective self-restraint.[47]

Green adopted similar arguments to justify Forster's 1870 Education Act. Not all liberals had agreed that the state should supplement the voluntary funding of schools. Nonconformists in particular, had been worried that it would lead to the Church of England having too great an influence in education. Although Green was considerably more Radical on this issue than most, wishing to open up the secondary and tertiary as well as the primary sector to talent rather than wealth as part of 'a reconstitution of society through that of education',[48] it provided him with his strongest case for interference since all the relevant legislation had been passed by a reformed parliament and hence could be portrayed as emanating from the popular will.[49] In addition, compulsory schooling could be justified on entirely Millian grounds 'as the prevention of a hindrance to the capacity for rights on the part of children' whose parents neglected their moral duty towards them (*PO*, 209).

Analogous reasoning partly underlay his interpretation of the Factory and Employers' Liability Acts. The regulation of hours and conditions of work might appear, according to his third criterion, as a paternalistic interference with spontaneous benevolence and freedom of contract. As with temperance, Green's position was strongest with regard to the oppressed themselves. Their self-reliance was not endangered by laws securing them good housing, fair terms of employment and a healthy environment because they had none to lose. As all the 'authorized accounts' of royal and parliamentary commissions showed:

> Left to itself, or to the operation of casual benevolence, a degraded population perpetuates itself. ... Given a certain standard of moral and material well-being, people may be trusted not to sell their labour, or the labour of their children, on terms which would not allow that standard to be maintained. But with large masses of our population, until the laws we have been considering took effect, there was no such standard.[50]

Among the poor, enlightened self-interest, if not a directly moral will, would provide an adequate incentive for self-improvement once they had something worth striving for.

Green found it more difficult to explain why the successful capitalist should sacrifice a personal advantage for the benefit of others. C. B. Macpherson in particular sees the difficulty as insuperable because of Green's view of property.[51] Green certainly regarded some private possessions as basic to an individual's capacity for self-realization (*PO*, 213) and justified inequalities of property-ownership as indications of people's different talents and tastes and of the divergent forms personal development could take (*PE*, 191; *PO*, 223). However, Green denied that the accumulation of goods within capitalist relations inherently produced a destitute mass of wage labourers possessing nothing beyond the means of subsistence (*PO*, 220, 227). Once more, his thinking followed a largely traditional route. Green distinguished conspicuous consumption from the employment of goods as part of a rational plan of life. He assumed the former inherently involved enslavement to impulse, 'the wild beast in man' (*PO*, 217), which the progress of society gradually brought into check through the growing consciousness of a rational will common to all people's projects. Since only social recognition secured an individual's rights, 'there result[ed] a common interest in the free play of the powers of all.' An individual's 'positive condition' of possession rested on the correlative 'negative condition' of respecting the power of appropriation of others (*PO*, 221), Green contended that in an ideal free market property would be treated as an aspect of the common good and the possibilities for possession as part of one's self-realization would be open to all.

Green granted 'the many characteristics of the institution of property, as it actually exists, which cannot be derived from the spiritual principle which we have assigned as its foundation' (*PO*, 217). Following Mill and Radical opinion generally, he treated these aberrations as products of the lawless feudal era, evidence of a period when impulse had ruled over the will, and associated them almost entirely with the landed wealth of the aristocracy. The poor character of the urban proletariat, 'whose ancestors ... were trained in habits of serfdom' (*PO*, 229) could be attributed to the demoralizing influence of this degenerate period as well. Green ascribed the present low condition of the masses to 'this debased population' that 'gluts the labour market and constantly threatens to infect the class of superior workmen'. Their servile habits made them easy prey for unscrupulous employers seeking a cheap source of labour, for they lacked the moral backbone to combine for better terms, thus undermining the bargaining power of those who did.[52] The situation was further exacerbated by the continued existence of the aristocratic landlords themselves, whose inherited wealth derived from no effort of their own and, unlike industrial capital, remained largely unproductive. Adopting a quasi-Lockean proviso based on his view of property as an aspect of the common good, Green opined that one's right to non-renewable natural resources such as land depended upon rendering them 'more serviceable to society as a whole ... than if they were held in common'. For '[t]he capital gained by one is not taken from another ... if it is compensated by the acquisition of other wealth on the part of those extruded from the soil' (*PO*, 229). With Irish landlords particularly in mind, Green thought the descendants of feudal barons, whose acquisition came from conquest rather than labour, as hereditarily corrupted as their former dependants. They used the land for game and sport rather than cultivating it, and in innumerable ways had 'taken away the interest, and tied the hands, of the nominal owner – the tenant for life – in making the most of his property'. The Ground Game Act was thus a measure of considerable moral force for Green, although recent commentaries on his writings frequently pass over his defence of it in bemused silence. Green surmised that a genuinely free market in land, rather than the system of entailed estates, combined with an adequate protection of the interests of tenants, would remove the problem and encourage 'the formation of that mainstay of social order and contentment, a class of small proprietors tilling their own land'[53] (*PO*, 228).

Thus blame for the chief abuses of the contemporary economic system lay not with 'capitalism or the free development of individual wealth' but 'the violent manner in which rights over land have been acquired and exercised' (*PO*, 230). Only the historical accident which caused Britain to miss the clean sweep of the French Revolution accounted for the continued influence of 'unrestrained landlordism' (*PO*, 226) and its attendant evils of 'exaggerated luxury at the top. flunkeyism in the middle and recklessness at the bottom'.[54] The wealth generated by the successful capitalist, in contrast, was 'constantly distributed throughout the process in the shape of wages to labourers and of profits to those who mediate in the business of exchange' (*PO*, 226). The 'large masses of hired labourers' required by the mines and manufacturing industries did not risk sharing the fate of their forefathers the 'landless countrymen', because they could become 'small-scale capitalists themselves'. The better paid workers owned houses and furniture, and even clubbed together in benefit societies in order to match the investment power of the 'great' capitalists (*PO*, 227). Green, in true liberal spirit, imbued the market with the ethical purpose of moulding character and eroding unearned privilege – the main source of moral laxity. He assumed that the accumulation of the 'great' capitalist went beyond mere material gain, reflecting instead the moral impulse for self-development. In consequence, he foresaw no clash between individual attempts at self-realization, for all were aspects of the same spiritual principle. Green's view of the likely contours of a fully evolved industrial system was therefore very similar to Mill's and Spencer's. Like them he envisaged it tending towards the voluntary co-operation of individual producers, grouped together in associations for mutual advantage. The new industrial enterprises would operate on the model of friendly societies as workers' co-operatives. The resulting domestic harmony would be mirrored at the international level. One of the chief proofs of the benevolence of capitalism within the liberal catechism was the supposed unifying effect of free trade between nations and its pacifying influence (*PO*, 174). Green fully supported the unpopular position of Cobden, Bright, and ultimately Gladstone on foreign affairs, condemning, for example, British involvement in the Crimea. He saw 'special class interests' lurking behind all wars, evidence of the continued predominance of 'old *dynasteiai*' (*PO*, 173).[55]

Green's acceptance of the liberal characterization of the market blinded him to its potential failings. The capitalist worked for the challenge involved, ploughing profits back into the system for the benefit of everyone rather than retaining them for personal uses. Yet even assuming a society of altruists, problems of scarcity and divergent views of the good life, or simple misinformation about other people's requirements, can give rise to incompatible priorities for the use of available resources.[56] Green skirted around these and other difficulties because he assumed a harmonious moral order existed between rational individual goals. Since autonomy tended to shade into an overcoming of material pleasures, he did not envisage the distributional disputes between caviar addicts and those with more modest demands beloved of modern welfare economists. He regarded market distribution as a correct reflection of individual desert, overlooking the way it disproportionately rewards those talented in money-making rather than in other directions (*PO*, 223). Green made no provision for a planned redistribution of goods to remedy these defects. In any case, he thought welfare measures undermined individual independence and charitable impulses (*PO*, 17). Similarly, he thought the common ownership of property 'incompatible with that highest object of human attainment, a free morality' (*PO*, 223), although an unpublished manuscript suggests that, like Mill and Spencer,[57] he did not rule out the possibility that human 'sympathy' might voluntarily bring this about in a distant future.[58]

Despite the conventionality of many of Green's opinions, they were not without their subversive aspect once liberalism failed to live up to its lights. According to Green's theory, societies improved in their internal organization as the possibilities for self-development were extended to larger numbers of people (*PO*, 142; *PE*, 206–7). Once this right became generally recognized, then any attempt by an entrenched 'powerful class' to resist it would ultimately justify revolution (*PO*, 142, 144). Green supported the North in the American civil war and Mazzini in Italy for these reasons, and even countenanced force in 1867 should further suffrage reform be blocked.[59] Yet if this latter issue demonstrates the impeccable democratic and liberal nature of his intentions, it also illustrates the shaky foundations on which they rested. Green claimed that:

> enfranchisement of the people was an end in itself ... that citizenship only makes the moral man [and] gives that self respect, which is the true basis of respect of others, and without which there is no lasting social order or real morality.[60]

However, the ensuing election result of 1874 bitterly disappointed him. Characteristically, he sought the explanation in the servility of the working classes, their 'lack of moral progress', which had made them unable to cope with an 'unexampled commercial prosperity' so that 'political enthusiasm' was lost 'in what I may call a general riot of luxury' in which 'the money and the beer flowed freely'.[61] Once again, Green was forced into finding mitigating circumstances to bolster his belief that freedom and enlightenment naturally brought a common morality.

IV

The aims and limits of Green's advocacy of state intervention were summed up by a colleague at Balliol, the economist Arnold Toynbee, in an 1882 lecture to working men, entitled 'Are Radicals Socialists?'. He told them:

> We have not abandoned our old belief in liberty, justice and self-help, but we say that under certain conditions the people cannot help themselves, and that then they should be helped by the state representing directly the whole people. In giving this state help, we make three conditions: first, the matter must be one of primary social importance; next, it must be proved to be practicable;

thirdly, the state interference must not diminish self-reliance. Even if the chance should arise of removing a great social evil, nothing must be done to weaken those habits of individual self-reliance and voluntary association which have built up the greatness of the English people.[62]

Green sought to foster the Victorian ideal of self-improvement, not to challenge it. Within an intellectual environment in which such ideas were generally accepted, and where the people could be expected spontaneously to adopt such behaviour, his views had genuinely progressive implications. For they entailed the extension of opportunities to ever greater sections of the community to participate in a form of life which met with widespread support, However, his position risked becoming intolerant and even coercive once the system of beliefs which it rested upon came to be questioned, and its coherence and desirability for much of the population called into doubt. Given the implausibly optimistic conception of human nature underlying Green's philosophy, such criticisms seemed inevitable. When citizens failed to act 'responsibly', Green was led to devise sophistic arguments to justify why they should be obliged to do so. As a result, Green's approach to social reform increasingly served a conservative purpose, that of so structuring society that only certain types of conduct brought success. A point which prompts the concluding and topical reflection, that to propagate Victorian values when they have ceased to command common assent, and in social conditions which have rendered them even more contestable than they were in nineteenth-century Britain, will necessarily involve the resort to illiberal and authoritarian measures to enforce their adoption.[63]

Notes

1   This view was typical of the older textbooks, e.g. R. C. K. Ensor, *England 1870–1914* (Oxford, 1936), pp. 162–3; H. J. Laski, *The Decline of Liberalism* (London, 1940), pp. 11–12; A. Bullock and M. Shock (eds), *The Liberal Tradition* (Oxford, 1956), p. xliv; and still resurfaces in more recent ones, e.g. W. H. Greenleaf, *The British Political Tradition*, 4 vols (London, 1983–), II, pp. 124–41.
2   M. Richter, *The Politics of Conscience: T.H. Green and his Age*, (London, 1964), ch. 9.
3   Richter, *Politics of Conscience*, pp. 201–7; I. Berlin, 'Two Concepts of Liberty', in *Four Essays on Liberty* (Oxford, 1969), p. 133 n.
4   e.g. C. B. Macpherson, *Democratic Theory: Essays in Retrieval* (London, 1973), pp. 5–6, 50–1, 114, 130, 156, 175. I. M. Greengarten, *Thomas Hill Green and the Development of Liberal-Democratic Thought* (Toronto, 1981) systemizes Macpherson's scattered comments.
5   P. Clarke, *Liberals and Social Democrats* (Cambridge, 1978), pp. 22–7; and A. Vincent and R. Plant, *Philosophy, Politics and Citizenship: The Life and Thought of the British Idealists* (Oxford, 1984), pp. 26, 94–5.
6   This approach naturally reflects an indebtedness to S. Collini's important monograph, *Liberalism and Sociology: L. T. Hobhouse and Political Argument in England 1880–1914* (Cambridge, 1979), esp. ch. 1.
7   The desire to revive Green in order to mount a defence of social-democratic politics lies behind many recent studies. See my review article, 'A Green Revolution?

Idealism, Liberalism and the Welfare State', *The Bulletin of the Hegel Society of Great Britain*, X (1984), pp. 34–9 for criticisms of this project.

8 The quotes, from Bright and Cobden respectively, come from A. Briggs, *Victorian People* (London, 1954), p. 51; and I. Bradley, *The Optimists: Themes and Personalities in Victorian Liberalism* (London, 1980), p. 52. In addition, for this picture of Victorian liberalism I have drawn on, J. R. Vincent, *The Formation of the British Liberal Party 1857–68* (London, 1966), esp. ch. 3; R. Shannon, *The Crisis of Imperialism 1865–1915* (London, 1976); C. Harvie, *The Lights of Liberalism: University Liberals and the Challenge of Democracy* (London, 1976); and M. Pugh, *The Making of Modern British Politics* (Oxford, 1982). For Green and Bright, see R. L. Nettleship, 'Memoir', in *Works of T. H. Green* (London, 1888), III, pp. xx, xxiv.

9 The following discussion draws heavily on S. Collini, 'The Idea of "Character" in Victorian Political Thought', *Transactions of the Royal Historical Society*, 5th series, 35 (1985), pp. 29–50.

10 S. Smiles, *Self-Help, with Illustrations of Conduct and Perseverance* (London, 1859, 1925), p. vi.

11 Vincent, *Liberal Party*, p. xxix. See J. Burrow, *A Liberal Descent: Victorian Historians and the English Past* (Cambridge, 1981) for a full discussion of this historical vision. Green's own version of it can be found in his *Four Lectures on the English Revolution*, in *Works*, III, pp. 277–364.

12 Sidney Webb, in the *Nineteenth Century*, September 1901, quoted in Pugh, *Modern British Politics*, p. 22.

13 M. Richter, 'T. H. Green and his Audience: Liberalism as a Surrogate Religion', *Review of Politics*, 18 (1956), pp. 444–72; Richter, *Politics of Conscience*.

14 Herbert Spencer, *The Principles of Ethics* (London, 1893), II, p. 251, cited by Collini, 'The Idea of "Character"', p. 31.

15 J. S. Mill, *On Liberty*, in *Utilitarianism, On Liberty and Considerations on Representative Government* (London, 1972), p. 16.

16 J. S. Mill, *Principles of Political Economy, Collected Works* (Toronto, 1965), II, p. 367.

17 J. S. Mill, *System of Logic, Collected Works* (Toronto, 1974), VIII, pp. 904–5.

18 See T. H. Green, 'Popular Philosophy in its Relation to Life', in *Works*, III, pp. 92–125.

19 T. H. Green, *Prolegomena to Ethics* (1883), ed. A. C. Bradley (Oxford, 1924), para. 1. Note: All further references to this work appear in the text as *PE* followed by the paragraph number.

20 Green, 'Popular Philosophy', p. 124.

21 Mill, *Logic*, p. 842.

22 e.g. D. Nicholls, 'Positive Liberty 1880–1914', *American Political Science Review*, 57 (1962), pp. 114–28; and more recently J. Gray, *Liberalism* (Milton Keynes, 1986), p. 32.

23 T. H. Green, 'Lecture on "Liberal Legislation and Freedom of Contract"' (1881), reprinted in his *Lectures on the Principles of Political Obligation and other writings*, ed. P. Harris and J. Morrow (Cambridge, 1986), p. 202.

24 T. H. Green, 'On the Different Senses of "Freedom" as Applied to Will and to the Moral Progress of Man' (1879), reprinted in *Principles*, para. 17.

25 e.g. G. C. MacCallum, 'Negative and Positive Freedom', *Philosophical Review*, 76 (1967), pp. 312–34; W. E. Connolly, *The Terms of Political Discourse*, (Oxford, 2nd edition, 1983), pp. 143–6; T. Baldwin, 'MacCallum and the Two Concepts of Liberty', *Ratio*, 23 (1984), pp. 125–42; J. Gray, 'On Negative and Positive Liberty', *Political Studies*, 28 (1980), pp. 508–26.

26 e.g. D. Miller, 'Constraints on Freedom', *Ethics*, 94 (1983), pp. 66–86, and the

ensuing debate with F. Oppenheim, *Ethics*, 95 (1985), pp. 305–14.

27 Collini, *Liberalism and Sociology*, pp. 28–9, 46–9.

28 Mill, *Logic*, p. 841.

29 Alfred Marshall, *Principles of Economics* (London, 8th edition, 1920), p. 528; and idem, *Industrial Remuneration Conference* (1885), pp. 173–4, quoted in G. Stedman Jones, *Outcast London: A Study in the Relationship between Classes in Victorian Society* (Oxford, 1971), pp. 7, 9. On Marshall's moralistic economics, see Winch and Collini's essay, 'A Separate Science: Polity and Society in Marshall's Economics', in S. Collini, D. Winch, and J. Burrow, *That Noble Science of Politics: A Study in Nineteenth Century Intellectual History* (Cambridge, 1983), pp. 309–37.

30 Gladstone, quoted in Bradley, *The Optimists*, p. 153.

31 Green, *Lectures on the Principles of Political Obligation* (1886), paras 5–7. Note: Hereafter referred to in the text as *PO* followed by paragraph number.

32 J. Raz, *The Morality of Freedom* (Oxford, 1986), ch. 8. I have found Raz's argument generally useful for understanding Green's view of freedom.

33 For the influence of Mazzinian nationalism on Victorian Liberalism, see Harvie, *Lights of Liberalism*, ch. 5; and Bradley, *The Optimists*, ch. 5.

34 For an interesting comparison of the views of I. Kant, *Political Writings*, trans. H. Nisbet, ed. H. Reiss (Cambridge, 1977), p. 74, and for Green's views, see H. Williams, *Kant's Political Philosophy* (Oxford, 1983), pp. 129–37. Note too the analogous ideas of Mill in *Representative Government*, Ch. XVI and in the essay on Coleridge in *Dissertations and Discussions*, 3 vols, (London, 2nd edition, 1867), I, pp. 419–21.

35 A. Milne, 'The Idealist Criticism of Utilitarian Social Philosophy', *Archives Européennes de Sociologie*, 8 (1967), p. 322.

36 F. Hirsch, *Social Limits to Growth* (London, 1976). Compare the rather different criticism of Plant and Vincent, *Philosophy, Politics and Citizenship*, pp. 177–8, from whom I have borrowed this example. I spell out my differences in Bellamy, 'A Green Revolution?', p. 38.

37 H. Sidgwick, 'Green's Ethics', *Mind*, 9 (1884), pp. 183–4.

38 Green, 'Liberal Legislation', p. 196.

39 My understanding of this issue owes much to the excellent article by P. Nicholson, 'T. H. Green and State Action: Liquor Legislation', *History of Political Thought*, 6 (1985), pp. 517–50.

40 Speech at Oxford, 1872, quoted in Nicholson, 'Green and State Action', p. 539.

41 Nicholson, 'Green and State Action', pp. 525–7; Green, 'Liberal Legislation', p. 209; Nettleship, 'Memoir', p. cxvi.

42 T. H. Green, Speech to Oxford Board of Hope Union, *Alliance News*, 12 April 1879, p. 230, quoted by B. Harrison. 'State Intervention and Moral Reform in Nineteenth Century England', in P. Hollis (ed.), *Pressure From Without in Early Victorian England* (London, 1974), p. 305.

43 Green, 'Liberal Legislation', pp. 210–11.

44 Green, Letter to Harcourt, January 1873, quoted in Nicholson, 'Green and State Action', p. 542.

45 Nettleship, 'Memoir', p. cxviii; Nicholson, 'Green and State Action', pp. 520–5.

46 e.g. Mill, *On Liberty*, p. 140; H. Spencer, *Social Statics* (London, 1851), pp. 280–1, 322–6.

47 Green, 'Liberal Legislation', pp. 210, 212.

48 T. H. Green, 'The Grading of Secondary Schools' (1887), in *Works*, III, p. 387.

49 Green, 'Liberal Legislation', pp. 197–8.

50 Green, 'Liberal Legislation', pp. 203–4.

51 C. B. Macpherson, *Property: Mainstream and Critical Positions* (Toronto, 1978), pp. 203–4. My discussion follows the fine analysis of J. Morrow, 'Property and Personal

Development: an Interpretation of T. H. Green's Political Philosophy', *Politics*, 18 (1983), pp. 84–92.

52 Green, quoted in Nettleship, 'Memoir', p. cxii.

53 Green, 'Liberal Legislation', p. 205.

54 Green, quoted in Nettleship, 'Memoir', p. cxii.

55 Nettleship, 'Memoir', p. xxiv; and the views of Cobden and Bright, cited in Briggs, *Victorian People*, pp. 223, 224.

56 See S. Lukes, 'Taking Morality Seriously', in T. Honderich (ed.), *Morality and Objectivity* (London, 1986), pp. 98–109.

57 Mill, *Principles of Political Economy*, pp. 793–4; Spencer, *Social Statics*, p. 123.

58 Morrow, 'Property', p. 90, quotes the relevant passage from Green's marginal annotations of Plato, *The Republic*, Book V 464–D to this effect.

59 Green, Speech to the Oxford Reform League, reported in the *Oxford Chronicle*, 30 March 1866, and cited in Harvie, *Lights of Liberalism*, p. 118.

60 Nettleship, 'Memoir', p. cxii.

61 A. Toynbee, *Lectures on the Industrial Revolution in England* (London, 1884), p. 219.

62 For a fine study of this ambiguous Greenian legacy, with especial reference to the Charity Organization Society, see Stedman Jones, *Outcast London*, esp. Part 3.

63 Mrs Thatcher's advocacy of Victorian values is notorious, e.g. *The Standard*, April 1983. Somewhat odder has been the use made of Green by members of the Labour Party in an effort to challenge her on her own ground, e.g. R. Hattersley, *The Observer*, 24 January 1988 – an attempt I believe to be misguided.

* I am very grateful for the comments of Raymond Plant, John Morrow, Peter Nicholson, Tim Gray, and Michael Freeden on an earlier version of this paper.

Chapter nine

Gladstonianism, the provinces, and popular political culture, 1860–1906

Christopher Harvie

> [He has] a fervent imagination which furnishes facts and arguments in support
> of them: he is an audacious innovator because he has an insatiable desire for
> popularity, and in his notions he is a far more sincere republican than Bright,
> for his ungratified personal vanity makes him wish to subvert the institutions
> and the classes that stand in the way of his ambition.[1]

> The political future, or rather the future of politics, is one I look forward to
> with some want of heart. Mr G marks the close of a political era. It will be not
> only new men, but new ways of looking at things, which will mean
> unsettlement of men's minds, and an uneasy and troubled fermenting of ideas
> until they take new shape.
>
> Things point to a reconstruction of the parties, and to an entirely new view
> of things. Land, Church, Parliament, the relations of labour, our whole social
> system seems to be in the crucible.[2]

The first of these quotes dates from the beginning of Gladstone's formal membership of the Liberal Party; the second from the aftermath of his resignation in
1895. The odd thing is that the dates could almost be reversed. Charles Greville's
vision of Gladstone as a disruptive, demagogic force seemed the conventional
wisdom of the English political and administrative elite in the 1880s and 1890s,[3]
while in the 1860s Charles Roundell, then in charge of the campaign to repeal the
University Tests Act, found the former Burgess of the University the same deeply
entrenched conservative who 'would rather see Oxford level with the ground than
its religion regulated in a manner which would please Bishop Colenso.'[4]
This ambiguity makes any discussion of the intellectual content of Gladstonianism very difficult. The elite reacted with predictable hostility to Gladstone's
declaration in 1886 that his policy of Irish Home Rule implied a struggle between
'the classes and the masses', yet the same Gladstone could write, six years later:

> The natural condition of a healthy society is that governing functions should
> be discharged by a leisured class. In matters where the narrow interests of that
> class seem to be concerned, it has its besetting sins and dangers. But for the
> general business of government it has peculiar capacities; and whatever

control a good system may impose, by popular suffrage, by gathering representation from all classes, by tradition, or opinion, or the press, yet, when the leisured class is depressed, that fact indicates that a rot has found its way into the structure of society.[5]

This was the man whose portrait stared down from millions of artisan parlour walls, and whose memory, more than that of Keir Hardie (or, I suspect, Queen Victoria) was cherished in working-class homes into the second half of the twentieth century.[6] 'The greatest man', the Scottish miners' leader Bob Smillie – not a 'Lib-Lab' but a pioneer socialist – had ever met was Gladstone, followed by Sir Henry Campbell-Bannerman.[7] Yet the Gladstone cult was not a 'national' but a northern and western phenomenon, and was muted in London and the south-east.[8] Gladstonian Britain, after 1886, corresponded to anti-Thatcher Britain in 1988: a fact – as I hope to prove – of more than coincidental interest. [9]

Gladstone could be described in European terms as a nationalist politician, comparable with Bismarck or Cavour, but only so far. Although Colin Matthew writes that 'his acute sense of organic and historicist nationality ... meant that the acceptance of nationality was his starting-point',[10] he admits that his ultimate beliefs, as stated in 1870, were supra-national:

> The greatest triumph of our time, a triumph in a region loftier than that of electricity or steam, will be the enthronement of (the) idea of Public Right, as the governing idea of European policy; as the common and precious inheritance of all lands, but superior to the passing opinion of any.[11]

Was it this moralism which made Bismarck repeatedly summon up a 'Gladstone ministry' as a phantom with which to threaten his conservative Prussian allies in the 1880s?[12] Or was he more realistic in discounting it?

> If reactionary measures are to be carried, the Liberal party takes the rudder, from the correct assumption that it will not overstep the necessary limits; if liberal measures are to be carried, the Conservative party takes office in its turn from the same consideration.[13]

Contemporary English Conservatives were less complacent. Echoing Greville, bureaucratic ex-liberals like Sir Henry Maine saw the 'new radicalism' which Gladstone had helped create as 'entirely fluid, taking all shape and direction from the accidental and temporary pressure of great masses of ignorant and impulsive men'.[14] This pioneering, elite-oriented, interpretation regarded Gladstone essentially as a demagogue whose ambitions might ultimately be both autocratic and socialistic; it passed via the Liberal Unionist intellectuals of 1886[15] (many of whom had always had their doubts) to the sociological study of the Liberal Party by Mosei Ostrogorski in 1899, and via him to that fundamental text of 'British' descriptive political analysis, Graham Wallas's *Human Nature in Politics*, in 1908. In Ostrogorski's view, Gladstone both goaded and was goaded by the electorate to overthrow the old Whig–Liberal oligarchy:

The tone of profound emotion and the fiery passion ... supplied the masses with the strong sensations which they thirst for, and his fighting temperament ... flattered even the less elevated instincts of combativeness common to all English crowds more than any others.[16]

Wallas, writing his unpublished *Prolegomenon to Politics* (1899), fitted Gladstone's career into the pessimistic interpretations of mass politics adumbrated by Ernest Renan and Gustave le Bon:

Ordinary human nature stood revealed as undynamic and incompetent, politically helpless without the leader and the expert. Government appeared an art relying on advertisement and acting, rather than a clear and reasonable proceeding. Gladstone's great popular success, for example, appeared in this light to have rested more on his ability as an actor and self-advertiser, than on his politics.[17]

Gladstone himself was oblivious to all this. The Oxford dons who entertained him in 1890 found him amiably reactionary,[18] asserting that 'the country had never been better governed than in the period preceding the first Reform Bill', and that the unreformed House of Commons would have carried all the great measures of 1830 to 1880.[19] Seven years later, communicating with the editors of *Essays in Liberalism*, 'by Six Oxford Men', he assured Hilaire Belloc, F. W. Hirst, J. L. Hammond, and their friends that

I regard the design formed by you and your friends with sincere interest, and in particular wish well to all the efforts you may make on behalf of individual freedom and Independence as opposed to what is termed Collectivism.[20]

Social reformers were correspondingly annoyed by a leader who purposively distanced himself from their 'New Liberalism'. 'Socialism was, to Gladstone, an abomination', wrote G. W. E. Russell.

Endeavouring to parry a question which must leave revealed my own guilt, I feebly asked if by Socialism my venerable Leader meant the practice of taking private property for public uses, or the performance by the state of what ought to be left to the individual; whereupon he replied, with startling emphasis: 'I mean both, but I reserve my worst Billingsgate for the attack on private property'.[21]

Professor John Vincent has drawn from this a portrait of an aristocrat, deeply imbued with the values of landed society, whose greatest success, in 1886, was to stop Radicalism in its tracks and preserve the autonomy of a parliamentary politics which habitually disregarded the rank and file.[22] But although Gladstone remained on good terms with serious-minded aristocrats and Treasury civil servants 'of the old school' after 1886, his popularity among Liberal activists nevertheless transformed an unpopular cause like Irish Home Rule into a weapon which disposed of many of his most articulate rivals. The Radical-Unionist

Leonard Courtney wrote to Mrs Millicent Fawcett that no matter how sceptical about Home Rule his Cornish electors were, Gladstone's advocacy of it would keep them loyal to Liberalism.[23]

In 1893, A. V. Dicey denounced Gladstone's Home Rule Bills as an 'alliance with revolutionists or conspirators' which had 'imbued respectable English statesmen with revolutionary doctrines and revolutionary sentiment'[24] and party activists later regretted that they had been imbued with too much Gladstone. In the disaster year of 1923, Ramsay Muir was to write to H. A. L. Fisher:

> I believe we have thought too much about leaders and organisation, and enquired too little: this has been the malady of the Liberal party for a long time – I put it down to the tremendous personal ascendancy of Gladstone, which was mischievous in the long run.[25]

Granted this situation, did the paradox of Gladstone the social reactionary and political revolutionary contribute to the failures in cohesion which were to exclude the Liberals from power from 1886 to 1905? We have to remember that, when Liberalism finally made its landslide breakthrough, in 1906, it was not on a collectivist programme but by exploiting the reaction against imperial aggrandizement in South Africa, and opposition to unsound finance in the shape of Joseph Chamberlain and tariff reform. And such Gladstonian texts, all the more telling because of the absence of a Gladstone to preach them, were to preface a period of near-revolutionary political transformation.

II

It is not only difficult but actually unhelpful to disentangle 'Gladstonianism' from the personality of Gladstone himself, and the quality of his political praxis. John Vincent wrote of him that, in the 1860s,

> So quickly did he evolve, that differing impressions, mutually exclusive in the long run, but all favourable, were coexistent in the minds of great classes, and Gladstone obtained that support of the general interest he looked for, from a party which was a confederation of all classes, each acting in their own interest. By the velocity of his evolution towards many-sidedness, he temporarily squared the political circle.[26]

And D. A. Hamer, in his study of the later phase of Liberalism, assessed his outstanding quality as the ability to fuse the form and content of policy out of a complex range of highly differentiated ingredients.[27] Gladstonianism without Gladstone is as improbable as Italian unification without Cavour or German nationalism without Bismarck. But although Gladstone occupied a comparable position in the evolution of his own country's polity, the result was not liberalism or nationalism but something deeply personal.

Who, for example, were Gladstone's legatees? The Liberal Imperialists exclude themselves almost by definition; that removes Rosebery, Asquith, Arthur

Acland, and Haldane. Harcourt and Granville accepted Home Rule, but were otherwise Whigs. Morley, as biographer, helped to create the tabernacle but parted from the master as an agnostic and an explicit elitist (which accorded ill with an unsuitable private life). Goschen shared the financial expertise but, by 1886, had become deeply reactionary and bellicose. Campbell-Bannerman had most of the Gladstonian qualifications, but in a very effete form. Lord Acton and James Bryce, two men of equivalent intellect, were both destined to remain on the political fringe. In fact, Gladstone's ideological successors are to be found among what A. J. P. Taylor called the 'high-minded' who wrote for the *Manchester Guardian*, agonized over the First World War, and aligned themselves with the Bryce Memorandum and Woodrow Wilson's attempt to inject 'the idea of Public Right' into international relations. These included those post-war 'converts to Labour', C. P. Trevelyan, Sir George Young, Arthur Ponsonby, Philip Noel-Baker, and indeed Acton's heir, Richard.[28] Gladstonian moralism also seems to have proved stronger than any residues of collectivist New Liberalism in keeping stalwarts of post-Asquithian Liberalism, like G. M. Trevelyan, Gilbert Murray, and Ramsay Muir, attached to such institutions as the Liberal summer schools and the League of Nations – an impulse which drew in another High Church Conservative-turned-foreign policy moralist, who was to become a fixture on centre-left platforms, Lord Robert Cecil.

But if we attempt to tease out an ideology from this, what do we find? In a famous statement of 1891, recorded by Morley, Gladstone declared impeccably Millite sentiments:

> I can truly put up all the change that has come into my politics into a sentence; I was brought up to dislike and distrust Liberty, I learned to believe in it. That is the key to all my changes.[29]

Yet Morley constructed in the *Life* a much more symmetrical progress towards democracy than the evidence really suggested. D. M. Schreuder suggests that even in the 1890s, '"Gladstonian Liberalism" was as much atavistic and conservationist in its content as progressive and "liberal"'[30] – a commitment to the 'masses' not just contradicted by conservative table-talk but by, say, positions of principle on such questions as woman suffrage,[31] something which brought him closer to Morley's former Positivist colleagues than to Millite principles.

This does not, however, augur for a Spencerian, or Hayekian, version of non-democratic liberalism. Gladstone had no conception of absolute rights in property. In contradistinction to Vincent's portrait of a landed aristocrat, he deplored inheritance and, like his friend Thomas Carnegie, regarded individual property as a trust to be stewarded, and ultimately donated, for the public good.[32] Herbert Spencer found Gladstone distinctly over-susceptible to the lure of democracy and state action;[33] indeed, the powers reserved to the state in his railway legislation of 1844, when he was a Tory at the Board of Trade, were considerable, in what was more a controlled system of private regional monopolies than a competitive structure.[34] Although subsequent development was limited, apart from some extension of Post Office powers, the 'right' of popular control remained, exemplified by the 1881 Irish Land Act, to distress 'old Liberals' of the type of Sir Henry Maine, who believed that:

> The sociological rule which affirms that the progress of society is from status to contract only expresses one aspect of the truth that societies in time become civilised and free because the individuals contained in them learn to manage their own affairs, instead of requiring other persons to manage for them.[35]

The Land Act prompted from T. H. Green an address on 'Liberal Legislation and Freedom of Contract', which became influential when published in 1885, three years after his death. Green, a solid party Liberal and pillar of the Oxford Caucus (the prototype of the 'Lecturer-in-Social-Policy-as-Minutes-Secretary' type that holds the contemporary Labour Party together) was providing an *ex-post facto* argument for Gladstone's measure, which was subsequently prospected for useful justifications of 'New Liberalism' of the Hobhouse–Beveridge sort.[36] He argued that freedom of contract must be constrained by the state, to establish some parity of opportunity between the parties:

> not indeed directly to promote moral goodness, for that, from the very nature of moral goodness, it cannot do, ... but to maintain the conditions without which a free exercise of the human faculties is impossible.
> ... given a certain standard of moral and material well-being, people may be trusted not to sell their labour, or the labour of their children, on terms which would not allow that standard to be maintained.[37]

In comparison with his anti-collectivist rhetoric, it is difficult to find any 'positive' formulation of Gladstone's which is as clear-cut. In *A Chapter of Autobiography* he wrote:

> the action of man in the State is moral, as truly as it is in the individual sphere; although it be limited by the fact that, as he is combined with others whose views and wills may differ from his own, the sphere of the common operations must be limited, first, to the things in which all are agreed; secondly, to the things in which, though they may not be agreed, yet equity points out, and the public sense acknowledges, that the whole should be bound by the sense of the majority.[38]

As political philosophy this is meaningless but, for Gladstone the politician, usefully flexible. In the case of land reform, as later over miners' working hours, he was able to make up his mind on the specific circumstances of the situation, and an intuitive empathy with Irish peasants or miners, rather than let doctrine wrong foot him.[39]

The third element, Gladstone's political Christianity, may mirror the religiosity of Victorian Britain; but in the elite, the older loyalties of family and sexual relationships, patronage, caste expertise (within such groups as the diplomats), and atavistic patriotism, still personified by men like Melbourne, Palmerston, and Hartington, weighed as heavily as upper-class piety. Nonconformity created a new, popular force, but its parliamentary representation remained low until the 1880s. It tended to sectarianism, and no sooner had it repaired the damage of the 1857 election when Palmerstonian patriotism saw off Bright and Cobden, than the 1870 Education Act sent it into sulks, leaving it to Gladstone, in his campaigns on foreign policy in the late 1870s, to forge a religious alliance broad- and high-minded enough to be spiritually generous – a political analogue to, as well as an organizational development from, the ecumenical evangelizing of the Americans Moody and Sankey in 1873–4.

Even this, however, was not straightforward. The politics of organized dissent, maturing by the 1890s, were imperialistic, and Robertson Nicoll, their chief press publicist in *The British Weekly*, expressed deep hostility to Gladstone – 'the greatest curse of the country ... while he lingers on plotting and scheming'.[40] In 1914 he still could not understand

> how anyone who has studied Gladstone's career can fail to see that he regarded Dissenters with something like loathing. He knew that he was mainly indebted to them for his political victories; he knew that they took his side and made it possible for him to prevail in causes that lay nearest his heart. Under extreme exigencies he would even compliment them and tolerate their company. But he never made a real friend, so far as I know, of any Dissenter.[41]

More sympathetic figures appreciated his political support and his endorsement of nonconformist aims. They remained puzzled about how he attained this position.

III

Any attempt at an ideological analysis of what L. T. Hobhouse defined as 'a moral rather than an intellectual force'[42] can only yield meagre results. The young Oxford essayists of 1897, even with Gladstone's blessing, found it very difficult to say much about his contribution to Liberalism. Nevertheless, Robertson Nicoll could acknowledge the effect of Gladstone in action:

> If I had not heard Gladstone in Midlothian I should have lived and died without the faintest conception of what human speech can do. At that time Gladstone simply maddened his audiences. He welded them into a unity, wild with passion, ready to follow him even to the death.[43]

Nicoll substantiates a plethora of claims about Gladstone's political personality: his 'superhuman qualities', the remarkable eyes 'as may be seen in a bird of prey', his physical strength, exemplified in walking and tree-felling at Hawarden, his powers of endurance, linguistic ability, and mental concentration.[44] Goldwin Smith, a virulent opponent for the last twelve years of Gladstone's career, paid tribute to his enormous stamina, recollecting a day in 1855 when Gladstone spent six and a half hours working with him on the Oxford University Bill, and one and a half hours at a Privy Council, then went to spend the evening at the Commons and, as Chancellor of the Exchequer, reply to the debate at 1 a.m.[45] 'The voice', Smith admitted, 'the manner, the bearing of the orator were supreme, and filled even the most adverse listener with delight.'[46]

Such tributes do more to recreate the man than speeches in cold print – although print still shows the skills which 'brought facts into touch with humanity' and flattened the young Lloyd George in 1890. The new MP, on a day trip to Hawarden, had tried to browbeat Gladstone into declaring himself on Welsh disestablishment:

> Could Mr Lloyd George, obviously an authority on Welsh nonconformity, tell him how many nonconformist chapels there were in Wales in 1742? The answer, 105, Lloyd George did not have.[47]

But this reverential anecdotage embellishes technical accomplishments in British politics which were both fundamental and definitive. From the 1860s onwards parliament functioned in a frame created by Gladstone as Chancellor in which public expenditure and inter-departmental relations were governed by strict and transparent rules laid down by the Treasury and enforced by the Public Accounts Committee of the Commons.[48] In the early 1880s, he elaborated this by establishing the Cabinet's authority over the Commons, and the Prime Minister's authority over the Cabinet. In 1892, Sir Henry Campbell-Bannerman could write that 'the government is being formed for the special purpose of enabling Mr Gladstone to carry out his ideas: it is in an unusual degree *his* government.'[49] This proposition, confirmed by what actually happened when Gladstone stood down in 1894, was unthinkable in the 1860s, when the Cabinet was assumed to be a committee of equals, any one of whom could summon it, or in the 1870s, when extra-parliamentary political organizations challenged the autonomy of the elite.[50]

J. L. Hammond regarded these achievements as contradictory: the Treasury technician frustrated the magnanimous statesman who might have settled the Irish problem.[51] Yet, in the first place, Colin Matthew has pointed out that Gladstone's departmental reforms both responded to, and furthered the shift away from, patronage as the main activity of government,[52] something which inevitably brought further demands for legislation as groups which could no longer be ignored or bought off had to be 'incorporated'. Under pressure from the crises thus provoked, 'Gladstonianism' could be remarkably elastic, stretched to its limits in regard to Ireland. As he rose to dominance in the 1880s, Gladstone the moralist perceived malfunctions and injustices in the structure of the British state, and evolved conceptions of liberty and equity beyond the customary values of Westminster: a'European sense' which led him to the pluralism implied by Home Rule.

The intellect was converted even if the technician was frustrated. Both phases suggest – and certainly suggested to Gladstone – a symbiotic, intuitive relationship between personality and doctrine. In 1876, following controversies with Herbert Spencer and Frederic Harrison, he criticized positivism in an article on 'Courses of Religious Thought' in the *Contemporary Review*:

> Schemes, then, may suffice for the moral wants of a few intellectual and cultivated men, which cannot be propagated, and cannot be transmitted; which cannot bear the wear and tear of constant re-delivery; which cannot meet the countless and ever-shifting exigencies of our nature taken at large; which cannot do the rough work of the world.[53]

Gladstone did not, however, substitute the cyclical pattern of the real conservative that Disraeli preached in his novels, *Tancred* in particular. Gladstone believed that progress was linear. In 1868, defending his change of mind on the Irish Church, he argued, in terms not far from those of Saint Simon, Comte, and Mill, that the transition 'from a stationary to a progressive period' inevitably promoted 'instances of what is called political inconsistency'. The mark of the statesman was intuitively to abstract what made for justice from 'the seething public mind'.[54] In other words, he accepted the 'positivist' notion of progression in history, but regurgitated it in an idiosyncratic, personal form.

Gladstone invested the role of the statesman-orator in this process with a mystical gloss:

> [The work of the orator] is cast in the mould offered to him by the mind of his hearers. It is an influence principally received from his audience (so to speak) in vapour, which he pours back upon them in a flood.

Beneath which he was realistic:

> The sympathy and concurrence of his time is, with his own mind, joint parent of the work. He cannot follow nor frame deals: his choice is, to be what his age will have him, what it requires in order to be moved by him; or else not to be at all.[55]

Gladstone was very careful to prepare his era for himself. His rise in the 1860s owed much to careful cultivation of the new middle-class daily press; and Mid-lothian was, at one level, a brilliant use of the railway system, which delivered crowds and newspapers, and enabled a 'whistle-stop' triumph on American lines. The key to Gladstonianism as a phenomenon in British Liberal politics thus lies in his appreciation of 'transition' – the tension between a fluid political public (or publics) and a more rigid parliamentary machine, rather than in the internal logic of the ideas he mediated. Although Gladstone functioned in a stable constitutional monarchy, Max Weber's concept of 'charismatic leadership' has a particular relevance to his extra-parliamentary politics, where the

> *extraordinary* quality of a person, regardless of whether this quality is actual, alleged or presumed. ... to which the governed submit because of their belief

in the extraordinary quality of the specific *person*. ... rests upon the belief in magical powers, revelations and hero worship ...

Weber went on to argue that

> Charismatic rule is not managed according to general norms, either traditional or rational ... and in this sense is 'irrational'. It is 'revolutionary' in the sense of not being bound to the existing order.[56]

The terms are very similar to those employed by Gladstone's critics in the 1880s. But the quality of Gladstone's persona was only part of the myth. Just as significant was the problematic political community he addressed, which registered not simply the impact of industrialization and reform, but the peculiarly complex civil society of a multinational state whose components operated at different levels of political development.

IV

'The Grand Old Man', 'the People's William', 'the Old Parliamentary Hand': among the appellations of Gladstone's 'revolutionary' decades, the last suggests less charismatic features. For John Vincent, in his study of the politics of Home Rule, the idol of the Treasury and the magus of the provinces were triumphantly combined in 1886, when 'a sane, balanced, good-humoured but old-fashioned old gentleman' saw off both the Whig and the Radical challenges to what really mattered: his hegemony in the Liberal Party. He limited the damage that the dissidents could do, manoeuvred the Home Rule issue to confine the most dangerous of them, and kept the majority of the party loyal.[57] The threat of Chamberlain and the Caucuses, embodied in the 'Unauthorized Programme' of 1885, ended with centralization actually being enhanced. An elite from both political parties combined to concentrate public attention on the sort of issue it enjoyed coping with: 'The Irish issue kept the economy out of politics. It enabled the politicians to avoid making any response to the real aching crisis of the mid-1880s'.[58] In the conspectus of *The Governing Passion*, a key text of the 'High Politics' or 'High Tory' school of historical interpretation, Home Rule itself (a programme which Vincent regards as never having got past the 'discussion stage') was a battle Gladstone never intended to win.

Gladstone was always an adroit performer, one of whose standard tactics was to crush an opponent, and then generously adopt his cause. The university reformers had learned this in the 1860s; Lloyd George would do so in the 1890s. Goldwin Smith certainly wrote that Gladstone sponsored Home Rule because he 'was a party leader; a full believer in the party system; and his party wanted to prevail over its rival. It is only by contention for power that party government can be carried on.'[59] This would bear out Vincent's line, had it been articulated in 1886; in fact, Goldwin Smith's propaganda for the Unionist cause reached a pitch of frenzy which cost him most of his Gladstonian friends.[60] He was not alone.

G. M. Trevelyan, then a mature ten-year-old, recollected that his father, George Otto Trevelyan, who, after a brief period as a Unionist had returned to the Gladstonian fold, had to face

> The violence of the upper-class reaction against the Liberals, the common abuse of our Irish fellow-subjects employed as common stock-in-trade, the nascent 'Imperialism' of the revised Tory party. ... The intellectual and literary society of London and the Universities which he had lived and moved in all his life had been mainly Liberal; it now became mainly Unionist, nourishing hot detestation of Gladstone and moral reprobation of his fellows.[61]

The younger Trevelyan was enough of a Home Ruler to sign his letters GSI – 'God Save Ireland'.[62] Was he duped by an issue that, Vincent assures us, was rarely treated seriously by political professionals (although he admits an inability to record the daily political pabulum of non-diary-keeping politicians)?[63] If so, the deception went wide. Labour men with an interest in politics were overwhelmingly sympathetic. The Catholic Irish in mainland Britain were decisively won over to the Liberals, and the Scots, Welsh, and Northerners stayed loyal. Thereafter, calling oneself a Home Ruler was an explicit declaration of Radicalism, while the notion of a 'radical Unionist' vanished within a couple of years.[64]

If Gladstone did not take Home Rule seriously, the secret was effectively kept from publicists and literary men whom he had habitually treated with respect.[65] Their propaganda was remarkable for the emotion expressed by men who usually advertised their dispassionate qualities. The geologist John Tyndall wrote to *The Times* in June 1887:

> A former worshipper of the ex-Prime Minister said to me some time ago 'Never in the history of England was there such a consensus of intellect arrayed against statesmen as is now arrayed against Mr Gladstone. What a fall. I rejoice to find this unanimity of judgement so specially illustrated among scientific men.'[66]

This was par for the course. Matthew Arnold, in 'The Nadir of Liberalism', assaulted Gladstone as 'fantastic', 'unsound', 'unsuccessful', 'dangerous',[67] much inferior to Bismarck: a man with no foresight 'because he has no insight' leading 'a party of bounded and backward mind'.[68] This was typical of the anti-liberal tone of the English metropolitan *literati* from Swinburne to Spurgeon. Vincent dismisses this as a diversion from main political business. It was not. Academic and intellectual endorsement is important in the formation of even the lower levels of 'public doctrine' (Professor Vincent has done his bit for Mrs Thatcher in his column in the *Sun*) and the defeat of Home Rule marked, as Trevelyan implied, a rightward shift which endured more or less until the Boer War, and incubated the authoritarian imperialism of W. E. Henley, W. H. Mallock, Rudyard Kipling, Benjamin Kidd, and J. A. Cramb.

V

1886 was a defeat for Gladstone and Liberalism, and Gladstone felt it. He believed he would win the 1886 election handsomely, and was surprised when (probably because of unexpectedly inept management in the recently redistributed constituencies which enabled many Unionists to be returned unopposed) he did not.[69] This suggests a much less ideological explanation of the Liberal split than that recently proffered by J. P. Parry, who sees 1886 as a final parting of the ways between a moderate 'Whig-Liberalism', essentially Erastian in its religious view, which 'did not believe it was desirable to sweep away all the securities for order which many radicals wished to destroy',[70] and a Gladstonianism which had sold out to sectarian Radicalism. But by substituting ideology for family and patronage, Parry's 'Whig-liberalism' is ultimately less precise than John Roach's 'old liberalism'. Among university intellectuals, for instance, the division over Home Rule was less ideological than situational, with those integrated into the party system much more likely to follow Gladstone than those who remained in academic or literary life.[71] Matthew Arnold's description of Gladstone as 'a captivating, a fascinating personality' presents a more plausible clue to the state of 1880s Liberalism than ideological fissure or conspiracy theory.

A. P. Thornton has written, not wholly flippantly, that the humourlessness of the new generation of imperialist, self-consciously elitist politicians set them apart from the charm and informality of Gladstone.[72] This approachability may have been the signature of supreme confidence, or it may have been the shrug of a man conscious of the mismatch between the task before him – the taming of the Lords – and his own failing powers. But there are two things to be said about it. First, Gladstone stood apart from the 'scientistic' racialism which, with its 'national efficiency' correlates, became pervasive at this time in British politics, especially in imperial and Unionist circles. 'The Anglo-Saxon stereotype of the Irish Celt', L. P. Curtis argues, 'really killed Home Rule in 1886 and 1894';[73] *The Times*, *Punch*, and the *Spectator* in the 1880s and 1890s do not make pleasant reading. Secondly, Gladstone's 'public doctrine' had come to represent a concept of nationalism which, sincerely and confidently held by him and reciprocated by his public, still distanced him from the political elite and its proconsular style.

Viewed as a 'captivating' extension of personality in London, Gladstone's politics take on an altogether sharper profile in the areas which provided his strongest support at the end of his career. According to Kenneth Morgan his outlook shows

> that the dominating influence upon him, in Wales as in Ireland, Italy or Bulgaria, was the mighty force of nationalism. More sensitively and more passionately than any other figure in political life, he responded to the cries of struggling nationhood.[74]

This has to be located in the context of a multinational Britain, and in a Scottish identity which has, in the biographies, a curious, flickering quality. Goldwin Smith and Bryce granted it importance; Morley went back as far as he could into the family antecedents.[75] Others, like J. L. Hammond and Erich Eyck, ignored it altogether, and most of the rest followed Morley in implying that any such imprinting did not matter very much ('we may perhaps find a sort of explanation') after Gladstone had gone through the mill at Eton, Oxford and High Church Anglicanism.[76]

There are two reasons why this should be revised. Gladstone's upbringing occurred at a peculiar juncture and was uncharacteristic of the English elite. Raised in the inter-married Scottish exile community of Liverpool, he was the result of a union of Highland and Lowland Scots: half-Celt, in an age peculiarly sensitive to race; evangelical and liberal (Morley implies) on his father's side; Episcopalian and Jacobite on his mother's.[77] The family evolution into Toryism made sense when, under pressure of Jacobinism and the Napoleonic War, the provincial bourgeoisie was co-opted – indeed, demanded that it be co-opted – into the governing elite. But an evangelical like John Gladstone was probably more at home as an evangelical Anglican than under the 'moderate', Erastian Kirk,[78] and befriended Dr Thomas Chalmers, the leader of the Evangelical party in the Kirk, *after* 'going over'. Chalmers stayed with the Gladstones in Liverpool in 1817 and became an important influence on William, who spent some time in theological study in Edinburgh in 1828, before matriculating at Oxford, at a time when Chalmers' defence of establishment was at its most strenuous.[79]

Chalmers, who occupied a position in Scotland cognate with that of O'Connell in Ireland, was comparable as a political personality, and Gladstone's description of him has an autobiographical ring:

He has a mind keenly susceptible of what is beautiful, great and good; tenacious of an idea when once grasped, and with a singular power of concentrating the whole man upon it.[80]

But Chalmers, like Gladstone profoundly influenced by Bishop Butler, was also preoccupied with 'the Godly Commonwealth', in which the relationship of church and state embodied the role of conscience in the conduct and organization of social life. When Gladstone regarded disestablishment as removing 'the one great anti-septic element'[81] from the profession of the politician, Chalmers could only have given unqualified assent.

Although it was Gladstone's dissent from Chalmers' 1838 London lectures on the equality of Presbyterian and Episcopalian establishments – he described them as 'a jumble of church, un-church and anti-church principles' – that spurred the writing of *The State in its Relation to the Church*, or most of Gladstone's formal contribution to political theory (the rest being devoted to repudiating it), Gladstone and Chalmers had more in common, in both faith and practice, than what separated them.[82]

Rather than the Tractarian movement, it was Chalmers' economic ideas –

economic freedom together with the transformation of individual benevolence into charity organization and social casework – that worked themselves deeply into Gladstone's life. The night missions in London to rescue prostitutes made as much sense in Chalmers' doctrine as in Freudian psychology, and what Matthews regards as the apogee of Gladstonian 'retrenchment', his partnership in 1869 with Goschen at the Local Government Board in helping set up the Charity Organization Society, had a direct Chalmersian pedigree.[83]

In this context even Gladstone's transition to High Church Anglicanism in the 1830s, which preceded by two years Keble's Assize Sermon from which the Oxford Movement is usually dated, can be seen, in part, as a Scottish response to the political crisis. Within his circle at Oxford Henry Moncrieff and James Hope provided a strong Scottish element; after 1829, the Gladstone 'home base' was Fasque and Edinburgh;[84] and his Toryism – 'rather melancholy and severe, than violent or ultra in the ordinary sense of these words'[85] – emerged at a time when the Conservative order in Scotland was in the process of utter destruction. Later, Gladstone would characterize the 1832 Reform Act as a 'political birth, the beginning of a duty and a power, neither of which had attached to the Scottish nation in the preceding period'.[86] At the time, the dissolution of the old Scottish political system must have seemed as appalling as it did to both of Gladstone's coadjutors in Scottish affairs, Sir Walter Scott (whose novels he read constantly) and Chalmers, who moved across to the Tories in response to the Whig-Radical threat to disestablish the Kirk.[87] Gladstone can be seen, in short, as one of a group of Scots (Carlyle and Edward Irving were others) entrapped and bewildered by a sequence of political changes which, for good or ill, destroyed the society they knew.

How much did this threat of Durkheimian anomie provoke a therapeutic, if predominantly intellectual, transfer of nationality to the larger, English unit?[88] The resulting dualism would explain both the extreme length of his justification of Anglicanism, and the speed with which it was abandoned when it outlived its political purpose: over Oxford University reform in the 1850s and the Church of Ireland in the 1860s. The other face of Gladstone's acclimatization was his real mastery, inculcated by Sir Robert Peel, of parliament and administration, the secular arm of the English establishment – an intellectual conversion, but one soon legitimated by his own competence.[89]

'The key to my position', he later commented, 'was that my opinions went one way, my lingering sympathies the other.'[90] These 'sympathies' are usually understood to refer to Anglicanism, yet the Fasque- and Edinburgh-based Gladstone was, in a very real sense, a member of the Scottish Episcopalian church and deeply alert to other developments in Scottish church politics. The large files of correspondence with Bishop Skinner, Bishop Forbes, and Dean Ramsay, among others, are the bulkiest and most neglected parts of Gladstone's papers, but they contain significant indicators to his ultimate political position. Shortly before the traumatic year of 1845, when Newman 'went over', Gladstone paid a tribute to the Free Church of Scotland, which in 1843 Chalmers had led out of the Kirk:

here are great masses of men ready to offer the sacrifices of faith according to their power, and beyond their power: with one heart and with one soul; and that for the sake of a system, with regard to which we contend that its appeal, however elevated and touching it may be, has not the Divine authority which we know to belong to the Body of Christ.[91]

To turn from this to the poverty and poor education of the Episcopalian clergy was salutary: 'Can there be found on the face of the earth a more disgraceful contrast?'[92] Gladstone's anti-Erastian argument, which reserved to the church its own corporate and spiritual identity, endorsed in part Chalmers' claim that the Church of Scotland should have its own legislative authority, separate from that of the state. Gladstone had been familiar with this argument in the 1830s, when Chalmers had frequently consulted him on the issues of lay patronage and parliamentary supremacy. In 1851, with the example of the Free Church clearly in mind, he sketched out to Bishop Skinner of Aberdeen the reform of the Scottish Episcopalian church in terms which, more than any other pronouncement of the period, show his openness to political reform. Given that the churches had in general 'made a composition with the world for half a gospel':

They herewith present this peculiar feature that, as in civil so in spiritual matters, they tend to devolve on the governed a portion of the work of government. It is that tendency which working without method or control that makes the period revolutionary: but which, when kept within due bounds and trained to act within stable and well-adjusted laws, seems capable of being so used as to give increased vigour to legitimate authority along with increased scope to reasonable freedom.[93]

From this there followed a plea for 'a constitutional system' as 'the great Providential instrument for effective resistance to anarchical designs'.[94] But what sort of constitution? For Morley this was plainly an endorsement of parliamentarianism, but 1851 was an early station on Gladstone's pilgrimage to Liberalism. The essentially aristocratic reforms of the universities and the civil service were still to come. 'On the Functions of Laymen' assumed, rather, that political activity was diffused among institutions, of which the Churches were as important as parliament. This concept was later to be used by Harold Laski, along with the political theory of the Oxford Movement, as an important argument for political pluralism, which could have provided philosophic justification for the ultimate Gladstonian millennium of 'Home Rule all round'.[95] The intellectual processes of both essays may be tortuous, but the emotions they convey foreshadow the appeal to be made, forty years later, to the 'masses' against the 'classes'.

The second 'Scottish' element in Gladstone's politics, while less tangible, stems from the same religious tradition. The church conflict was, on one level, a catastrophe which distorted party conflict into religious wrangling and retarded

Scotland's political development for sixty years; but on another, it educated a people long divorced from political participation, and provided the first issue for a century to unite Lowlands and Highlands. The Free Church's publicists and academics both enhanced the Celtic element in Scottish history and restored to the Calvinist tradition a status lost in the eighteenth century. While they stressed the inspired nature of scripture, they also demanded a high standard of exegesis as part of a rigorous academic preparation for a ministry skilled enough to defend religion against the assaults of secular science.[96] The result was an intellectual community as close to Gladstone as it was remote from the British secular intelligentsia. Not only did the Free Kirk's anthropological research on the Old Testament soon attain a European reputation, the folklorist and editor, Hugh Miller, the Free Kirk's leading publicist, saw the evangelical revival and the 'Ten Years' Conflict' causing legends of supernatural power akin to those of the early Celtic saints to cling to the 'men', the religious laymen who had stood up against the lairds and 'moderate' ministers in the Highland parishes.[97] This suggests that the later mutual regard of Gladstone and the 'masses' may have had deeper roots in such quasi-mystical definitions of an 'inspired community' as the 'men', the Welsh 'gwerin', the 'folk' of Lowland Scotland, than in any anticipation of class politics.

To consider Gladstonianism retrospectively is to realize that between 1800 and 1832 party politics within the British Isles had suddenly been extended to communities whose consciousness was religious, or legendary, whose traditions were (or had recently been) conveyed orally, and whose first language was often not English. During Gladstone's political apprenticeship the Celtic fringe – 45 per cent of the total population in 1841 – was bidding to overtake the English, so it was quite appropriate that, while one part of his synoptic mind mastered parliament and administration, another registered the Scottish Church question, and a third 'Ireland, that cloud in the west, that coming storm, the minister of God's retribution upon cruel and inveterate and but half-atoned injustice'.[98] Moreover, in his Homer and Dante studies, he explored what seemed a valid mode of communication, a 'communal homeland'[99] of epic that the nineteenth-century statesman could still share with the oral tradition.

Gladstone's Homeric studies were not unique among Victorian statesmen reared as they were in the public schools, although they seem peculiarly Casaubon-like in their rejection of modern classical scholarship in favour of an attempt to combine the Greek epics with Christian revelation. Yet to him Homer was alive. The epics were 'a world of religion and ethics, of civil policy, of history and ethnology, of manners and arts'[100] full of precepts for contemporary issues. He admired their 'intense political spirit':

> It is the very picture before our own eyes in our own time and country, where visible traces of the old patriarchal mode still coexist ... with political liberties of more recent fashion, because they retain their hold on the general affections.[101]

Nor was he one to resist being cast as patriarch himself, representing, in communities which lacked political institutions, an 'heroic' force around which the people could rally.

From Dante, whom he regarded as the bridge between the mythic and the modern, Gladstone adopted a concept of nationality which was subordinated to a European ideal of Christendom – supposedly inhering in the Holy Roman Empire – rather than a narrow British patriotism.[102] This allowed him to involve himself in Scots, Welsh, or Irish politics while also representing a 'constructive' engagement in foreign affairs, promoting national self-government 'upon what remains of the ancient and venerable fabric of the traditional civilizations of Europe'.[103] The fluid nature of his definitions and his audience – let alone his personality – made Gladstone's 'European sense', his quest for justice in international relations obtained through a concert of the European powers, threaten to turn into the unstable compound of high-mindedness and casuistry condemned by A. J. P. Taylor.[104] But in peripheral Britain 'great moral issues' of this sort, far from serving elitist ends and inhibiting social politics, were essential in order to create any sort of radical identity.

Ieuan Gwynedd Jones has written that in Wales in the 1860s Irish Church disestablishment

> was virtually the only aspect of politics which the body of electors and the populace in general could understand as an issue of principle, and to which they could engage themselves. The fact that the Liberal party as such, under the leadership of Gladstone, was committed to such a measure helped to break down that feeling of isolation and parochialism which had hitherto characterised them.[105]

The stimulus that this gave to absorption in other, more secular issues helped create a new mythic age: 'The 1860s remained a kind of contemporary politics, a romantic memory, matter for peroration and eloquence'[106] among the cadres – 'the preacher, the college lecturer, the chapel deacon'[107] – who came to dominate the Liberal Party. Gladstone's Midlothian campaign was to perform a similar function for Scotland in the 1870s, and, G. M. Trevelyan maintained, for those areas of England like the northern counties which had seen 'the continuance of warlike habits among a sparse population'.[108] In other words, politics could in such areas still be dramatized into a type of heroic and improving myth, in the same terms as those with which the Welsh had approached the Irish Church issue, as

> supremely a question of justice, of morality, of the fitness of things ... they voted as they did because they felt the analogy between themselves and the Irish, between *that* system and *these* blatant inequalities, to be profoundly true. ...The fruit of all this in process of time was a new culture, radical, humane, and democratic.[109]

VII

Was the Gladstonian effect obtained by deception, boosting the naive self-esteem of peripheral communities to recruit representatives for a purely metropolitan struggle? Was it an unscrupulous use of the politics of charisma in the interests of absolute parliamentary sovereignty? In one respect this accusation strikes home. In the Midlothian campaign Gladstone admitted that parliament was 'overweighted ... overwhelmed', and implied that 'secondary and subordinate authorities' could be created as part of a comprehensive settlement: 'I will consent to give to Ireland no principle, nothing that is not upon equal terms offered to Scotland and the different portions of the United Kingdom'.[110] But if he attempted to work out such a commitment in his abortive schemes for 'devolution' through Grand Committees in 1880, and Provincial Councils in 1882,[111] it seems to have been technically obviated by his increasingly efficient control of the Commons after that date, and then eliminated by his supremacy in the party after 1886.

Cooke and Vincent argue thus in *The Governing Passion*, but their self-congratulatory account of metropolitan 'high politics' coincided with the reappearance of 'that cloud in the west'. Brutal and persistent conflict and the real possibility of the break-up of Britain have, since then, made the failure of Gladstone's *démarche* more regrettable. Yet much of the Hammond version still stands open to question. Gladstone knew Scotland and Wales well, but visited Ireland only twice and took no interest in its cultural or religious development (being equally alienated from the 'low' Church of Ireland and the ultramontane Catholic hierarchy). He endorsed Home Rule for Scotland without furthering it, while Scottish seats were colonized by English carpetbaggers. Where a positive Scottish policy might have detached some Unionist supporters, Gladstone tolerated a steady leakage of activist support to the imperialist right and, after 1888, to the left, in the shape of the Scottish and later the Independent Labour Parties.

As he approached eighty, Gladstone reduced his workload, effectively devolving limited authority to the provinces of the Liberal Party while supervising Metropolitan political business himself, a centralization confirmed by a competent senior civil service, the management of parliamentary politics, and the Liberal Imperialists' promotion of a new range of social policies.[112] The constitutionalist-revolutionist confrontation had positioned itself in the metropolis: the confrontation with the regions was postponed for at least twenty years.

Cooke and Vincent treat Gladstone as an archaism. But he was much less of one than Disraeli, whose novels show him far more isolated from industrial society.[113] But Gladstone was perplexed and ultimately entrapped by the centralized system which he created from the residue of aristocratic government. A present-day political commentator, Neal Ascherson, compared the Home Rule debates in 1886 with those on Scottish devolution in 1977:

How elastic and sovereign Gladstone was, compared to politicians today! The problems were so similar. But the confidence in change and innovation was so much greater. The central doctrine of the sovereignty of Parliament was of course an obstacle to Gladstone. But ... what was only a general principle in 1886 has become a fixed taboo today.[114]

It could be argued that this 'taboo' dates *precisely* from 1886, when Dicey's *Law of the Constitution*, publishing the dogma of parliamentary sovereignty, was promptly confirmed by the defeat of Home Rule. From being only tentatively convinced of his own case, Dicey became a lucid, fanatical upholder both of the Union and of parliamentary sovereignty. Gladstone somewhat embarrassingly, congratulated him on *England's Case against Home Rule*. As an old parliamentary hand, he had every reason to do so.

Gladstone in London was a parliamentary chief rather than a Liberal, on the periphery he was a charismatic 'priest-king' rather than a Mazzinian democrat. By 1890 he seemed to have tamed nationalist and nonconformist alike. But the end-result was peculiar. When nonconformity, turned respectable, metropolitan, even imperialist, bayed for the adulterer Parnell's blood at the National Liberal Federation Conference in November 1890, Gladstone conceded to it. The result of the turmoil that followed was the creation of a hero whose posthumous charisma was to cast a shadow over the next three decades of Irish history. If Gladstone's declaration for Home Rule in 1886 fired the idealism of a whole Irish generation for an 'attainable' autonomy, Gladstone the Homeric scholar's 'betrayal' of Parnell would send another Cuchullain stalking through the Dublin GPO.

Notes

1 Charles Greville 1860, quoted in Sir Algernon West, *Recollections, 1832–1886*, (Walton-on-Thames, 1908), p. 283.

2 C. S. Roundell to the Earl Spencer, 5 May 1895, in Peter Gordon (ed.), *The Red Earl: Papers of the Fifth Earl Spencer, 1835–1910* (Northampton, 1986), II, p. 254.

3 See the present writer's *The Lights of Liberalism: University Liberals and the Challenge of Democracy, 1860–1886* (Harmondsworth, 1976), pp. 90ff.

4 Quoted in John Morley, *William Ewart Gladstone* (London, 1903), Lloyd's two vol. edn, 1908, pp. 709–10.

5 Quoted in G. M. Young, *Mr Gladstone*, the Romanes Lecture, 2 June 1944 (Oxford, 1944), p. 27.

6 See G. T. Garratt, *The Two Mr Gladstones* (London, 1936), p. v.

7 Bob Smillie, *My Life for Labour* (Richmond, 1926), p. 242.

8 Garratt, *The Two Mr Gladstones*, p. v.

9 See Henry Pelling, *Social Geography of British Elections* (London, 1967), p. 416.

10 H. C. G. Matthew (ed.), *The Gladstone Diaries, Vol. VII, January 1869 to June 1871* (Oxford, 1982), p. xxix.

11 'Germany, France and England', in *The Edinburgh Review*, October 1870, quoted in Matthew, ibid.

12 See A. J. P. Taylor, *Bismarck: the Man and the Statesman* (London, 1955), pp. 209, 216, 232.
13 Ibid., p. 161.
14 Sir Henry Maine, 'Radicalism Old and New', in *St James' Gazette*, 25 June 1881, quoted in George Feaver, *From Status to Contract: a Biography of Sir Henry Maine, 1822–88* (London, 1969), p. 217; and see John Roach, 'Liberalism and the Victorian Intelligentsia', *The Cambridge Historical Journal*, XIII (1957), p. 71.
15 Cf. Leslie Stephen on Gladstone, in *The Nation*, I, (1865), p. 586.
16 Mosei Ostrogorski, *Democracy and the Rise of Political Parties* (1899), trans. Frederick Clarke (London, 1902), p. 180.
17 Martin Weiner, *Between Two Worlds: a Study of the Political Thought of Graham Wallas* (Oxford, 1971), p. 77.
18 C. R. L. F[letcher], *Mr Gladstone at Oxford, 1890* (1908), p. 43.
19 Ibid., p. 42.
20 *Essays in Liberalism*, ed. J. S. Phillimore and F. W. Hirst (London, 1897), p. vii.
21 G. W. E. Russell, *Fifteen Chapters of Autobiography* (1912; London, 1914), p. 272.
22 John Vincent, *The Formation of the British Liberal Party, 1857–68* (1966; Harmondsworth, 1972), pp. 244–5. Alastair B. Cooke and John Vincent, *The Governing Passion* (Hemel Hempstead, 1972), pp. 15, 457–8.
23 Courtney MSS, London School of Economics, Leonard Courtney to Millicent Fawcett, 4 July 1886.
24 A. V. Dicey, *A Leap in the Dark, or the New Constitution* (London, 1893), p. 190.
25 Fisher MS., Bodleian Library, Oxford, Muir–Fisher, 9 February 1923.
26 Vincent, *The Formation of the British Liberal Party*, p. 228.
27 D. A. Hamer, *Liberal Politics in the Age of Gladstone and Rosebery* (Oxford, 1972), p. xiii.
28 A. J. P. Taylor, *The Trouble Makers* (1957; 1969), p. 172.
29 Quoted in D. M. Schreuder, 'The Making of Mr Gladstone's Posthumous Career: the Role of Morley and Knaplund as "Monumental Masons", 1903–1927', in Bruce Kinzer (ed.), *The Gladstonian Turn of Mind* (Toronto, 1985), p. 107.
30 Ibid., p. 199.
31 Ann P. Robson, 'A Bird's Eye View of Gladstone', in Kinzer, *The Gladstonian Turn of Mind*, pp. 63–96.
32 Sir Philip Magnus, *Gladstone* (London, 1954), pp. 384–5.
33 See Spencer's introduction 'From Freedom to Bondage', in Thomas MacKay (ed.), *A Plea for Liberty* (London, 1891), p. 10.
34 H. C. G. Matthew (ed.), *The Gladstone Diaries, Vol. VII, 1869–71* (Oxford, 1982), p. xxvi; and Henry Parris, *Government and the Railways in Nineteenth Century Britain* (London, 1965), pp. 77, 223.
35 Feaver, *From Status to Contract*, p. 215.
36 G. W. E. Russell dated the concept from an article of his in 1889, Russell, *Fifteen Chapters of Autobiography*, p. 361.
37 Green, *Works*, ed. R. L. Nettleship (London, 1885), III, pp. 374, 376.
38 *A Chapter of Autobiography* (London, 1868), p. 58.
39 See Clive Dewey, 'Celtic Agrarian Legislation and Celtic Revival', *Past and Present* (1974); and Michael Barker, *Gladstone and Radicalism: the Reconstruction of Liberal Policy in Britain, 1885–94* (London, 1975), p. 255.
40 T. H. Darlow, *William Robertson Nicoll* (London, 1925), p. 108.
41 *British Weekly*, 9 July 1914, quoted in ibid., pp. 375–6.
42 Hobhouse, *Liberalism*, p. 105.
43 Darlow, *William Robertson Nicoll*, p. 38

Christopher Harvie

44 D. A. Hamer, 'Gladstone: the Making of a Political Myth', *Victorian Studies*, 22 (1978), p. 35.
45 Goldwin Smith, *My Memory of Gladstone* (London, 1904), pp. 3–5.
46 Ibid., p. 37.
47 Walter Besant, *The Master Craftsman* (London, 1896), II, p. 98; B. B. Gilbert, *Lloyd George, the Architect of Change* (London, 1987), p. 79.
48 Henry Roseveare, *The Treasury: The Evolution of a British Institution* (Allen Lane, 1969), p. 139; and see H. C. G. Matthew, 'Disraeli, Gladstone and the Politics of Mid-Victorian Budgets', *Historical Journal*, XXII (1979), No. 3.
49 John Mackintosh, *The British Cabinet* (1961; Wellingborough, 1977), p. 291.
50 Ibid., pp. 155, 194.
51 Hammond, *Gladstone and the Irish Nation*, p. 72.
52 H. C. G. Matthew, 'Introduction' to *The Gladstone Diaries, 1868–71* (Oxford, 1982), p. xxx.
53 Quoted in Hammond, *Gladstone and the Irish Nation*, p. 544.
54 Gladstone, *A Chapter of Autobiography*, p. 10.
55 Morley, *Gladstone*, I, p. 191, quoted by D. A. Hamer 'Gladstone: the Making of a Political Myth', *Victorian Studies* 22 (1978), p. 46.
56 'Die Wirtschaftsethik der Weltreligionen: Einleitung' (1915), trans. H. H. Gerth and C. Wright Mills, in *From Max Weber: Essays in Sociology* (New York, 1946), pp. 295–6.
57 Cooke and Vincent, *The Governing Passion*, pp. 54–5. This was an extreme version of the High Politics interpretation; subsequently this has been modified and somewhat replenished with ideology in Maurice Cowling, *Religion and Public Doctrine in England* (Cambridge, 1981, 1986), and in J. P. Parry, *Democracy and Religion: Gladstone and the Liberal Party 1867–1875* (Cambridge, 1986).
58 Ibid., p. 458.
59 Goldwin Smith, *My Memory of Gladstone*, p. 66.
60 There is, for instance, a three-year gap in his correspondence with James Bryce after a letter of 10 March 1886, in which Smith described Morley's conduct as 'vile'.
61 G. M. Trevelyan, *Sir George Otto Trevelyan* (London, 1930), p. 121.
62 Mary Moorman, *George Macaulay Trevelyan* (London, 1980), p. 25.
63 Cooke and Vincent, *Governing Passion*, pp. 164–5.
64 See P. C. Griffiths, 'The Caucus and the Liberal Party in 1886', *History*, 61, 202 (June 1976), pp. 195–7.
65 Cf. Rait, *Memorials of A. C. Dicey* (London, 1925).
66 Quoted in Hammond, *Gladstone and the Irish Nation*, p. 532.
67 In *The Nineteenth Century*, 19 (May 1886), pp. 645–60.
68 Ibid., p. 654.
69 Russell, *Fifteen Chapters of Autobiography*, p. 279.
70 Parry, *Democracy and Religion*, p. 46
71 See Harvie, *Lights of Liberalism*, ch. 9.
72 Thornton, *The Imperial Idea and its Enemies*, p. 88.
73 L. P. Curtis, *Anglo-Saxons and Celts* (Bridgeport, 1968), pp. 103–4.
74 Kenneth O. Morgan, *Rebirth of a Nation, Wales 1880–1980* (Oxford, 1981), p. 56.
75 Smith, *My Memory*, p. 5; Bryce, *Studies in Contemporary Biography*, pp. 402–5; Dicey, *The Nation*, XXXV (1882), p. 219; Morley, *Gladstone*, I, pp. 6ff.
76 Erich Eyck, *Gladstone* (1938; London, 1968); Morley, *Gladstone*, I, p. 14.
77 Morley, *Gladstone*, I, p. 15; Sydney Checkland, *The Gladstones: a Family Biography* (Cambridge, 1971), pp. 29–30.

78 Butler, *Gladstone, Church, State*, p. 11; and see Linda Colley, 'Whose Nation: Class and National Consciousness in Britain, 1750–1830', *Past and Present*, 113 (1985), p. 110.
79 Ibid., p. 19; and see A. C. Cheyne, 'Introduction', *The Practical and the Pious: Chalmers Bicentenary Essays* (Edinburgh, 1984), p. 21.
80 Morley, *Gladstone*, I, p. 128.
81 Quoted in Butler, *Gladstone, Church, State and Tractarianism*, p. 46.
82 Morley, *Gladstone*, I, pp. 127–33.
83 Matthew, *Gladstone Diaries*, VII, p. xxvii; and see C. L. Mowat, *The Charity Organization Society* (London, 1961), p. 70.
84 E. J. Feuchtwanger, *Gladstone* (Harmondsworth, 1975), p. 32; Morley, *Gladstone*, I, p. 80.
85 Butler, *Gladstone, Church, State and Tractarianism*, p. 40.
86 Morley, *Gladstone*, II, p. 582.
87 Ibid., p. 498; and Stuart J. Brown, *Thomas Chalmers and the Godly Commonwealth in Scotland* (Oxford, 1982), p. 274; and see the present writer's 'Scott and the Image of Scotland', in Alan Bold (ed.), *Sir Walter Scott: the Long-Forgotten Melody* (London, 1983).
88 Cf. Emile Durkheim, *Suicide, A Study* (1895); for the 'dual identity' of nineteenth-century Scots intellectuals, see Karl Miller, *Cockburn's Millennium* (London, 1975), especially ch. 12, 'Caledonia's Orphans'.
89 Bryce, 'Gladstone', pp. 409, 452.
90 Quoted in J. L. Hammond and M. R. D. Foot, *Gladstone and Liberalism* (1952), p. 2.
91 W. E. Gladstone, 'The Thesis of Erastus and the Scottish Church Establishment', in *The Foreign and Colonial Quarterly Review* (1844), repr. in *Gleanings of Post Years* (London, 1879), III, p. 38.
92 Ibid., p. 39.
93 British Museum Add MSS. 44300, folio 178, dated Fasque, December 1851: 'On the functions of Laymen in the Church'.
94 Ibid.
95 Harold Laski, *Studies in the Problem of Sovereignty* (Yale University Press, 1917), p. 208; and W. E. Gladstone, *Lessons of the Election* (London, 1886), pp. 36–7.
96 William Hanna, *Life and Writings of Thomas Chalmers* (Edinburgh, 1852), IV, pp. 418ff.
97 See Richard Dorson, *The British Folklorists* (London, 1968), pp. 137–52.
98 To Mrs Gladstone, 12 October 1845, quoted in Hammond, *Gladstone and the Irish Nation*, p. 51.
99 Ibid., p. 698; Gladstone carried on a long correspondence with picturesque Scottish Greek and Celtic Scholar Professor John Stewart Blackie, and Dr Kenneth Morgan informs me that while at work on his Homeric researches in 1875, Gladstone corresponded with the Welsh bard 'Morien' (Owen Morgan, 1836–1921), a disciple of the great Druidic myth-maker, Iolo Morganwyg.
100 Richard Jenkins, *The Victorians and Ancient Greece* (Oxford, 1980), p. 201.
101 Ibid.
102 Kleinknecht, *Imperiale und Internationale Ordnung*, p. 105; and see D. M. Schreuder, 'Gladstone and Italian Unification, 1848–1890: the Making of a Liberal', *English Historical Review*, 85 (1970), p. 482.
103 *Examinations of the Official Reply of the Neapolitan Government* (1850), in *Gleanings*, IV (London, 1878), p. 113.
104 Taylor, *The Trouble Makers*, pp. 62ff.
105 Ieuan Gwynedd Jones, *Explorations and Explanations: Essays in the Social History of Victorian Wales* (Gomer, 1981), p. 159.

106 Ibid., p. 269.
107 Ibid., p. 293.
108 G. M. Trevelyan, *English Social History* (London, 1944), p. 19.
109 Jones, *Explorations and Explanations*, pp. 297–8.
110 Speech at the Corn Exchange, Dalkeith, 26 November 1879.
111 Hammond, *Gladstone and the Irish Nation*, pp. 200, 259.
112 Cf. H. C. G. Matthew, *The Liberal Imperialists* (Oxford, 1973).
113 See William Stafford, 'Romantic Elitism in the Thought of Benjamin Disraeli', *Literature and History*, 6, 1 (1980), p. 43.
114 Neal Ascherson, 'Devolution Diary': Tuesday, 15 February 1977, *Cencrastus*, 22 (1986).

Chapter ten

The new liberalism and its aftermath

Michael Freeden

In their heyday – during the half-century preceding the 1880s – the Liberal Party and liberalism appeared to be one, incorporating a moral code of generalized appeal, buttressed by a confidence nourished on class, culture, and a belief in progress that offered clear directives for political action. Of course, tensions and disputes abounded, as they do in any political movement. But the clearing-house for defining and realizing the aims of political liberalism was situated within the party, and never better epitomized than in the person of Gladstone himself.[1] From the 1890s onwards this was no longer the case. Advanced Liberals had been disappointed with the failure of the 1891 Newcastle Programme to take root in the party. Gladstone was perceived by many as a hindrance that prevented the party's political and ideological modernization. The Liberal administrations of 1892–5 fell little short of a disaster. If one wishes to look for vital and innovative elements within the liberal movement in the late nineteenth and early twentieth centuries, it is initially the intellectual development of liberalism, rather than its political prowess and acumen, that deserves most attention. Its centre of gravity was located on the periphery of the party, not at its core; its impact, though noticeable in Edwardian legislation, was decidedly not on liberalism exclusively, but on a wider range of progressive thought that forged a social welfare ethos embellished by future generations. For political theorists, this intellectual development, resulting in a set of beliefs termed the new liberalism, is an exciting metamorphosis of the liberal tradition, fashioning new vessels to contain an historic creed, and occasionally replenishing their contents, though not unrecognizably. For historians of the period, the problem is different: How important a lever for change was the new liberalism? How popular and widespread was its political programme? What was its relation to the Liberal Party, and could it have prevented the impending demise of that ailing institution and the rise of Labour? It is hence quite clear that any assessment of the new liberalism depends on the setting in which it is viewed and the ends against which its performance is measured.

The contention of this chapter is to suggest that the new liberalism significantly changed the nature of British political discourse and thinking; that it introduced new concepts and arguments concerning the structure of society and the role of the state; that, although its immediate bearing on political action fell short of its own aspirations, it permeated those institutional forums that constituted left-of-centre progressivism; and that, *à propos* current scholarly debate, its historical influence cannot be calculated merely in terms of immediate electoral and party support, or even short-term party policy (though there is a reasonable amount of evidence for all of these),[2] but rather as a broad ideological and cultural phenomenon. The problem of analysing the new liberalism is further compounded by three different connotations the term has acquired in modern scholarship. The first refers to the closely reasoned ideological reformulation of liberal theory undertaken by theorists and reformers in the generation prior to the First World War. The second relates to the wider body of progressive liberal argument that proceeded on the path of liberal-Radicalism. This Radicalism was reformist in spirit, espousing causes such as political reform, free trade, land, education, and temperance but, as we shall see, removed from the collectivist and organicist features of the first variant. The third – New Liberalism – denotes the policies of the Liberal Party and, specifically, the Liberal administrations between 1905 and 1914. These distinctions are not always maintained, and confusions tend, therefore, to creep into the lively exchanges of views on turn-of-the-century liberalism that have now persisted for over two decades.[3] This chapter will discuss the first variant – new liberal ideology – while recognizing the existence of interlinkages with the other two. Rather than merely restate the gist of the more extensive analysis undertaken by me in the past,[4] I have chosen to assess further evidence, especially with reference to the Rainbow Circle and the land question, and to sharpen the focus on a few issues, in particular the role of the state.

The two main exponents of the new liberal theories were L. T. Hobhouse, social philosopher, political theorist, and occasional journalist, and J. A. Hobson, economist, social theorist, journalist, and lecturer. They became close friends and heavily influenced each other's writings, minor differences notwithstanding. The new liberalism was not, however, the creation of a few individuals, but the product of a loosely attached group of likeminded people who exchanged ideas and formulated common views through a number of shared forums, the membership of which overlapped in an unusually consistent pattern. Indeed, the development of the new liberalism bears witness to the importance of small, urban coteries in the formation of modern political ideologies that, irrespective of their mass appeal, instilled a social-liberal ethos in a new generation of progressive reformers and sympathizers. The world of journalism, especially that revolving round the weekly *Speaker* (later the *Nation* under the redoubtable H. W. Massingham), as well as the ideological spearhead provided by C. P. Scott's *Manchester Guardian*, was a key focus. The ethical societies were another, as was the Settlement Movement, inspired by a sense of mission among Oxford graduates and owing much to T. H. Green's appeal to the social conscience. Prominent new liberals also included J. M. Robertson, rationalist, writer, and Liberal MP; Herbert Samuel, rising Liberal politician; and a host of lesser figures that intersected with the above groups as well as with the Liberal Party. Philosophical Idealism supplied some of the intellectual tools utilized by New Liberals, though not so much through Green as through D. G. Ritchie, who effected a singularly apposite fusion of Idealism, Darwinism, and utilitarianism. The Rainbow Circle, as we shall see, was another major crucible of new liberal thinking. H. Scott Holland, C. F. G. Masterman, R. B. Haldane, and Seebohm Rowntree were further contributors, albeit from different perspectives, to the new body of thought.

It is rare to find political thinking occurring as a hermetically sealed intellectual exercise, and the new liberalism was no exception. It developed as a reaction to the perceived costs of the industrial revolution: the dehumanization that accompanied the growth of cities, the increasing inequalities of wealth that divided employer and worker and made a mockery of the implicit equality of the *laissez-faire* model that political economists subscribed to. It also recognized the claims of the underprivileged to a say, through greater political participation, in the governing of their lives. It was not merely an immediate reaction to social and economic facts, though, but one that specifically rechannelled the precepts of liberalism to allow the flow of new currents in late nineteenth-century thought. It attempted this in particular through a reconciliation of the dual social goals of welfare and liberty, achieved by a subtle redefinition of both notions. Welfare was largely dissociated from the obsession of Victorian capitalism with wealth-making as a panacea to social evils, and was linked instead to a qualitative appreciation of life-enhancing goods and services essential to human development.[5] Liberty was reformulated to take account of a more sophisticated appreciation of the nature of human action and the constraints operating on it. The new liberals successfully proved their intellectual vitality by thinking through liberal tenets in the light of changing facts and fashions. In the course of this complex and sustained endeavour, they integrated new terms such as social reform, intervention, and community into the historical liberal tradition. *Soi-disant* liberals such as Lecky and Spencer, who refused to make the necessary adjustments to their beliefs, remained stranded in an obsolescent Individualism that rejected the new ideas emanating from science and from social philosophy as aberrations of mind and of history, or sought to interpret them in conventional terms. However, the very rationalism and incremental perfectionism of liberalism dictated a continued critical self-assessment of the liberal tradition itself, whereas those liberals who rested on the laurels of nineteenth-century achievements were in danger of defaulting on the intellectual commitments of the creed that had nourished them.[6]

The new liberals had to address a plethora of issues. The permeation of a non-partisan concept of socialism into political discourse, as in Sir William Harcourt's 'we are all socialists now', signalled a general acceptance among progressives of the advantages, and not merely the necessity, of human interaction. As a minimum statement, it reflected the duty that the privileged had towards the poor and the disadvantaged, but it was a duty that replaced the older conceptions of charity and trusteeship with a recognition both of the ethical responsibility and of the greater social efficiency involved in social reform. Socialism was seen as a spirit of co-operation that would contribute towards the utilitarian end of the benefit of all.[7] The essential interdependence of people was presented both as a sociological fact and as a philosophical argument, a message transmitted by many Positivists, Idealists and Evolutionists. For the new liberals, however, socialism meant more than the tidying up of areas that individual initiative had failed to cope with. They attempted to take into account the latest teachings of science and theories of society, and to apply both rational and ethical analysis to solving social problems. The result was an advanced notion of a community that, especially on Hobson's understanding, displayed a life and purpose of its own that complemented and sustained the ends of individuals. The new liberals emphasized a developmental and socially-oriented conception of human nature,[8] the enhancement of which could only be achieved through assisting the growth of the shared and socially beneficial elements of human behaviour. From this perspective individualism and socialism appeared not as opposed ideas; rather, mutual aid became the necessary precondition for a continuing respect for human rights and individual excellence. The new liberals could assert that 'the contrast between Liberalism & Socialism is beside the mark: the real contrast is between Socialism & Individualism.'[9] They argued that the components of social structure were interdependent and mutually sustaining, and that human beings had to be regarded as amalgams of physical, psychological, mental and moral needs, desires, and attributes. Co-operation, integration, and collective organization were the logical concomitants of that position. These theoretical fundamentals had immediate consequences for political action, as the changing attitude of new liberals to property illustrates. Beyond mounting objections to monopolies – always a prime target for liberals opposed to concentrations of social power – the newly-discovered notion of community prompted Hobhouse to argue that 'if private property is of value ... to the fulfilment of personality, common property is equally of value for the expression and the development of social life.'[10] Private and social property, on this understanding, could coexist. Likewise, Hobson extended his socioeconomic theories by locating a surplus that was formed by current social inequalities and by superior bargaining power in the hands of some capitalists. This surplus appeared as profits unnecessary to economic motivation, and could be claimed for society, as the latter was a prime partner in the creation of individual wealth and property.[11] The practical proposals linked to these analyses eschewed nationalization (new liberals felt it denied the value of individual personality and activity) and opted instead for steeply graduated taxation, accompanied by other measures of economic redistribution, such as pensions and a minimum wage, measures that accepted that wealth was a product of combined individual and social effort.[12] Such proposals were geared to immediately attainable social and political reform that was neither utopian nor revolutionary, nor at a cost unacceptable to recalcitrant sections of society. Typically, they combined a strong appeal to ethical principles with economic and social arguments that presented such reforms as socially expedient.

From another perspective, new liberal views were sustained and refined through the adoption of evolutionary and biological theories. Contrary to the prevailing interpretation of 'nature as red in tooth and claw' and natural selection as ensuring, in Spencer's words, the survival of the fittest, the new liberals read into evolution the proof of an ethical progression towards a rationally co-operating society or, as Hobhouse put it, regarded evolution as orthogenic and as establishing harmonious patterns of interaction.[13] Competition was being replaced by social responsibility and altruism, and social institutions would be successful in as much as they reflected these advanced manifestations of human nature. Collectivism could be seen in the dual light of an expression of purposive morality and of a natural and efficient organization of human beings. Both Ritchie and Hobhouse believed that the emergence of consciousness on the evolutionary scene indicated a shift in the evolutionary process itself, now able – through human agency – to plan and direct future social development[14] and to do so while recognizing the importance of the community as the central social unit. Regulation by the community of its members was an act of rational self-control of the socially inclined individuals who composed it. Hobson took this mode of analysis further by viewing society as a social organism that arguably existed as a separate psychical, ethical, and even physical entity. At any rate, the welfare of the parts was inextricably bound up with the health of the whole, but – and here the totalitarian conclusion mercifully failed to follow – the well-being of society (or to use a neo-Benthamite phrase, social utility) depended on the full development of individual personality and respect for the rights and interests of its members.[15] The significance of this liberal organicism lay not only in the quasi-scientific status it accorded to the concept of community, but in its emphasis on the interconnections among various spheres of social activity and the subsequent necessary close relationships that were now accepted as linking specific social reforms in areas such as health, unemployment, and poverty.

The institutional incarnation of these ethical and evolutionary developments was the state, for as Ritchie wrote: 'it is as a State, *i.e.* as an ordered political society, that a social organism becomes most distinctly conscious of its existence as an organism and consequently most capable of regulating the tendencies, which if left to themselves, would make its history a merely natural process.'[16] One of the most interesting contributions of the new liberals to the political theory and practice of their generation was a notion of the state that, for a short time in British history, hailed that institution as the main agency of social improvement and of the pursuit of the common good. To appreciate that development, a distinction needs to be drawn between the state as an impartial institution and a neutral one. For much of the nineteenth century that distinction did not apply. Liberals preferred the state to be neutral both in thought and in deed, an organization whose direct services were required mainly as a fall-back when individual initiative did not materialize.[17] Concurrently, most advanced liberals looked to the state as the champion of the impartial non-sectionalism that they espoused, a state that was not prejudiced or biased in favour of one social group or another, but that could act as a fair arbitrator among competing social groups. Towards the end of the century, however, a different attitude to the state emerged among progressive liberals, one that detached the idea of neutrality from that of impartiality. Liberals now felt they ought to reject the notion of a neutral state[18] while preserving that of an impartial one. Far from being ethically neutral, the state was regarded as a benevolent, rational organization, the product of a purposive evolutionary process, and committed to the realization of a total and morally specific conception of the general interest. Assimilating the notion of the common good, the impartial conception of the state stressed the *common* element, whereas the non-neutral, ethically committed, conception emphasized the *good* as a specific set of communal ends to be served by the state. This latter version viewed the state as the catalyst, implementor and protector of those values that underlay the social theories espoused by the new liberals;[19] it is hence a useful corrective to a theory of a liberal state as a non-participatory umpire or, as in some recent analyses of liberalism, to regarding it as a political theory that is neutral among different notions of the good.[20]

The recent availability of the Rainbow Circle minutes [21] has corroborated with unprecedented clarity the spread of new liberal attitudes beyond its most noted theorists. True, Hobson was a key figure; Hobhouse, however, failed to take up the place to which the Circle elected him.[22] Yet both the range of subjects and the substance of Rainbow Circle discussions attest to the well-honed abundance of sophisticated and socially relevant new liberal discourse, and its filtration to political elites – eight of its members were elected to the 1906 parliament.[23] Even if some members of the Circle had other, often compelling, allegiances to Fabianism, moderate socialism, or a cautious liberalism, there is no question that its frequent debates coloured their views and that the Circle was a very powerhouse of broad new liberal thinking. From the very start, Circle members insisted on differentiating themselves from the older Radicalism by according the state a central role in their philosophy. The Liberal MP J. A. Murray Macdonald found in the state and in the state alone the conditions of a 'virtuous and noble life', and was urged by another Member to define the state 'as the communal personality not as a formal expression of government'.[24] Samuel, though by no means the most advanced liberal member of the Circle, rejected the older Benthamite liberalism in favour of a new liberalism whose 'root idea must be the unity of society – complex in its economic, co-operative, ethical, and emotional bonds'. He too advocated 'a very positive view of the State as "a partnership in every virtue & all perfection"'. Samuel nevertheless appeared to return to Benthamism. Weighing liberty against communal interest, he asserted that 'old beliefs must be left. To coerce a minority may be to free a majority. The greatest liberty of the greatest number is the motto of the New Liberalism.'[25] Samuel failed to realize that the support he lent coercion was couched in language quite consonant with utilitarian analysis, even if it would have been rejected by

Bentham himself. That was not, as shall be seen, the typical New Liberal stance towards justified coercion. Samuel had an opportunity to correct himself a few years on, when he observed, in a significant reflection of the influence of the Oxford curriculum on social reformers: 'Now a day we have gone back from B[entham] to Aristotle & say that the State exists to promote the best life of its members rather than their happiness, if by "happiness" we mean their pleasure as judged at the moment by themselves.'[26]

Evolutionary and biological metaphors also prevailed widely in the Circle. The ethicist and journalist G. H. Perris, for example, dismissed the 'crude Darwinist' approach to politics as Individualistic and Malthusian, and called for a revision of evolution to 'be conducted from the assumption that liberty tends to progress only when it is subject to authority. Here we have to lean upon, at least as a utility in thought, the organic analogies in social life.'[27] Hobson, discussing the question 'to what type of organization does society correspond?', in which he expounded his radical organistic model, elicited both support and dissent from his audience. He was followed by the journalist J. H. Harley on the same subject, reinforcing Hobsons's analysis by remarking that 'in the social organism growth is less limited, changes are more various, & interdependence is closer, than in a biological organism. Society is a super organism.' At the following meeting, Ramsay MacDonald, ever a supporter of the analogy, talked of the necessity for the three factors of production – land, capital, and labour – to be 'coordinated as are the tissues in a biological organism.'[28] And W. H. Crook, liberal editor, journalist, and one-time secretary of the Liberal Eighty Club, described the English state as an organism, defined the present tendency as being towards increased state regulation, and concluded, in language reminiscent of Hobson's distinction between the uniformities of machinery and the individuality of art: 'Let us have Socialism for all that concerns the organic side of human nature, & individualism for the supra-organic.'[29] The real significance of the prevalence of biological and evolutionary language is to demonstrate the highly consensual thinking that lay behind the new conceptions of human nature, of the state, and of the demand for interlocking paths of social reform.

A good illustration of an emerging, if limited, consensus among Circle members was a debate on the formation of a Progressive Party in 1899. Samuel identified the movement for such a force as a convergence between demands emanating from the deprived classes and sensitive public conscience. He called for a policy that would at the same time 'express full knowledge and sympathy with labour demands' and conciliate the employer and the commercial classes generally by proving that the changes it contemplated would benefit the latter. Ramsay MacDonald, from a position of relative hostility to the topic, summed up the ensuing debate by observing: 'No one disputed the truth of the general terms but their application would raise dissension rather than make harmony at the present time.' An interesting, if slightly premature, remark during that debate was that 'one of the greatest impediments in the way of reform was the attempt made to keep the Liberal Party together.'[30] This was an acute realization that progressive liberalism was redrawing ideological maps so as to cut across existing political organizations. Hobson reiterated that very insight:

> The principles upon which such a party must be based are already in existence in the form of widely held intellectual affinities which as a matter of fact place the leaders of the Radical, the Socialist & the Labour groups much nearer to each other than their followers imagine.

Indeed, the Rainbow Circle was a prime instance of the formation of consensus at the top. In practical terms, democratic reform of the House of Lords, increased local self-government, old age pensions, and measures of economic justice and redistribution, as well as – in view of the South African situation – a clear rejection of expansionist imperialism, were some of the issues that Hobson identified as the basis for the Progressive Party's platform.[31] If the political achievements of the new liberalism were limited, the reasons for that do not lie in its ideological and intellectual capacity, but in its inability to relax the inflexibilities of existing party structure, or to penetrate beyond its natural urban professional base and arouse the type of mass enthusiasm that had become an essential ingredient of any recipe for political success.

Liberalism had, of course, always benefited from the impetus and initiative of its Radical wings; but the new liberalism, while radical, was not identical with Radicalism. This latter activist strain had sought to express individual dignity and independence by extending access to the political process and diminishing some of the starker inequalities of English society, and in so doing had frequently latched on to what contemporaries unkindly referred to as 'fads'. In the last quarter of the nineteenth century, liberal-Radicalism had been bolstered by an accretion of nonconformists, who came to constitute its dominant component. Indeed, when the Rainbow Circle was launched as a permanent discussion group in 1894, its first chosen topic was to distinguish its position from the older Manchester Radicalism that was still thought to prevail among liberal circles. Ramsay MacDonald, summarizing the debates, depicted the latter as 'essentially a revolt and not primarily a positive contribution to social philosophy', having 'no positive idea regarding the meaning & scope of' individualism. He went on to write:

> The general results of the discussion had been an agreement on the following main positions[:] that the conception of the individual as independent of society is false; that economics of the quantitative kind must be supplemented by economics of the qualitative kind;[32] that formal political democracy is not sufficient in itself to secure good government; that Trade Unionism cannot be made the basis of a great political movement; that co-operation is equally narrow; & fundamentally that the politics of the past corresponded to the economic problem of production & in the future that they must correspond to the problem of use.'[33]

By the turn of the century the divergence between the collectivist tendencies of new liberals and the individualist platforms of some Radicals was evident.[34] The shifting nature of class support for political parties meant that the Liberal Party was losing – if it had ever enjoyed – the backing of actual and potential voters from the working class, while its traditional middle-class supporters were fragmented, among others, into a number of professional groups that maintained their progressive drive, and a growing component of property-holders whose creed became increasingly bound up with the preservation of acquired rights, non-intervention in economic affairs, legal encouragement for the profit motive, and the virtues of individually-based character and initiative. The Radicalism that survived had in the main become a fringe liberal phenomenon, not only in the Celtic sense of the term, but as a motive-force for moral and political improvement. Nonconformist evangelicalism may, in terms of personal, moral, and psychological motivation, account for the passion and consciences of a number of individuals,[35] but there is little evidence for its direct influence on increasingly secular modes of political thinking. Instead, both Radicalism and nonconformity made way, at least in terms of zeal and vision, for a more highly integrated, communitarian, and theory-laden approach, based on comprehensive social doctrines that looked for their inspiration to scientific teachings, to philosophy, and to developments in the social sciences.

The land question is an edifying illustration of this growing divide between communitarian new liberals and liberal-Radicals.[36] Because the industrial revolution and its costs were predominantly urban issues, land was not a prime object of New Liberal concern. The decline of the economic importance of agriculture, the diminishing rural population and peasant class, suggested that the land question was 'old-worldish' and largely irrelevant. Nevertheless, the single taxers – the Henry Georgeites[37] – who campaigned for one tax to eliminate the entire unearned increment; those socialists who pressed for land nationalization; and – more commonly – those conservatives and progressives alike who wanted the break-up of estates and the spread of peasant proprietorship, kept the issue at the forefront of politics. The new liberals were in sympathy with these issues, but did so peripherally. What is of interest here is the relative attitude of different liberal groups to what clearly remained an important issue of New Liberal politics. In as much as the new liberals were radical reformers – and they were – they lent a vigorous voice to the demands for land reform. Crucially, however, they assimilated the land question into their general theory. Their attack on land was not in the name of a panacea, nor did it appear to most of them to require top priority as a vital element of a social reform programme. Land simply symbolized a blatant instance of the concentration of wealth and power in the hands of an insignificant proportion of the nation's population. Landowners represented three evils: they controlled an economic monopoly, they exercised unjustifiable social supremacy locally and nationally, and, as a class, they used their political power to oppose the national will and interests. In this respect new liberals did not differ from most other Radicals. The existence of monopolies offended their sense of social justice and engaged their practical espousal of redistribution.

183

Many reformers saw land as an extreme, particular case of social wrongs which were evident wherever one looked. As Hobhouse wrote: 'The attack on the land monopoly could be carried much further, and might lead the individualist ... to march a certain distance on parallel lines with the Socialist enemy.'[38] Elsewhere, he remarked that people who adopted this position 'do not draw the line either at the land or at monopoly in general ... the problem of poverty goes beyond the problem of the land.'[39] From another angle, Hobson accepted the Radical argument that equal access to land would underpin personal liberty, but extended such equality of opportunity to all natural resources and, importantly, refused to call a halt at that point, insisting that 'most persons, on reflection, will perceive that full liberty of self-development involves other opportunities, some of which are not related even remotely to the ownership or use of land.'[40]

The critique of monopolies, however, encompassed different ideological perspectives. The unearned increment that landowners unjustly appropriated could belong to the peasant or tenant that worked the soil or – at least in part, as Hobhouse and Hobson maintained – to society as the creator of the conditions that enabled the existence of private property. Here was one significant divergence between new liberals and liberal-Radicals. As Hobson explained,

> Land Nationalization stands upon two widely different and philosophically inconsistent bases. To those who take their stand upon the 'natural rights' of the individual it is the coping-stone of a free-trade policy. Equal access to the resources of nature seems essential, if liberty to labour and to accumulate property is to be equally secured to all ... let each man own himself and have an equal use of nature with every other man, and all will be well ... The other basis of Land Nationalization [was] the recognition not of the rights of the individual, but of the definitely social origin and character of land-values.[41]

Hence the official Liberal policy demanding an extensive system of peasant proprietorship was unacceptable to new liberals.

Not that they wished to do away with private property in land: G. F. Millin, a writer and journalist member of the Rainbow Circle, did not think advanced progressives would

> deem it necessary to assume an attitude of mere antagonism to the private ownership of land, or to the commercial employment of private capital. Nor will they think of disregarding anybody's actual rights; but they will put the public rights and interests in the first and foremost place ... [42]

Some new liberals, such as the author and politician C. F. G. Masterman, saw limited private ownership of land as a counterweight to the rapid deterioration of urban living conditions, and called for an 'attempt to counteract the magnetism of town by the magic of ownership'.[43] The 1907 Small Holdings Act was a move in this direction but lacked provisions to make the legislation compulsory, a typical omission by the more cautious and pragmatic New Liberals, unwilling to overwork the communitarian interventionism of new liberal theorists.

Alternatively, Hobhouse suggested to establish 'a class not of small landlords but of small tenants ... [which would] guarantee to the individual a certain share in the common stock'. Rather than reinforcing the voting strength of property, Hobhouse aspired 'to establish a State tenantry from whose prosperity the whole community would profit'.[44]

Ultimately, unlike Radical land reformers, the new liberals did not claim that the land was the root of all industrial and social evils. Nor did they rest content with the assertion that the country was a way of life, an education, and a repository of values dear to the hearts of Englishmen. Instead, as Millin put it, they preferred the organic perspective that saw land as one of a series of interconnected ills such as housing, poverty, unemployment, and health which necessitated a co-ordinated approach.[45] This also led to the 'urbanization' of the land problem, especially over the taxing or rating of site values of undeveloped urban ground – a transplantation of the issue that explains the continual role it played in Edwardian as well as Victorian times. The new liberal *Nation* regarded the land issue as an aspect of social reconstruction in which different elements – local taxation, rural depopulation, and housing – were combined, and presented it both as a question of redistribution (fair shares in national assets), and a concrete expression of the dominant interest of the community and its national and regional agencies in the regulation of socio-economic life.[46] By the end of the Edwardian era, Lloyd George had involved the Liberal administration in a land campaign.[47] It included proposals for a living agricultural wage, cottages for labourers, security of tenure, powers of compulsory land purchase by local authorities for purposes of development, a land valuation scheme with rating reform, the possibility of a national land tax to serve as a fund for national services (an echo of the Development Grant, introduced alongside the 1909 Budget, which new liberals had seen as a vindication of their insistence on the creation of funds for general communal needs), even a Ministry of Lands as an instrument for implementing social and industrial policy. All these were welcomed by new liberals as being in line with their integrated onslaught on the social problem.[48] Indeed, many of these proposals reversed the traditional flow of argument: instead of according primacy and separate treatment to the land question, they constituted an extension of urban new liberal concerns to rural issues. Naturally, though, the campaign attracted the interest of those Radicals who were still obsessed with land reform as a panacea.[49] But by the advent of the First World War, two basic liberal approaches to land had crystallized: the Radical liberal one that saw it, in the words of a liberal supporter of Lloyd George, as appealing to the imagination of the country, for the yearning for land was a 'natural instinct' or 'natural right' that necessitated equal opportunity for all in access, and on it depended the development of national liberty and patriotism;[50] and the new liberal one that regarded land as one particular social problem that could be solved only by a reformulation of social relationships to express mutual responsibility, solidarity and collective regulation. Official New Liberalism eclectically straddled the two, but failed to implement its proposed land reforms. As the new liberals had suspected, the issues the land campaign had addressed were, on their own, too marginal to capture the imagination of the general public.

The land question is an instance both of the collectivist and organic nature of the new liberal thought and of the practical impact of its ideas, however difficult it may be to quantify that influence. New liberals always preferred to stress the ethical content of their positions, whereas Liberal politicians, not surprisingly, found ethics too flimsy a garb in which to cloak their policies, and resorted to further justifications for pensions, minimum wages, and social insurance that incorporated arguments from national efficiency or industrial productivity. Nevertheless, the new liberalism bequeathed to British political culture a general conception of social structure and ends as well as modes of action needed to realize them. In particular, it enhanced public appreciation of specific social needs while demonstrating that these were compatible with, indeed conducive to, the demands of individual development. It was a strong supporter and refiner of the arguments for old age pensions and national health and unemployment insurance. The new liberals presented pensions as an act of communal recognition of individual effort, and they applauded the insurance measures that shared out responsibility among those three stalwarts of modern civilization: the citizen, the producer, and the state.[51] In particular, the financial philosophy of the new liberalism bore fruit in the 1909 'People's Budget', which Hobson welcomed as a vindication of the policies for which he and others had been campaigning for twenty years.[52] A perusal of Edwardian social legislation undisputedly reflects new liberal themes such as the ultimate moral responsibility of the state in conjunction with individual activity, the linkages among social problems, and the redistribution but not total elimination of private wealth.

If the practical result of the new liberal theories was a partial endorsement of communal intervention in individual life, a dehumanizing compulsion did not follow. Idealist thought had long accepted the possibility of a reconciliation between compulsion and freedom, in as much as the law was a proper reflection of the moral will of its maker: a rational citizenry. Although this metaphysical explanation was espoused by British as well as continental thinkers, the new liberals did not resort to it because they feared that most Idealists submerged the individual within the whole.[53] Instead, they engaged in a demonstration that individual liberty would not be harmed by social regulation, thus evading the complications that the negative/positive liberty distinction entailed. This demonstration was twofold: intellectually, new liberals held that their theory of evolution was non-determinist and did not undermine the notion of free will; practically, this was buttressed by their view that irresponsible power was a constant danger against which individuals would always have to be institutionally protected. Although they later adopted a more cautious position, the new liberals were persuaded, at the height of their optimism, that the course of rational evolution could render these latter safeguards unnecessary. Their conception of liberty was consequently dominated by the scientific evolutionary perspectives they had assimilated, and which wedded them to a developmental theory of human nature. Any impediment to that purposive course of development was perceived as a hindrance to the natural realization of human potential. A deterministic theory of evolution was dismissed because the evolutionary process itself resulted in the exercise of human choice and will.[54] The ability to make conscious choices was thus a demonstrable attribute of being human. At the same time, it was accompanied by the emergence of a human personality that exhibited, as Hobson saw it, both individually unique and socially-shared orientations.[55] Hence any notion of liberty had to allow both for the unhindered growth of a purposive, socially-oriented human being *qua* member of a community *and* for a choice-making, unconstrained individual. True, rational choices of such individuals would further communal ends (including communal ends best served by individual self-development). But those choices had to emanate from *individuals* and would do so by the grace of evolutionary logic. Hobhouse's idea of harmony mediated between any possible tension between the individual and the communal good. Granted the harmonious interaction of members of a society, and granted the development of individual personality expressing itself among others *in* collective activity, a common good would emerge, and consequently

> there is nothing in the doctrine of liberty to hinder the movement of general will in the sphere in which it is really efficient, and nothing in a just conception of the objects and methods of the general will to curtail liberty in the performance of the functions, social and personal, in which its value lies.

Hobhouse was secure in the belief that 'liberty and compulsion have complementary functions, and the self-governing State is at once the product and the condition of the self-governing individual.' This 'positive conception of the State' was necessary to the realization of individual freedom.[56]

The First World War demonstrated the defectiveness of the new liberal theory of the state. Its weaknesses did not lie in the subordination of the individual to the whole. Nor were they, conversely, located in the granting of absolute licence to the individual. Rather, they related to an over-reliance on the uninterrupted improvement that the evolutionary process itself seemed to offer. Ritchie had already warned that

> an adequate theory of the State must rest upon a philosophy of history; and steady progress in political and social reform cannot be made unless there is a willingness to learn the lessons of experience, and a reasonable reverence for the long toil of the human spirit in that past from which we inherit not only our problems, but the hope and means of their solution.[57]

Many new liberals were over-sanguine about the growth of the ethical, purposive, and impartial state and about the removal of human and social impediments in its path. Their experiences during the war may not have changed their *concept* of the state, but their faith in its practicability and in its historical imminence, as well as their enthusiasm for facilitating its realization, suffered. Their ideological predisposition had enabled them to accept, even welcome, intervention whose sole purpose was to promote human improvement and individual welfare. Paradoxically, it did not equip them to condone wholesale intervention to areas where the state had traditionally claimed supremacy: the exercise of power as force. When new liberals had resorted to compulsion, they did so secure in the knowledge that a non-sectional view of the social good was available for all who cared to observe it, and that the task of the social reformer was simply that of speeding up the process – to serve as pioneer of the emerging social consciousness, not as wielder of tyrannical methods or harbinger of an elitist vision of the philosopher's truth. But the rational idea of the state to which they subscribed could apply only while it appeared to be the benevolent and impartial agent of the community. State compulsion was acceptable to Hobhouse only as long as 'the function of State coercion is to override individual coercion'. Not even coercing a man for his own good was justified for, like Green, Hobhouse asserted that 'to form character by coercion is to destroy it in the making'. The task of the state was to reorganize restraints, for 'the object of compulsion is to secure the most favourable external conditions of inward growth and happiness so far as these conditions depend on combined action and uniform observance.'[58]

The war changed all this. The state as warrior was associated for many new liberals with what Campbell-Bannerman had referred to, in the context of the South African war detested by most of them, as 'methods of barbarism'. Moreover, the ends to which the force of the state was put were reprehensible as well. The new liberals resisted conscription as an unwarranted infringement of individual liberty, both because its aim was the employment of physical force – a means that undermined their appeal to reason – and because the state no longer acted as an impartial agent for the general good, but pursued – so they believed – a policy that favoured specific social groups at the expense of others. Censorship, the curtailment of trade union rights, the powers of secret arrest and trial, and massive intervention in the economy brought forth protests from those liberals who had previously applauded the extension of the internal boundaries of the state. Their belief system now on the defensive through the force of external circumstances, the new liberals were impelled to restructure the internal emphases of their arguments. The values they cherished were perceived to be under a dual threat: they were attacked by policies arising from sectional interests, as well as divested of an ethical basis. Hobson returned to a favourite theme when he condemned the war as a collaboration of militarists, capitalists, and conservatives who sought to foist their private, profiteering, and anti-social interests on the nation,[59] and did so while trampling upon cherished individual rights of their own people. Hence he found in the activities of the British state an element of the Prussianism it was ostensibly fighting.[60] Hobhouse pessimistically sought refuge from this new omnipotent state in an earlier liberalism, commenting on the bitter lessons of the war that experience of state control has given renewed life to the idea of liberty, mounting both popular and scholarly attacks on Idealist conceptions of the state, and envisaging a retreat to a Spencerian anti-statism. Eventually he contemplated a return to a severely restricted definition:

> after a prolonged course of Fabian economics and Hegelian metaphysics one departs wishing that one could never hear the word 'State' again. But I think we ought to control the sense of nausea due to repletion for the sake of the many who use the term 'State' in all innocence for the supreme legal authority.'[61]

Clearly, these responses had emotional as well as rational dimensions. Though the disillusionment with the promises of social evolution was one from which the new liberals never quite recovered, they did not entirely renege on the hopes they had pinned on the state as protector, regulator, and enabler. But henceforth they treated it with circumspection, as a repository of the potentially dangerous power they had previously hoped to eliminate through ethical and institutional progress. The new liberals' assumption that power would virtually 'wither away' under a blanket of rational and harmonious co-operation was unsuited to the political realities of the post-war period. The need for industrial reconstruction and efficiency, and the increasing stress on the direct political initiatives of, and relationship between, capital and labour left little room for their pre-war hopes of a collectivist communitarianism aimed at individual growth – a formula whose internal balance relied essentially on the evolution of an overarching benevolent state. In post-war liberal thought, when it came to discussions of social and economic policy, the state had to take its place among other types of social organization, such as those envisaged in the Liberal 'Yellow Book'. The responsibility for controlling political power and representing diverse interests could no longer be its preserve alone; the harmony it should have provided was therefore not ensured. The state became part-problem, part-solution.

Nevertheless, the new liberalism left an important heritage for future progressives. It was a political theory that supplied a succinct operative ideology, much of which was implemented. The state *had* permanently claimed a stake in extensive areas of human activity, and one that, unlike some socialist options, allowed for a large measure of co-operation with private and voluntary energies, while retaining a monopoly on the larger perspective that social needs demanded. Questions of democratic participation and of individual development were accepted as entirely compatible with the requirements of social welfare and human equality. Even when the Labour Party moved into the vacuum left by the partial demise of the Liberal Party, it adopted a complex and sophisticated balance of those values that, upon close analysis, can only be described as adherence to a new liberal formula. Ultimately, it bequeathed to the British political tradition an awareness that a defence of communal ends need neither hark back to a corporate and conservative feudalism nor anticipate an imposed socialist uniformity. The common good and social welfare were attainable through collective action, but such action was entirely consonant with, indeed dependent upon, the pursuit of individual development, liberty, and dignity.

Notes

1 See chapter 9, this volume.
2 P. F. Clarke. ' The Electoral Position of the Liberal and Labour Parties, 1910–1914', *English Historical Review*, 90 (1975), pp. 828–36; H. C. G. Matthew, R. I. McKibbin, and J. M. Kay, 'The Franchise Factor in the Rise of the Labour Party', *English Historical Review*, 91 (1976), pp. 723–52.
3 See, e.g., T. Wilson, *The Downfall of the Liberal Party 1914–1935* (London, 1968); N. V. Emy, *Liberals, Radicals and Social Politics 1892–1914* (Cambridge, 1973); M. Freeden, *The New Liberalism: An Ideology of Social Reform* (Oxford, 1978); P. Clarke, *Liberals and Social Democrats* (Cambridge, 1978). More recently, see D. Powell, 'The New Liberalism and the Rise of Labour, 1886–1906', *Historical Journal*, 29 (1986), pp. 369–93; G. L. Bernstein, *Liberalism and Liberal Politics in Edwardian England* (London, 1986); R. A. Rempel, 'Conflicts and Change in Liberal Theory and Practice, 1890–1918: the case of Bertrand Russell', in P. J. Waller (ed.), *Politics and Social Change in Modern Britain* (London, 1987), pp. 117–39. For recent overviews of the various problems exercising scholars, see M. Bentley, *The Climax of Liberal Politics: British Liberalism in Theory and Practice 1868–1918* (London, 1987); and K. Rohe, 'Sozialer Liberalismus in Grossbritannien in Komparativer Perspektive: Zu Gesellschaftstheorie des New Liberalism 1880–1914', in K. Holl, G. Trautmann, and H. Vorländer (eds), *Sozialer Liberalismus* (Goettingen, 1986), pp. 269–92.
4 In Freeden, *The New Liberalism*; and idem, *Liberalism Divided: A Study in British Political Thought 1914–1939* (Oxford, 1986).
5 Here Hobson's redirection of Ruskinian thought into progressive channels of social utility was instrumental. See J. A. Hobson, *John Ruskin Social Reformer* (London, 1898) and *Work and Wealth* (London, 1914).
6 See chapter 7, this volume.
7 J. Chamberlain, 'Favourable aspects of State Socialism', *North American Review*, 152 (1891), pp. 536–8.
8 C. G. E. Gaus, *The Modern Liberal Theory of Man* (London, 1983).
9 Rainbow Circle Minutes, British Library of Political and Economic Science, 8 January 1908.
10 L. T. Hobhouse, 'The Historical Evolution of Property, in Fact and in Idea', in C. Gore (ed.), *Property, its Duties and Rights* (London, 1913), p. 31.
11 J. A. Hobson, *Problems of Poverty* (London, 1891), p. 198: *The Social Problem* (London, 1901), pp. 146–7. For a general discussion of Hobson, see M. Freeden (ed.), *J. A. Hobson: A Reader* (London, 1988), pp. 1–27.
12 L. T. Hobhouse, *Liberalism* (New York, 1964. 1st edn 1911), p. 98.
13 L. T. Hobhouse, *Social Evolution and Political Theory* (New York, 1911); *Development and Purpose* (London, 1913).
14 Cf. the interest New Liberals expressed in eugenics: M. Freeden, 'Eugenics and Progressive Thought: A Study in Ideological Affinity', *Historical Journal*, 22 (1979), pp. 421–43.
15 Hobson, *Work and Wealth*, p. 304.
16 D. G. Ritchie, *The Moral Function of the State* (London, 1887), p. 6.
17 See, e.g., A. Bullock and M. Shock (eds), *The Liberal Tradition* (Oxford, 1967); and H. G. C. Matthew, *The Liberal Imperialists* (Oxford, 1973), pp. 245–6.

18 In the *COD* sense of indefinite, vague, or indeterminate.
19 See, e.g., D. G. Ritchie, *The Principles of State Interference* (London, 1891).
20 See, e.g., R. Dworkin, 'Liberalism', in S. Hampshire (ed.), *Public and Private Morality* (Cambridge, 1978).
21 Unavailable to me when writing *The New Liberalism*.
22 Rainbow Circle minutes, 9 December 1903.
23 See congratulatory resolution in ibid., 7 February 1906.
24 Ibid., 7 November 1894.
25 Ibid., 6 November 1895.
26 Ibid., 1 May 1901.
27 Ibid., 2 October 1895.
28 Ibid., 4 October 1905, 1 November 1905, 6 December 1905.
29 Ibid., 2 May 1906.
30 Ibid., 3 May 1899.
31 Ibid., 7 June 1899.
32 A clear reflection of Hobson's developing views on the subject from the early 1890s onwards. See, e.g., *The Social Problem* (London, 1901), pp. 45–50.
33 Rainbow Circle minutes, 19 June 1895.
34 For an interesting account of the differences between liberal-Radicalism and New Liberals, see Emy, *Liberals, Radicals and Social Politics*, pp. 47–8, 52, 64–71. For an examination of the roots of middle-class, non-collectivist radicalism, see G. Claeys, 'Liberalism as Radicalism: The Problems of Class and the Limits of Collectivism in 19th Century British Reform Movements', in K. Rohe (ed.), *Englischer Liberalismus im 19. und Frühen 20. Jahrhundert* (Bochum, 1987), pp. 67–100.
35 See S. Koss, *Nonconformity in Modern British Politics* (London, 1975).
36 Many of this latter group are referred to as New Liberals in the second sense discussed at the outset.
37 See, e.g., H. George, *Progress and Poverty* (London, 1881).
38 Hobhouse, *Liberalism*, p. 52.
39 L. T. Hobhouse, 'The Contending Forces', *English Review*, 4 (1909–10), pp. 367, 369.
40 J. A. Hobson, *The Crisis of Liberalism* (London, 1909), pp. 97–9.
41 J. A. Hobson, 'The Influence of Henry George in England', *Fortnightly Review*, 67 (1897), p. 842.
42 G. F. Millin, *The Village Problem* (London, 1903), p. 6.
43 C. F. G. Masterman, 'Towards a Civilization', *Independent Review*, 2 (1904), p. 502.
44 Hobhouse, *Liberalism*, pp. 91–2.
45 G. F. Millin, 'The New Liberalism', *Fortnightly Review*, 69 (1901), pp. 634–42.
46 *Nation*, 20 April 1907, 27 April 1907.
47 Emy, *Liberals, Radicals and Social Politics*, pp. 216–24.
48 *Nation*, 25 October 1913. Cf. also [L. T. Hobhouse], 'The Land Campaign', *Manchester Guardian*, 1 February 1913.
49 Emy, *Liberals, Radicals and Social Politics*, p. 276.
50 L. M. Phillips, 'Mr. Lloyd George and the Country', *English Review*, 12 (1912), p. 638.
51 Cf. Freeden, *The New Liberalism*, pp. 229–38.
52 J. A. Hobson, 'The Significance of the Budget', *English Review*, 2 (1909), pp. 794–805.
53 See, e.g., L. T. Hobhouse, *The Metaphysical Theory of the State* (London, 1918).
54 Cf. L. T. Hobhouse, *Social Evolution and Political Theory* (New York, 1911), pp. 155–6.
55 Hobson, 'Character and Society', in P. L. Parker (ed.), *Character and Life* (London, 1912), pp. 72–6; and Hobson, *Towards Social Equality* (London, 1931).

56 Hobhouse, *Liberalism*, pp. 71, 81.
57 D. G. Ritchie, *Natural Rights* (London, 1894), p. 286.
58 Hobhouse, *Liberalism*, pp. 76–8. See also chapter 8, this volume.
59 J. A. Hobson, *Democracy After the War* (London, 1917). This was reminiscent of his attack on the South African war. See especially his *The Psychology of Jingoism* (London, 1901).
60 J. A. Hobson, 'The War and British Liberties. III. The Claims of the State Upon the Individual', *Nation*, 10 June 1916.
61 L. T. Hobhouse, 'The Future of Liberalism', *Manchester Guardian*, 5 September 1919; 'Herbert Spencer', *Manchester Guardian*, 1 May 1920; 'The New Democracy', *Manchester Guardian*, 19 April 1920; and *The Metaphysical Theory of the State* (London, 1918). For a more detailed discussion, see Freeden, *Liberalism Divided*, chapter 2.

Chapter eleven

From liberal-Radicalism to Conservative corporatism: the pursuit of 'Radical business' in 'Tory livery'

Joseph Chamberlain, Birmingham, and British politics, 1870–1930

Alan Hooper

I

In seeking to explain the demise of Liberalism as an organized political force in the early twentieth century, historians have stressed both the imperatives arising from economic and social processes and the manoeuvres pursued by the practitioners of 'high politics'. While George Dangerfield recorded with sardonic pleasure the 'strange death' of Liberal England during what he considered the terminal years of 1910–14, two recent historians, A. B. Cooke and J. Vincent, narrating the Home Rule crisis of 1885–6, seem equally delighted by the 'deliquescence' of Liberal convictions they discover in events often considered to mark the onset of Liberal decline. Neither a rationalistic emphasis on 'politics' as a 'connected wholeness', in Cooke and Vincent's phrase, nor an empiricism which stresses the 'political realities of the moment', as the same authors express their preferred approach, are adequate to explain a process as complex as the decline of a major political force, and with it a political order, over a forty-year period.[1] Rather, it is necessary to weigh the opportunities and the constraints, identify the tractable and the ineluctable, in the circumstances confronting British politicians during the years between the 1880s and the 1920s.

Such has been the achievement of those involved in the historical debate under way since the early 1970s concerning the attempted Liberal renewal known as the 'new liberalism'. It is not my intention to review the relevant issues in detail, that has been done elsewhere and, as contributions to this volume indicate, the debate continues. It is important to note, however, that the discussion opened by P. Clarke, and pursued more recently by a number of historians, has advanced consideration of the degree to which it was possible for liberalism to renew itself *to the left*, creating what Clarke has called 'social democracy'.[2] What has been less evident in the argument concerning liberalism's prospects at the turn of the century is consideration of its relationship with the *right*. With a few exceptions, notably E. Halévy, N. Harris, and recently S. Hall and B. Schwarz, the manner in which liberalism fed into new 'rightist' currents and reshaped, rather than simply reinforced, conservative priorities has been neglected.[3]

Such neglect seems the more surprising when the involvement with the Conservative Party of two of the outstanding figures, not only of liberalism but of early twentieth-century politics, Joseph Chamberlain and Lloyd George, is recalled. Those for whom politics is at once an 'arcane and esoteric craft' and a merry-go-round may consider the issue misconceived, an explanation to be divined in the political exigencies surrounding the political crises of 1886 and 1916, or worse still, given the only too-evident ambitions of two political adventurers, a symptom of 'political virginity'.[4] It is the contention of this essay that pursuing the subject more closely provides an opportunity to investigate the fate of a political current within liberalism whose significance is in danger of disappearing in the face of a critical, even condescending, historical scholarship.

The current in question is Radicalism. On a number of occasions during the years between the 1832 Reform Act and the First World War Radicals seemed poised to achieve the momentous transformations in British society whose desirability they so clamorously proclaimed. Each time, however – 1832, 1868, 1885 – the hopes proved illusory. By the turn of the century, not only was a radical transformation of society improbable but no coherent Radical Party seemed possible. Radicalism's disarray in the late nineteenth century led D. A. Hamer to describe the 1885 'Radical Programme' of Joseph Chamberlain and his associates as 'one of the outstanding dead-ends in British political history'. Hamer goes beyond noting the obstacles presented by constituency reorganiz-ation and Home Rule to imply that Radicalism lacked the resources to develop a programme relevant to the social and economic problems which were to dominate early twentieth-century politics. It is a judgement that has found support among other historians of early twentieth-century Radicalism who have contrasted ' new liberalism', with its concern with the social problems of the twentieth century, with 'old radicalism', obsessed with issues like land reform which had preoccupied the nineteenth. By 1914, claims Paul Adelman, in his recent survey of middle-class Radicalism, 'the impulse of Victorian Radicalism ... was ... clearly exhausted'.[5]

Such obituaries gain credibility by underestimating Radicalism's nineteenth-century legacy and, consequently, overlooking its twentieth-century relevance. Nineteenth-century Radicalism was concerned not only with constitutional issues, but also with the economic problems that loomed large in early twentieth-century Britain. The political rhetoric of the nineteenth century and the political labels of the twentieth century have obscured such concerns, thereby preventing an accurate assessment of Radicalism's true potential and devious trajectory. Thus, while Chamberlain's and Lloyd George's links with the Tories were partly expedient, the association of Radicalism with Conservatism suggested an underlying affinity of outlook in the face of the British state's problems which made it possible to imagine, as Chamberlain observed in 1885, 'people in Tory livery' carrying out 'Radical business'. When, therefore, Keith Middlemas, in a discussion of Lloyd George's industrial policies after the First World War, describes him 'searching ... for a middle way in politics', shifting 'from Liberal radicalism towards ... corporatism' he would seem to overlook the extent to which Radicalism contained corporatist elements; not simply, as Alan Sykes notes, a rhetoric which involved the 'unity of all productive classes, employer and employed, in contrast to class conflict' but the practice of regulating relations between capital and labour in the context of competitive capital accumulation.[6]

Such practice, a 'new radicalism' as Sykes observes, was most evident in the town described in the second half of the nineteenth century as the 'capital of English Radicalism', Chamberlain's Birmingham. Here too, however, familiar labels have hidden new realities: in particular, the town's well-known history of class co-operation has obscured important developments in its political economy from the 1850s onwards which had dramatic implications for Radical practice. These changes made the familiar rhetoric increasingly misleading, but one writer who sensed the significant, as opposed to the superficial, continuities between 1877 and 1917 was Elie Halévy. In his study of the Whitley Councils, entitled 'The Policy of Social Peace in England', Halévy noted that the proposed worker–employer collaboration had already 'triumphed' in Birmingham in the form of the 'industrial alliances' of the 1890s. 'Triumph' as a description of the alliances was as much an overstatement as the Whitley Councils were to prove a disappointment, but Halévy had identified a key to understanding the coherence in Chamberlain's transition from 'the tribune of a sort of socialist radicalism ... [to] the leader of British neo-protectionism' and in the evolution of radicalism.[7]

Radicalism as practised in Birmingham and developed by Chamberlain and, to a lesser extent, Lloyd George, offered a distinctively British source for the corporatism that was generated elsewhere by ideologies as diverse as Catholicism in Italy and *solidarisme* in France. Such currents, it has been argued, were part of the development in leading industrial societies after the First World War, but prefigured before it, of a new 'political economy' of a 'corporatist' or, in contemporary German usage, 'organized capitalist' character. Radicalism's role as an incubator of corporatism helps to resolve a paradox registered by Otto Newman and Middlemas that while corporatist practice seemed to flourish in Britain, corporatist theory was, as Newman puts it, 'singularly undeveloped, derivative or second-hand', or that its impact was largely pragmatic and hidden.[8] If corporatism took the form of a 'bias' rather than a transforming force in British politics in the twentieth century, it was due less to the inadequacies of indigenous corporatist traditions than to the obstructions presented by economic and political circumstances.

'The real fissures in the political culture between 1880 and 1920 lay not in political parties', Robert Colls has recently suggested, 'but along a line to do with attitudes to the State'.[9] In this context a convergence of the Radicalism forged in Birmingham and of a Conservative Party which not only sought to resolve the state's problems in the years 1900–30 but aspired to be its 'natural' governing party seemed less improbable than long-standing political rivalries might have suggested. As events were to prove, nineteenth-century Birmingham could not conquer twentieth-century Britain and the 'new' Radicalism was no more successful in transforming state and society through the Conservative Party than had been the 'old' working through the Liberal Party. Before discussing the failure of Radicalism's alliance with Conservatism, it is necessary to consider more closely its potential and, in particular, its genesis within liberalism. For if Radicalism's impact has been obscured by the fact that its legacy was inherited by 'new' Tories rather than 'Old', or even 'New', Liberals, its potential has been underestimated because of a failure to comprehend the nature of the transformation which it underwent in the second half of the nineteenth century. The reason for this lies, in part, in the ambiguities in Halévy's writings. Therefore, given the perceptiveness I have claimed for his comments, these must be examined.

II

Halévy's insight concerning the evolution of the Radicalism of Chamberlain and his adopted city was the product of something more than inspired intuition. In his classic analysis, 'The Growth of Philosophical Radicalism', Halévy explored at length the meaning and potential of Radicalism. In the light of this achievement it is the more regrettable that, to the claim that Radicalism as a movement failed, recent historians have added the assertion that Radicalism as a concept is meaningless.[10] In opposition to such judgements – a reaction, perhaps, to the word's promiscuous use in historical analysis and contemporary politics – I would suggest that Halévy provides an indispensable foundation for understanding Radicalism as a concept and its relationship to the corporatist tendencies of the early twentieth century. Halévy's account was not without flaws, however, deriving from his distinctive methodological approach to the study of political theories, and these have prevented a full appreciation of the value of his insights.

'Why did this man with a passion for thought ... logic and ethics', asked Raymond Aron in 1970, 'find fulfilment in the narrative of subtle games of diplomacy, the intrigues of parliament, social movements and workers' control?'[11] It is a question which goes to the heart of any assessment of Halévy's writings on Radicalism, highlighting the tensions arising from his desire to explore the intricacies of formal theory and to identify the assumptions informing political practice. Noting that he was 'first a philosopher', a recent biographer, M. Chase, argues that Halévy brought to his work as an historian the belief, which he acquired during his philosophical period of the 1890s, that the 'moral idea of a people' was to be found in 'their basic institutions'. From this premise he developed a sense of dialectic, similar to the one he himself described as Platonic, that resolved contradictions into systematic dichotomies. It was this 'negative dialectic', considered by Chase 'fundamental to his treatment of all questions of ideology and even historical narration', which Halévy employed to link ideologies and material processes. Less positively, however, it produced a tendency, as Halévy himself admitted, to use ideas 'to stylize and schematize events' which, when coupled with a relish for the 'paradoxes of history', may be considered to have led to the imposition of a Gallic 'logic' upon British 'reality'. Such, indeed, has been the view of those who regard Halévy's identification within Radicalism of a fundamental dichotomy concerning the spontaneous or artificial conciliation of interests as a tendentious and misleading schematization.[12]

Assessing whether Halévy was mistaken in emphasizing the 'double way' in which those he described as the Philosophical Radicals 'understood the identification of interests', through the 'conscious artifices of the legislator' or 'spontaneously by the actions of the law of nature', by the juridical or the economic, raises questions concerning the nature and impact of ideology. In a recent study of British liberal thought, R. Eccleshall has argued that despite the views of 'some commentators ... liberalism is neither hopelessly multifarious nor split into two irreconcilable phases', and that 'polar concepts such as individualism and collectivism ... tend to conceal the continuities between earlier and later liberalism'. Rather, liberalism gained 'intellectual identity' from its 'continual endeavour to create a structure of equal liberties'.[13] This is a valuable, though not completely satisfactory, corrective to an only too evident tendency to identify allegedly disabling dichotomies within political ideologies. Such interpretations seem to misconceive the nature and effectivity of ideologies, a central feature of which, as writers from traditions as different as the neo-Gramscian and the liberal have stressed, is their ability to extend across a range of apparently incompatible positions and thereby, as J. Seed has put it, to assimilate 'a contradictory field of discourses'. Rather than being a handicap, this holding together of contradictions, of 'squaring the circle' as S. Hall calls it, is the secret of an ideology's capacity to generate the political space within which it is possible to establish a hegemonic position in societies and to construct, rather than merely adapt to, events.[14]

If Halévy's identification of the natural/artificial distinction within Radicalism highlighted just such a hegemonic potential, his emphasis on the essential theoretical source of this contrast reflected a failure to locate such positions in their material context. It was this that made Halévy vulnerable to the methodological charge that he had imposed reified schemes on to reality, while interpretatively it reinforced a sense of irreconcilable positions within liberal-Radicalism which, though part of the polemic of thinkers like Spencer and Dicey against 'new Tory' collectivism, or conversely of new liberals against *laissez-faire*, was implicitly, if not theoretically, contradicted by Halévy's conviction that Chamberlain and Birmingham were *developing*, rather than negating, elements implicit within liberal-Radicalism. To understand this aspect of Radicalism one must relate theory to what Seed calls its 'precise institutional matrices and social relations', or, more concretely, to the political agenda outlined by the Philosophical Radicals in the 1830s, and pursued by liberal-Radicals from Cobden to Chamberlain thereafter, to establish a party of the middle and working classes with the capacity to create and control a state compatible with the needs of capitalist accumulation.[15] In tracing the evolution of this programme in liberal-Radicalism's major centre in the second half of the nineteenth century, it will become evident that Radicalism's difficulties were to be found less in its internal contradictions than in the intractability of the external relations it sought to influence.

III

Birmingham's reputation as a liberal-Radical centre – a reputation well attested in the nineteenth century – has been strongly emphasized by subsequent historians. Established during the Reform agitation of the 1830s, it was sustained, it has been argued, by a multiplicity of small-scale workshops in a variety of trades employing well-paid and socially upwardly-mobile workers, producing the close and generally harmonious relations between masters and men that was a central aspiration of middle-class Radicalism. This account captures, at best, half the truth with respect to the town and its Radical traditions – and even that half is the subject of increasingly sceptical investigation – for it neglects a very different set of relationships which, while preserving the town's rhetoric of class harmony, substantially modified its socio-economic and political orientation.[16] Joseph Chamberlain played a major role in the second half of the nineteenth century in establishing a new pattern of political and economic relations in Birmingham whose impact was felt locally and nationally well into the twentieth century.

When, in 1906, Chamberlain justified his tariff proposals as a continuation of the programme of the 'Birmingham School', it reflected less the special pleading of the apostate than a belief, derived from the practical concerns and ideological reformulations of his early career, that a Radical legacy was available for deployment in the light of new circumstances. It was a 'school' he claimed, reshaping Thomas Attwood's proposals of the 1830s for an expanded home market to secure full employment, which had concerned itself with two major issues – social reform and Empire. Although in emphasizing the latter Chamberlain may have inadvisedly stretched the tradition to fit his current preoccupations, the interpretation he placed on 'Empire', describing it as an arrangement to enable Britain to meet the challenge of 'our competitors, in the constant struggle for existence', was especially interesting.[17] While, once again, the language echoes the Social Darwinism then so fashionable, the stress on competition reflects a preoccupation which marked Chamberlain's career from the outset. During his Birmingham years, as businessman and mayor, Chamberlain was concerned to reorganize the town's economy in the face of the intensifying competition which, it has been argued, represented a crisis for its established structures of production.[18] In invoking Birmingham's traditions, Chamberlain implied they could be Britain's precedent.

Birmingham's problems, which became pronounced from the mid-1850s, arose from competitive pressures stemming from two sources. The immediate challenge, and ultimately the more significant for Britain, came from foreign competitors and, especially in Birmingham's case, the Americans. Equipped with new metal-working technologies they posed a threat to the town's trades which had, as N. Rosenberg notes, 'by the middle of the nineteenth century ... gone about as far as possible given their reliance upon the speed, strength, precision and dexterity of the human hand'.[19] A more persistent challenge arose from concern that the pursuit of cheapness would result in poor quality goods, produced by an ill-educated, low-paid and under-productive labour force, inhabiting a deteriorating working and urban environment. This problem, inherent in the town's intensely competitive economic structure, was prompting growing concern by the mid-Victorian years among not only the working class but some of the middle class too.[20] The twin threat brought contrasting responses, but from Chamberlain and his followers they produced a new definition of Radicalism which posed a decisive challenge to conventional interpretations.

The traditional liberal interpretation, ironically, was given classic statement by an individual related by faith and family to Chamberlain and at the very time, the 1850s, when significant change was beginning. Robert Martineau, responding to questions from his aunt Harriet, during her investigations concerning trade unionism, stressed the weakness of unions in Birmingham, emphasizing the familiar constraint of 'a multitude of garrets and small masters' employing a few workers: 'thoroughly and entirely independent', he claimed, their concern was to produce goods as cheaply as possible for sale to merchants and factors. This was not simply a structural analysis; it also had powerful evaluative, even moral, connotations: Birmingham's system was superior to those elsewhere – Sheffield was a frequent point of comparison – and trade unionism (an 'evil', a 'tyranny', in Martineau's words) an obstacle to the workings of a system of competitive individualism that was not simply compatible with but, naturally and spontaneously, conducive to a dynamic economy and consensual society.[21] Such was the view, widely held at the time, of a prominent middle-class Radical, but in so far as it was employed in accounts of Birmingham in the second half of the century it ignores the major changes which occurred in the town in the face of intensifying competition from the 1850s onwards.

One response, described by J. R. Hay as 'revolutionary', was that of Chamberlain and large businessmen like him. As Chamberlain explained, in his first major public statement in 1866, this involved a ruthless restructuring of trades – metal wood screws, in his case – through the exploitation of techno-logical and market opportunities to create a dominant position for a single firm. Chamberlain's strategy for his firm, the future GKN, involved buying up or driving out competitors ('absorb or exclude' was the slogan of Arthur Keen, who was pursuing a similar strategy in the nut and bolt trade), vertically integrating production, and sharing out or forcefully entering foreign markets. It meant, Chamberlain claimed, a 'revolution' which, while 'certainly leading to the extinction of the small manufacturer' and therefore 'deplored by some' was, in his opinion, 'really an almost unmixed good'.[22] In dismissing so cavalierly the small master, hitherto considered the key to the town's prosperity and stability, Chamberlain proposed a new partnership between large-scale capital, equipped to meet the challenge of international competition, and well-paid workers, for whom secure employment would offset the loss of the uncertain prospects of small-scale entrepreneurship. A strategy which, if not fully paternalistic (though at Cadbury's Birmingham produced one of the outstanding examples of that breed), invited the positive identification of labour's needs with capital's interests. So total, indeed, was the identification, that many of the largest firms, including Chamberlain's, adopted a negative stance towards unions which had adverse implications for the application of Radical solutions to Britain's problems in the next century.

The arrangements which emerged from the second response to the competitive pressures revealed more favourable attitudes towards unions. This strategy, more 'defensive' in character than the first, drew on traditions of trade regulation to which many employers and artisans subscribed, and in which some degree of labour/capital organization was essential. This was most evident in the 'Industrial Alliances' adopted in the 1890s in a number of Birmingham trades and which challenged the conventional picture of the town's industrial organization as seriously as Chamberlain's activities. Thus, E. J. Smith, a leading proponent of the arrangements, was preoccupied not by intrusive, 'alien' trade unionism but by 'ruinous competition': small masters underselling were 'criminal', lowering prices not through invention and ingenuity but by 'ignorance and recklessness'. Such competitive energies should be subject to 'moral and scientific control', substituting competition arising from improvements in the quality of goods, based upon productive working and providing a fair return for both capital and labour, for the 'sweating' which threatened many of the town's trades with a downward spiral of low prices, wages and quality.[23]

Smith's theory formalized practices which were implicit in many Birmingham trades during the first half of the nineteenth century but which became increasingly influential during its second half as 'respectable' employers and organized workers struggled with the adverse effects of competition – domestic and, increasingly, foreign – and the economic uncertainties associated with the Great Depression of the 1870s and 1880s. The outstanding example prior to the alliances, and to some extent their inspiration, was the attempt by the Amalgamated Society of Brassworkers, under the leadership of W. J. Davis, to regulate its trade in the 1870s. The workers were forced to unionize and encourage collective organization among the employers in an attempt to sustain regulation of their trade at the expense of small masters. Though defensive in origin, this strategy had a dynamic thrust as workers, and Davis in particular, stressed that quality rather than price was the key to countering foreign competition. Such a strategy attracted not only well-established firms who favoured quality production ('Produce the best ... and then let everyone know it' was the slogan of the penmakers, Gillots), but also large firms from newer sectors, like Chamberlain's, that were sympathetic to the unions' attempts to regulate trades where intense domestic competition threatened to tarnish the reputation of all Birmingham's producers with the derisory epithet 'Brummagem'.[24]

Neither strategy, alone or together, could meet the competitive challenge faced by the town, however. Chamberlain exaggerated the demise of the small firm; at most, and crucially for the future of the town's economy, large firms dominated small ones while linked to them in the mutual supply of productive inputs. Smith and Davis's 'alliances' could not insulate them from the small firms whose activities undermined agreements. Even 'honourable' trades, including two of the town's staples, guns and jewellery, tended to drift into the 'sweated sector'. If unions and firms were successfully to influence their socio-economic environment they required the intervention of an external force, an agency which through political intervention could underpin the new patterns within the town's economy.[25] It was this force that Chamberlain, as mayor and leader of the town's liberalism, sought to provide. In doing so he transformed not only the town's government, but also, its liberal-Radicalism, linking it decisively with the reputation of Birmingham and the fortune of his own family.

IV

D. A. Hamer, otherwise so sceptical concerning Radicalism's impact in the nineteenth century, has noted, more favourably, that Chamberlain's aim was to 'forge a relationship between Radicalism and power', liberating Radicals from their suspicion of government and encouraging them in 'acquiring and using government power'. With such an objective went not only what Hamer calls a shift from individualistic to 'constructive' Radicalism and a positive attitude to state power, but, as R. Currie has noted in his comments on Chamberlain's 1885 'ransom' speech, a new perspective on social relations, superseding *laissez-faire* individualism by a 'corporatism' of groups, 'organized and set to bargain' in a 'higher sectionalism'. This emergent corporatism, though not without the ambiguities to be found in corporatist theory in general concerning the balance between state and society, represented a decisive shift from the traditional liberal-Radical emphasis (what Chamberlain himself came to describe as Cobdenite liberal) on the sanctity of the market towards the encouragement of collective agencies – large firms, trade unions, the state – to regulate competitive economies.[26] This corporatism which developed in Birmingham in the nineteenth century and became the basis of a distinctive style of politics that persisted there well into the twentieth century, can best be understood within the priorities of nineteenth-century Radicalism and the categories employed by Halévy to analyse Radical theory.

In reshaping the Radical tradition in Birmingham, Chamberlain appeared to resolve each of the issues concerning the role of trade unions, the creation of a political party for both middle and working class, and the nature of the state, which had troubled Radicals since the 1830s. Harmonious relations between the middle and the working classes were secured by the acceptance of trade unionism and arbitration in industrial affairs, while a Liberal–Labour alliance promised the hitherto elusive Radical Party in the political sphere. Overarching and underpinning both was the state, and in the 1870s and for some time thereafter, this meant the local state, whose regulation of the working and urban environment and provision of educational and leisure facilities equipped firms and workers to pursue successful, increasingly large scale, capital accumulation. A strategy which, in consolidating the transition from 'old' to 'new' Radicalism, in the Birmingham context from Martineau to Smith, involved what Halévy identified as the pursuit of social harmony through an 'artificial', as opposed to a 'natural', route. For while both Martineau and Smith employed the familiar rhetoric of harmony to describe the relations between masters and men, they differed profoundly in their analysis of the means by which that harmony was to be attained. In Halévy's terms, Martineau stressed a 'natural' harmony of interests arising from individual effort free from collective restraint, Smith a conscious – or 'artificial' – strategy for harmonizing the 'conflicting interests of employer and employed' through the institutional collaboration, or 'ordered combination' as Smith called it, of organized labour and capital. In other words while the rhetoric of Radicalism was preserved, its institutional basis and orientation were recast in a corporatist direction.[27]

The opening years of the twentieth century saw a dramatic extension of this pattern of corporatist regulation in Birmingham. It began with the reactivation of the Chamberlain tradition of municipal intervention, first by J. S. Nettlefold, son of Chamberlain's old business associate, and then Joseph's own son, Neville. Their activities, despite Nettlefold's differences with the party and a significant labour challenge in the 1920s, ensured that Birmingham remained a unionist stronghold through until 1945. Underlying these developments were the activities of the City's Trades Council and Chamber of Commerce: the former pressing for municipal action across a wide range of services from the late 1890s, while the Chamber argued for increased state intervention at the national level. The latter's activities have been highlighted by J. R. Hay who notes that 'from the late nineteenth century to around 1920, as foreign competition and labour unrest intensified, many influential employers began to argue for state welfare as a means of social control and as a contribution to economic efficiency', with the Birmingham Chamber to the fore in advocating state-provided labour-exchanges and social insurance. In these campaigns the employers received active support from organized labour, W. J. Davis joining with leading Chamber figure R. H. Best to advocate quality production to meet foreign competition, while the Trades Council's 1899 old age pensions campaign involved collaboration with a progressive employer like Cadbury.[28]

Such activities transcended party divisions, stemming as they did from the town's need, as Hay argues, to link 'technological, commercial and profit considerations' with 'social welfare' to meet the challenge not just of socialism but, the town's long-standing problem, 'unfair competition by groups of employers who did not provide welfare but exploited their workers to a greater degree'. They gave Birmingham 'conservatism' a distinctive emphasis. For only there was Liberal–Unionism 'a popular movement', reformulating Radical concern with the 'People' into the Disraelian pursuit of 'One Nation', as Hay puts it, but with a solid body of institutional achievement, rather than rhetorical gestures, to reinforce it.[29] Birmingham represented, therefore, not just good intentions but established institutional arrangements which, through Radical-Unionist adhesion to the Conservative Party, promised solutions to the 'twin challenge' of external competitive pressure, military and economic, and internal social uncertainty faced by early twentieth-century Britain. So close was the identification between politics and place that, for some Tories, Joseph and his son Austen were 'often simply referred to by the contemptuous epithet "Birmingham"'. While the town's approach may have troubled some of his would-be allies, for Chamberlain it provided such inspiration, at once rhetorical and practical, that it has been justly said of him that 'throughout his career the industrial society of Birmingham shaped' his 'conception of the needs of Britain and its Empire'. The Chamberlain challenge assumed, therefore, something of the character of a geopolitical drama as Birmingham fought for the soul of Britain in a 'struggle', as the French writer Bérard noted, 'of reform against complacent conservatism'.[30]

Not only did Birmingham provide lasting inspiration for the Chamberlains, but its corporatist practices continued to evolve, reaching a peak in the First World War and in the activities of businessman Dudley Docker, recently described as 'an unusually active and explicit exponent of British corporatism'. Docker, who in a series of mergers secured for himself a central position in the City's economy, articulated with passion Birmingham's philosophy of 'amicable relations' between labour and capital in the context of tariff reform, proposing a 'completely integrated society and economy, in which each industry would have its own organization of workers and managers'. Docker pursued this vision from the Midlands to the national arena only to be rebuffed as 'the collapse of post-war reconstruction politics' convinced him, according to his recent biographer, that 'Britain would never reorganize itself properly to regain industrial supremacy'.[31] Why liberal-Radicalism reshaped into conservative corporatism should have disappointed its most ambitious exponent leads, finally, to a consideraton of the impact of this strategy in the context of Britain's political economy in the opening quarter of the twentieth century.

V

When Elie Halévy attended the National Industrial Conference in 1919, he may have shared the belief of the Belgian Foreign Minister that there were two 'methods of making the revolution which we feel is happening throughout the world, the Russian and the British method'. In fact, the conference proved, in R. Lowe's words, 'virtually barren of positive results', repeating the experience of its 1911 predecessor and foreshadowing the outcome of similar initiatives in 1927 and 1931.[32] R. H. Tawney's judgement that 1919 saw 'the last spasm of nineteenth-century individualism' may not be applicable to Europe, as he claimed, but when applied to inter-war Britain it has much plausibility. Notwithstanding Middlemas's discovery of a developing 'corporatist bias' in British politics in the 1920s and 1930s, the failure of corporatism, the absence of a 'New Deal', seems the more striking.[33] It is beyond the scope of this essay to account for this failure, a matter which is the subject of a growing literature, but it is appropriate to consider its implications for the fortunes of Radicalism in the twentieth century.

It has been the contention of this essay that the elements Middlemas identifies in Lloyd George's 'corporatism' of 1919 – industrial consent through employer–union collaboration under the auspices of the state, based on working-class affluence and managerial profit, and achieved by increased productivity and unrestrained competition – represented (with the partial exception of the last, unless the competition is understood to be international) not the negation of liberal-Radicalism but its transformation into twentieth-century conservative corporatism. Arthur Steel-Maitland, seeking to inspire fellow Tories at the end of the First World War with the vision of a 'community of interests between masters and men ... making the latter feel they are a corporate part of a mutually beneficent organization', or Sir Basil Blackett, advocating corporatist rationalization in 1929 in terms of 'getting rid of individualism in industry, co-operation, amalgamation', might have been Docker, Smith, or Chamberlain at any time in the previous fifty years.[34] Can Radicalism be responsible for the failure to realize the corporatist programme?

In part it involved a failure of the Radical leaders to pursue reform effectively. While it has been argued that Lloyd George's 'pragmatic interventionist kind of radicalism' made him, like Chamberlain, willing to discard the individualism of the 'great Victorian Radicals', Middlemas's assertion that he lacked a 'grand design' and 'was not then [1919], perhaps never was the man to redress the balance' between capital and labour, seems justified. Though aware of the need for a 'national efficiency' orientation in British policy, and especially for state intervention to further labour's industrial and welfare needs and to aid industry to compete with foreign rivals, neither his background – rural and petty-bourgeois rather than urban and industrial capitalist – nor his temperament – mercurial and iconoclastic rather than strategic and committed – equipped Lloyd George to see through a sustained restructuring of state and society on corporatist lines; rather, corporatism was simply one of a repertoire of techniques available for short-term crisis resolution.[35]

With Chamberlain, by contrast, the 'grand design', if not unproblematic, was clearer, rooted as it was in Birmingham's traditions; it was his tactical sense that proved unsure, threatening to endanger his broader objectives. This became most apparent when Chamberlain identified protection, and specifically imperial preference, as a crucial component of his programme for reorienting British policy. For despite Chamberlain's claim that protection was an integral part of the Birmingham programme – a claim he justified by mobilizing the city's Radical rhetoric in his support, asserting one could not 'logically and consistently attempt to defend labour against unfair competition' through trade union activity, 'without defending at the same time and against the same unfair competition the products of that labour' – in practice, this protectionist turn deflected attention from his Radical goals. Thus, while B. B. Gilbert has rightly stressed that tariff reform had an 'infinitely larger purpose' than simply adjusting trade relations, this broader vision was lost as Chamberlain became entangled in the details of his imperial programme. Moreover, Chamberlain's failure to develop coherently his social reform programme and his 'frankly contemptuous' attitude to the trade union leaders, as J. Amery puts it, made an effectively organized as opposed to a speculatively populist appeal to the working class impossible. While, therefore, Beatrice Webb considered that protection opened up the possibility of 'deliberate collective regulation' for Britain – Chamberlain, perhaps sensing that only in a less open economy than Edwardian Britain's would such regulation be possible – the need to rebut the many objections of his powerful opponents became such a preoccupation that even a generally sympathetic historian like Robert Skidelsky has doubted whether Chamberlain 'moved beyond the conception of a protected system to the idea of an organised or managed one'. In Chamberlain's defence, it might be argued that, in seeking to fulfil his Radical objectives, his chosen means obstructed rather than aided their realization; certainly while the career of supporters like L. S. Amery 'demonstrated', as G. C. Webber puts it, 'the ease with which tariff reformers could drift into corporatism'. For others, the implication that corporatism presupposed a break with established liberal economic patterns was enough to disqualify it.[36]

The damage caused was especially evident in Chamberlain's dealings with the Conservative Party. Despite Halévy's claim its Disraelian legacy meant that 'of all the Conservative parties in Europe the British ... was in a better position than any other' to respond to the Bismarckian challenge of linking social legislation and imperial expansion, Chamberlain's imperialist programme simply intensified Tory reservations concerning the erstwhile Radical and his 'Birmingham' schemes. For if protection made the fortunes of Chamberlain's programme a hostage to the prospects of individual industries and fluctuations in the business cycle, linking it to food taxes proved not only internally divisive but electorally embarrassing for the Tories. As a result, Conservatism came to doubt not only whether Chamberlain's objectives could be harmonized with the electoral cycle but, more fundamentally, whether Chamberlain possessed the capacity, essential to any 'true Conservative', of distinguishing means – in this case, economic arrangements – from the overriding end of defending the social order.[37]

This was the more unfortunate as the mutual requirements of Chamberlain and the Conservatives pointed to the desirability of an alliance between them centred on the need to strengthen the state to meet the challenge of foreign rivalry and domestic discontent. While the Conservatives offered Chamberlain a strong but relatively flexible governing party – a *Staatspartei* – he promised the Tories a dynamic policy to resolve not only the 'sense of alarm' which many felt over Britain's prospects, but also the 'crisis of identity' which afflicted the party as the inadequacy of Salisbury's fatalism in the face of the problems of party and state became evident. In particular, by drawing on the proto-corporatist traditions of 'organic statism' to be found in Tory thinking and grafting on to them Radicalism's institutional experience in redirecting class conflict towards broader collective goals, Chamberlain provided the Conservatives with a plausible corporatist strategy for Britain. While such a prospect was attractive to many Tories, even the most sympathetic found tariff reform less a prerequisite for wider reform than an obstacle to it. By 1910, F. E. Smith of the Unionist Social Reform movement 'sought a social policy which did not depend on tariff reform'.[38]

If Chamberlain's imperial strategy was a serious hindrance to his effective collaboration with the Conservatives, not all the obstacles lay on his side: there is reason for doubting whether the Tories were, in general, willing to assume the broad responsibilities of 'a new governing class' which, Amery has suggested, Chamberlain's strategy required. Halévy shrewdly noted that having joined the Conservative Party Chamberlain's task was 'to make of it a party in many respects similar to the Republican party in the United States, the party of progressive capitalism and large-scale industry'. Chamberlain's Birmingham heritage disposed him towards the priorities of large-scale capital and contemporaries as well as historians have seen in his social and imperial policies during the Salisbury government of 1895–1900 evidence of such an orientation. The Tories, moreover, less inhibited than the Liberals by reservations concerning state intervention and without their concern to eradicate rather than institutionalize class-conflict, possessed distinct assets in responding to Chamberlain's appeal that they adopt a more national or 'aristocratic' attitude and treat Britain, as Chamberlain treated her colonies, 'as an estate to be developed, for profit, certainly, but also for its own sake'. In practice, however, Chamberlain's vision, like that of his transatlantic equivalent Theodore Roosevelt, failed as the Tories 'oscillated', as G. R. Searle notes, between stressing the 'defence of property' and the pursuit of 'social reform'. Chamberlain's appeal was riven by the contradiction that it appealed to those 'concerned with resisting capitalist modernisation and at the same time groups committed to greater industrial efficiency'; thus the radical right, which before 1914 were attracted towards Chamberlain, were among Lloyd George's leading opponents in the early 1920s.[39]

If the absence of a secure party base simply emphasized Radicalism's century-long failure in this respect – reflecting perhaps a fatal ambivalence as to whether change would come through or above party – wider state/society relations in Britain in the opening decades of the century proved unfavourable to Chamberlain's Birmingham solutions. The character of the British state, its structure – the weakness of interventionist ministries like Labour in the face of a traditional but increasingly powerful department like the Treasury – and the continued dominance of an ideology of non-interventionist liberalism, ensured that Radical change would be stifled when not rejected outright. While Chamberlain was able to create a state in Birmingham, Lloyd George, though not without developing structures of relevance to corporatist strategies, had, in general, to work through established agencies that were, at best, less than wholehearted in their commitment to Radical change.[40] This said, however, it has to be asked whether the pattern of social relations established under Chamberlain's leadership in Birmingham, was applicable to the circumstances confronting Lloyd George in post-war Britain. Neither class relations nor the structure and dynamic of the economy lent themselves to the Radical/corporatist remedies developed and advocated by Birmingham during the years 1870–1930.

Halévy had noted in 1919 that if industrial reform meant the fusion of classes à la Whitley, they entailed 'a utopia'; if they meant, as the National Industrial Conference seemed to suggest, that rather than 'denying the idea of the class struggle' it 'is organized to permit the struggle to go on' then it might be possible for England to bring about a 'new triumph'.[41] But neither the employers nor the state were prepared for such an understanding; collaboration was purely tactical so that once advantage was gained withdrawal followed, a response which could only intensify the divisive class relations produced by bitter labour disputes and mounting unemployment. While inter-war Britain, like late Victorian Birmingham, faced competitive pressures requiring economic restructuring, Chamberlain's protectionist proposals had nothing like the same attractiveness or coherence as the programme he had forged in Birmingham in the 1870s. Even there, as we noted, Chamberlain's blending of two responses to competitive pressures, a 'revolutionary' and a 'defensive', into a strategy favouring (local) state regulation and assistance to capital and labour to meet those pressures, left unresolved ambiguities concerning employers' attitudes towards unions. Chamberlain's proposal for protectionism compounded these divisions as employers differed over whether a protected home market with high wages and perhaps, for no more than at the local level was it universally seen as a corollary, collaboration with the unions, was preferable to an attempt to confront foreign competition aggressively, even if this meant wage-cuts and conflict with the unions. Given these divisions within industrial capital, it proved impossible to force radical change upon a state dominated by finance capital and political immobility. A state capitalist solution of the sort that developed elsewhere, and which the Birmingham programme entailed, needed a stronger coalition of forces committed to a more regulated economy than existed in the 1920s. Such an outcome awaited the development of an influential, home-based, large-firm sector and a reinvigorated trade unionism in the 1940s. Even then, it was a circumscribed corporatism which emerged, reflecting the continued commitment of key sectors of British society to an 'open' and liberal political economy.[42]

Nevertheless, what evolved in the 1920s and 1930s, though not corresponding to 'organized capitalism' or corporatism, was not 'a simple reassertion of the old forms of legitimacy' derived from Cobdenite-Gladstonian liberalism. Rather, as J. Cronin observes, it was a 'unique political settlement characterised by several, seemingly contradictory, factors', a 'bastardised liberalism or, looking forward, a form of corporatism ... without the state'. If Chamberlain's 1903 programme was introduced in the 1920s, with 'creeping protection, industrial harmony, carefully costed welfare reforms ... rationalisation and intervention' – perhaps with his son, Neville, belatedly redeeming his father's bequest – and this was, as Middlemas suggests, a 'British Revolution', it displayed 'an innate conservatism' which proved more successful in securing a 'competitive equilibrium' in industry and 'crisis avoidance' in politics than forwarding the dynamic, competitive rationalization based on labour–capital collaboration which radicals had envisaged.[43] Radicalism's legacy, ironically, was to bolster conservatism in Britain, not only in a party sense but also in the nation's socio-economic relations. But though Radicalism failed, it was a failure that arose from an inability to overcome contemporary realities rather than from an unwillingness to shed outdated concerns. Radicalism went down in the face of twentieth-century intractabilities rather than in the pursuit of nineteenth-century fantasies. What Chamberlain had claimed, in 1906, to have achieved in Birmingham – that it was 'a great city today because a generation ago men were found – practically all its citizens – who were willing to work, and, if necessary, make sacrifices in order to maintain and support its reputation' – had not proved transferable to Britain. Radicalism had met its limits: Birmingham, as Lord Melbourne had informed Thomas Attwood one hundred years earlier, was not Britain.[44]

Notes

1   G. Dangerfield, *The Strange Death of Liberal England* (London, 1984); A. B. Cooke and J. Vincent, *The Governing Passion. Cabinet Government and Party Politics in Britain, 1885–6* (Brighton, 1974), pp. 11, 161.
2   P. Clarke, *Liberals and Social Democrats* (Cambridge, 1981); M. Freeden, *The New Liberalism. An Ideology of Social Reform* (Oxford, 1979); idem, *Liberalism Divided. A Study in British Political Thought, 1914–1939* (Oxford, 1986); G. L. Bernstein, *Liberalism and Liberal Politics in Edwardian England* (London, 1986).
3   E. Halévy, *The Era of Tyrannies* (New York, 1965); N. Harris, *Competition and the Corporate State. British Conservatives, the State and Industry* (London, 1972); S. Hall and B. Schwarz, 'State and Society, 1880–1930', and B. Schwarz, 'Conservatism and Caesarism, 1903–22', in M. Langan and B. Schwarz (eds), *Crises in the British State, 1880–1930* (London, 1985); see also the useful discussion in N. O'Sullivan, *Conservatism* (London, 1976), pp. 126–9; see K. D. Brown, 'The Anti-Socialist Union, 1908–1949', in K. D. Brown (ed.), *Essays in Anti-Labour History: Responses to the Rise of Labour in Britain* (London, 1974), pp. 246–7.
4   Cooke and Vincent, *The Governing Passion*, pp. 19, 161.
5   D. A. Hamer (ed. and intro.), *The Radical Programme* (1885; Brighton, 1971), p. xxxix; P. Adelman, *Victorian Radicalism. The Middle-Class Experience, 1830–1914* (London, 1984), p. 154; see also A. J. A. Morris (ed. and intro.), *Edwardian Radicalism, 1900–1914. Some Aspects of British Radicalism* (London, 1974), pp. 2–4.

6 M. V. Bérard, *British Imperialism and Commercial Supremacy* (London, 1906), p. 31; K. Middlemas, *Politics in Industrial Society. The Experience of the British System Since 1911* (London, 1979), p. 151; A. Sykes, *Tariff Reform in British Politics, 1903–1913* (Oxford, 1979), p. 57.

7 T. H. S. Escott, 'The Future of the Radical Party', in Hamer, *The Radical Programme*, p. ii; Halévy, *The Era of Tyrannies*, p. 140.

8 C. S. Maier, *Recasting Bourgeois Europe. Stabilization in France, Germany and Italy in the Decade after World War I* (Princeton, 1975), pp. 9–10, 12; P. J. Williamson, *Varieties of Corporatism. A Conceptual Discussion* (Cambridge, 1985), pp. 4, 22; J. E. S. Hayward, 'Solidarist Syndicalism: Durkheim and Duguit, part I', *Sociological Review*, 8 (i), p. 18; W. Grant (ed. and intro.), *The Political Economy of Corporatism* (London, 1985), p. 6; O. Newman, *The Challenge of Corporatism* (London, 1981), pp. 13–14; K. Middlemas, *Power, Competition of the State: vol. I: Britain in Search of Balance* (London, 1986), p. 6; Harris, *Competition and the Corporate State*, pp. 17–18, also considers corporatism a European import conflicting with, rather than developing out of, liberalism.

9 R. Colls, 'Englishness and the Political Culture', in R. Colls and P. Dodd (eds), *Englishness, Politics and Culture, 1880–1920* (Beckenham, 1986), p. 50.

10 See, for instance, D. Nicholls, 'The English Middle-Class and the Ideological Significance of Radicalism, 1760–1886', *Journal of British Studies*, 24 (4), pp. 415–16.

11 R. Aron, 'Elie Halévy', *Government & Opposition*, 19 (4), p. 409.

12 M. Chase, *Elie Halévy. An Intellectual Biography* (Columbia, 1980), pp. 3, 29, 35; Aron, 'Elie Halévy', pp. 413, 416; J. Viner, 'Bentham and J. S. Mill: the Utilitarian Background', *American Economic Review*, xxxix (2), pp. 368–9; see also A. Briggs, Foreword to E. Halévy, *A History of the English People in 1815* (London, 1987).

13 E. Halévy, *The Growth of Philosophic Radicalism* (London, 1928), p. 498; R. Eccleshall, *British Liberalism. Liberal Thought from the 1640s to the 1980s* (London, 1986), pp. 7, 8.

14 For a stress on the dichotomous features of ideology, see W. H. Greenleaf, *The British Political Tradition, vol. II: The Ideological Heritage* (London, 1983); for a liberal approach to ideology, Freeden, *Liberalism Divided*, p. 3; for a neo-Gramscian, S. Hall, 'Variants of Liberalism', in J. Donand and S. Hall (eds), *Politics and Ideology* (Milton Keynes, 1986), pp. 41, 51; J. Seed, 'Unitarianism, Political Economy and the Antinomies of Liberal Culture: Manchester, 1830–50', *Social History*, 7 (1), pp. 2–3.

15 Ibid., pp. 2–3; P. Richards, 'State Formation and Class Struggle, 1832–1948', in P. Corrigan (ed.), *Capitalism, State Formation and Marxist Theory* (London, 1980), pp. 58–9.

16 A. Briggs, 'Social Structure and Politics in Birmingham and Lyons, 1835–48', *British Journal of Sociology*, I (March, 1950), pp. 67–80 represents one of the first formulations; I. R. Tholfsen, 'Origins of the Birmingham Caucus', *Historical Journal*, II (2), pp. 161–84 one of a number of elaborations of the Briggs thesis; for recent criticism see C. Behagg, 'Masters and Manufacturers: Social Values and the Smaller Unit of Production in Birmingham, 1800–50', in G. Crossick and H. P. Haupt (eds), *Shopkeepers and Master Artisans in Nineteenth-century Europe* (London, 1984), p. 142; E. Duggan, *The Impact of Industrialization on an Urban Labour Market. Birmingham, England, 1770–1860* (New York, 1985).

17 C. W. Boyd (ed.), *Mr. Chamberlain's Speeches* (London, 1974), vol. II, p. 368; A. Briggs, *The Age of Improvement, 1783–1867* (London, 1955), pp. 204–5; B. Hilton. *Corn, Cash, Commerce. The Economic Policies of the Tory Governments, 1815–30* (Oxford, 1977), pp. 91, 130, 175–6.

18 N. Rosenberg (ed. and intro.), *The American System of Manufactures* (Edinburgh, 1969), p. 79; P. J. Waller, *Town, City and Nation. England, 1850–1914* (Oxford, 1983), p. 93.
19 Rosenberg, *The American System*, pp. 78–9.
20 A. F. Hooper, 'Mid-Victorian Radicalism: Community and Class in Mid-Victorian Birmingham, 1850–80', unpublished PhD Thesis (London, 1978), chs I and II.
21 H. Martineau, M. S. Coll, Birmingham University Library, H. M. 1321, 1327.
22 J. R. Hay, 'The British Business Community, Social Insurance and the German Example ', in W. J. Mommsen (ed.), *The Emergence of the Welfare State in Britain and Germany: 1850–1950* (London, 1981), p. 120; J. Chamberlain, 'Manufacture of Iron Wood Screws', in S. Timmins (ed.), *Birmingham and Midland Hardware District* (Birmingham, 1866), p. 606; A. Keen, 'Midland Captains of Industry', *Birmingham Gazette and Express*, 1907–9 (Birmingham Reference Library, 217842), pp. 1–2.
23 E. J. Smith, *The New Trades Combination Movement* (London, 1899), pp. xii, xx, xxiii–xxiv, 8–9, 18; for earlier examples, S. R. H. Jones, 'Price Associations and Competition in the British Pin Industry, 1814–40', *Economic History Review*, xxvi, (2), pp. 237–53; and R. A. Church and B. D. M. Smith, 'Competition and Monopoly in the Coffin Furniture Industry, 1870–1915, *Economic History Review*, xix, (3), pp. 628, 640–1.
24 Hooper, 'Mid-Victorian Radicalism', ch. II, Gillot, *Great Industries of Great Britain* (London [n.d.], *c*.1878), vol. II, p. 314; for David, W. T. Stead (ed.), *Coming Men on Coming Questions* (London, 1905), pp. 451–2.
25 For decline in the gun trade, 'Artifex' and 'Opifex', *The Causes of Decay in a British Industry* (London, 1907); for leading Birmingham firms in the 1880s, see Royal Commission on Depression of Trade and Industry, 1886, vol. xxi, qq. 1520, 1527; for the city's great firms in the early twentieth century, C. Shaw, 'The Large Manufacturing Employers of 1907', *Business History*, xxv (1), pp. 52–3; J. R. Hay, 'Employers and Social Policy in Britain: the Evolution of Welfare Legislation, 1905–1914', *Social History*, 4 (1977), where the need for state intervention in areas of small-scale producers like Birmingham is stressed; see also P. Schmitter, 'Neo-corporatism and the state', in Grant, *The Political Economy of Corporatism*, p. 45, where the existence of small producers and the adoption of corporatism are linked.
26 D. A. Hamer, *Liberal Politics in the Age of Gladstone and Rosebery* (Oxford, 1972), pp. 51, 95–6; R. Currie, *Industrial Politics* (Oxford, 1979), p. 48; Boyd, *Mr Chamberlain's Speeches*, p. 368; Bérard, *British Imperialism*, p. 221.
27 Hooper, 'Mid-Victorian Radicalism', chs I–II.
28 J. H. Nettlefold, *Birmingham Municipal Affairs. A Message to the Citizens* (Birmingham, 1918), p. 16; D. Dilks, *Neville Chamberlain: vol. I, 1869–1929* (Cambridge, 1984), pp. 126–7; J. Corbett, *The Birmingham Trades Council, 1886–1966* (Birmingham, 1966), pp. 56–7, 63, 81–2, 85; J. R. Hay, *The Development of the British Welfare State, 1880–1975* (London, 1978), pp. 32, 35–6; Hay, *The Origins of the Liberal Welfare Reforms, 1906–1914* (London, 1975), p. 32; Hay, 'The British Business Community ... ', pp.109, 117–19, 120–1.
29 Ibid., pp. 109–10; Hay, *The Development of the British Welfare State ... ,* pp. 3, 5–6; C. Harvie, *The Lights of Liberalism. University Liberals and the Challenge of Democracy, 1860–86* (London, 1976), pp. 231–2; R. Jay, *Joseph Chamberlain: a Political Study* (Oxford, 1981), pp. 343–4.
30 For the 'twin challenge', R. J. Scally, *The Origins of the Lloyd George Coalition. The Politics of Social Imperialism, 1900–1918* (Princeton, 1975), p. 98; D. Dutton, *Austen Chamberlain. Gentleman in Politics* (Bolton, 1985), p. 51; M. Gilbert, *Churchill's Political Philosophy* (Oxford, 1981), pp. 33–4; J. Vincent, (ed.), *The Crawford Papers. The Journals of David Lindsay, twenty-seventh Earl of Crawford and tenth*

Earl of Balcarres, 1871–1940 during the years 1892 to 1940 (Manchester, 1984), pp. 90, 232, 305; P. T. Marsh, 'Joseph Chamberlain' in D. J. Jeremy (ed.), *Dictionary of Business Biography* vol. I. A–C (London, 1984), p. 648; Bérard, *British Imperialism*, pp. 6, 18, 51–2.

31 R. P. T. Davenport-Hines, 'Dudley Docker', in Jeremy, *Dictionary of Business Biography* vol. II, D–G (London, 1984), pp. 130–3; ibid., *Dudley Docker. The Life and Times of a Trade Warrior* (Cambridge, 1984); J. Cronin, *Labour and Society in Britain, 1918–1979* (London, 1984), p. 20; S. Blank, *Government and Industry in Britain. The Federation of British Industries in Politics, 1945–65* (Farnborough, 1973), pp. 13–14, 16, 20; *The City of Birmingham Official Industrial and Commercial Handbook* (Birmingham, 1919); R. H. Brazier and E. Sandford, *Birmingham and the Great War, 1914–1919* (Birmingham, 1921), p. 193.

32 R. Lowe, 'The Failure of Consensus in Britain: the National Industrial Conference, 1919–1921', *Historical Journal*, 21 (3), pp. 650, 674–5; G. M. McDonald and H. T. Gospel, 'The Mond–Turner Talks, 1927–1933: A Study in Industrial Co-operation', *Historical Journal*, 16 (4), pp. 822, 829.

33 N. Whiteside, 'Industrial Welfare and Labour Regulation in Britain at the Time of the First World War', *International Review of Social History*, xxv (3), p. 725; D. E. Ashford, *The Emergence of the Welfare States* (London, 1986), p. 79, interestingly contrasts British and French attitudes towards the state.

34 Middlemas, *Politics in Industrial Society* ... , pp. 151, 179.

35 C. Wrigley, *David Lloyd George and the British Labour Movement* (Brighton, 1976), pp. ix, 43, 48; J. Campbell, *F. E. Smith. First Earl of Birkenhead* (London, 1983), p. 360; Middlemas, *Politics in Industrial Society*, pp. 66–7; M. Cole (ed.), *B. Webb, Diaries, 1912–24* (London, 1952), pp. 161, 165, 168, 175.

36 Boyd, *Mr Chamberlain's Speeches*, p. 366; B. B. Gilbert, *David Lloyd George; a Political Life. The Architect of Change, 1863–1912* (London, 1987), p. 267; P. Cain, 'Political Economy in Edwardian England: the Tariff-Reform Controversy', in A. O'Day, *The Edwardian Age: Conflict and Stability, 1900–1914* (London, 1979), pp. 52–3; J. Amery, *The Life of Joseph Chamberlain*, vol. V, *1901–3: Joseph Chamberlain and the Tariff Reform Campaign* (London, 1969), pp. 269–70, 311; vol. VI, *1903–1968: Joseph Chamberlain and the Tariff Reform Campaign* (London, 1969), p. 794; B. Drake and M. Cole (eds), *B. Webb, Our Partnership* (London, 1948), p. 267; R. Skidelsky, *Oswald Mosley* (London, 1981), p. 57; G. C. Webber, *The Ideology of the British Right, 1918–1939* (London, 1986), p. 80.

37 E. Halévy, *A History of the English People, Epilogue, vol I: 1895–1905*, Book 2 (Harmondsworth, 1939), p. 158; R. Blake, *The Conservative Party from Peel to Churchill* (London, 1970), pp. 181, 189; M. Pugh, *The Tories and the People, 1880–1935* (Oxford, 1985), p. 171.

38 P. Kennedy, *The Realities Behind Diplomacy. Background Influences on Britain's External Policy, 1865–1980* (London, 1981), Ch. III: Webber, *The Ideology of the British Right*, p. 6; Lindsay noted in 1900, 'we face catastrophe', Vincent, *The Crawford Papers* ..., p. 64; A. Stepan, *The State and Society: Peru in Comparative Perspective* (Princeton, 1987), p. 46, for 'organic statism' and corporatism; Campbell, *F. E. Smith*, pp. 358–9 for F. E. Smith's views on Toryism and the state; J. Ridley, 'The Unionist Social Reform Committee, 1911–1914: Wets before the Deluge', *Historical Journal*, 30 (2), p. 393.

39 Amery, *Life of Joseph Chamberlain*, vol. v, 222; Halévy, *A History of the English People*, p. 183; Webb, *Our Partnership*, p. 140; W. C. Mallalieu, 'Joseph Chamberlain and Workmen's Compensation', *Journal of Economic History*, X (1), p. 46; H. A. Will, 'Colonial Policy and Economic Development in the British West Indies, 1895–1903', *Economic History Review*, xxiii (1), pp. 131, 142; Freeden, *Liberalism*

211

Divided ..., p. 171; Middlemas, *Politics in Industrial Society* ..., pp. 39, 60; J. M. Cooper, *The Warrior and the Priest. Woodrow Wilson and Theodore Roosevelt* (London, 1983); G.P. Searle, 'The Revolt from the Right in Edwardian Britain', in P. Kennedy and A. Nicholls (eds), *Nationalist and Racialist Movements in Britain and Germany before 1914* (London, 1981), pp. 36–7; R. Thurlow, *Fascism in Britain. A History, 1918–1985* (Oxford, 1987), pp. 4–5, 48.

40 B. Schwarz, 'Conservatism and Caesarism ...', p. 54; Lowe, 'The Failure of Consensus', pp. 661–2; R. Price, *Labour in British Society. An Interpretative History* (London, 1986), p. 158 for the development of an industrial relations bureaucracy in the Board of Trade as a result of the 1896 Conciliation Act; K. Burk (ed.), *War and the State. The Transformation of British Government, 1914–19* (London, 1982); R. Lowe, 'The Erosion of State Intervention in Britain, 1917–24', *Economic History Review*, xxxi (2), p. 286.

41 Halévy, *The Era*, pp. 156–7.

42 For the contradictions of tariff reform, see Halévy, *History of the English People* ..., Book 3, pp. 72–86; R. Shannon, *The Crisis of Imperialism, 1865–1915* (St Albans, 1976), pp. 359–62; M. Balfour, *Britain and Joseph Chamberlain* (London, 1985), pp. 285–8; for opposition to a high-wage rationalized economy, Schwarz, 'The Corporate Economy, 1890–1929', in Langan and Schwarz, p. 97; for anti-union actions by large-scale employers in Birmingham post-1926, R. P. Hastings 'Birmingham', in J. Skelley (ed.), *1926. The General Strike* (London, 1976), p. 224; for an interesting analysis of politicians' attitudes towards state-capitalism, Webber, *The Ideology*, pp. 73–86; Harris, *Competition and the Corporate State*, p. 226.

43 Cronin, *Labour and Society in Britain*, p. 40; Middlemas, *Politics in Industrial Society* ..., pp. 173, 230, 277; by the mid-1950s, cartels in manufacturing industry were estimated to cover 50–60% of output, *Financial Times*, 11 June 1986; for one Conservative's acceptance of this fact, Q. Hogg, *The Case for Conservatism* (London, 1947), pp. 109–11, 233.

44 Boyd, *Mr Chamberlain's Speeches*, p. 367; G. Ingham, *Capitalism Divided. The City and Industry in British Social Development* (London, 1984), p. 109; Bérard, *British Imperialism*, p. 132; the episode might be seen as one phase in the, continuing, conflict between north and south with Birmingham occupying a pivotal, if uncertain, position in between; see J. A. Hobson's pioneering analysis of the first General Election of 1910, Clarke, p. 137.

Index

References in italic denote main entries.